Wine, Networks and Scales

Intermediation in the Production, Distribution and Consumption of Wine

PETER LANG
Bruxelles • Bern • Berlin • New York • Oxford • Wien

Business & Innovation

Vol. 25

The creation of new activities, of news production and consumption modes, of new goods and services, of new markets and new jobs (etc.) depends as much on the heroic action of entrepreneurs as on the strategies of big corporations which develop their activities at a global scale. Innovation and business are interlinked. The main themes of the books published in this series are: Entrepreneurship, enterprise and innovation; Innovation strategies in a global context; Innovation policies and business climate; Innovation, business dynamics and socio-economic change. The synergies between innovative entrepreneurship, firms' strategies and innovation policies is of major importance in the explanation of technological paradigms change and of the transformations in economic and social structures of wealthy and less wealthy countries. In this series are published books in English or in French specialized in economics, management and sociology of innovation and also dealing with change and entrepreneurship in a local, national or international perspective.

This series is supported by the Research Network on Innovation.

Stéphanie Lachaud-Martin, Corinne Marache,
Julie McIntyre, Mikaël Pierre (Eds.)

Wine, Networks and Scales

Intermediation in the Production, Distribution and Consumption of Wine

Business and Innovation
Vol. 25

Information bibliographique publiée par "Die Deutsche Bibliothek".
"Die Deutsche Bibliothek" répertorie cette publication dans la "Deutsche National-bibliografie"; les données bibliographiques détaillées sont disponibles sur le site <http://dnb.ddb.be>.

With the support of:

Liquoreux d'Aquitaine

teresma

THE UNIVERSITY OF NEWCASTLE AUSTRALIA
Wine Studies Research Network

ISBN 978-2-8076-1416-1 • ISSN 2034-5402
E-ISBN 978-2-8076-1417-8 (ePDF) • E-ISBN 978-2-8076-1418-5 (EPUB)
E-ISBN 978-2-8076-1419-2 (MOBI) • DOI 10.3726/b17374
D/2020/5678/47

Éditions scientifiques internationales
Bruxelles, 2021
1 avenue Maurice, B-1050 Bruxelles, Belgique

Cette publication a fait l'objet d'une d'une évaluation par les pairs.

www.peterlang.com

Table of Contents

Part II Intermediaries in the Production, Marketing and Consumption of Wine

Part III Networks, Identity and Migration in the Wine World

Introduction

Stéphanie Lachaud-Martin, Corinne Marache
and Julie McIntyre

The globalisation of the wine trade since the 1990s has brought about wide-ranging changes in the perception of wine and purchasing and consumption practices depending on the people and the places being considered. In most major cities and in many parts of the world it is possible to buy and drink wine of any origin, sometimes made on the other side of the world. At the end of the 20th century, scientists specialising in wine and vines made available new kinds of knowledge and technologies for perfecting methods for cultivation, vinification and the transport of wine. These have revolutionised the age-old traditions of a product which had historically acquired a social and cultural position that was very particular and often imbued with luxury and prestige. This can be seen when studying the philosophy and the trade patterns of Europe in the past – when men of letters viewed the vineyards as symbols of beauty and civilisation and when wine was seen as nourishment, either sacred or dangerous according to how it was used – and in the present day. Since 2008 researchers in humanities and social sciences from different parts of the world have paid growing attention to the social and cultural meaning of wine according to the place and the people present. This field of research, which at first was reserved to certain disciplines such as anthropology, has grown over the past ten years to include all the humanities and social sciences in the English and French speaking worlds and beyond. This interest in studying vines and wine has led us to enquire into the links and the points of convergence between the different disciplines concerned by this topic, which is now known as *Wine Studies*. This research into wine is on the rise and in particular the studies on the production, commerce and consumption of wine constitute a particularly pertinent prism for understanding the new links being forged in a context of globalisation and for analysing the issues about the mobility of people, of objects and of ideas.

In this context, in 2013, historian Julie McIntyre and sociologist John Germov set up a network of research into *Wine Studies* at the University of Newcastle, in Australia. This initiative came in response to the clear absence of such a centre in the humanities and social sciences in comparison with research centres which serve the wine-producing industry and where work is based on wine sciences and on the wine economy. Economic and scientific research on wine is of interest to historians, sociologists, anthropologists, geographers, researchers in language studies and others who are not involved in the fields of economics and science. The *Wine Studies Research Network* also developed using epistemologies and methodologies that are different to those deployed by economists and scientists. The network members proposed the adoption of a critical analysis of the wine industry. They are interested in wine-producing areas as natural environments, in consumer politics and in the way in which the production, the trade and the consumption of wine define a social and cultural dimension as well as an economic value. They also analyse both the positive and the negative external factors in the relations between people and wine.

In 2016, the *Wine Studies Research Network* co-organised the first international conference on wine studies in the humanities and social sciences with the *Menzies Centre for Australian Studies* at King's College in London. The meeting brought together over 30 researchers who, in particular, questioned the links between *Wine Studies* and *Food Studies*. Should *Wine Studies* be attached to these or should they develop their own lines of questioning, their own methods and their own literature? The conclusion of these discussions was that *Wine Studies* constitutes a historiographical field that is very specific and different from *Food Studies*[1]. This first scientific gathering resulted in two publications: a special edition of the review *Global Food History*, co-edited by Julie McIntyre and Jeffrey Pilcher, entitled "Worlds in a Wine Glass: Rethinking the Global and the Local"[2]. This series of articles showed that wine "has

---

1 McIntyre J., "Wine Studies in the Humanities and Social Sciences: A Report on Symposia and the State of the Field", *Journal of Wine Research*, vol. 28, no. 2, p. 159-164.

2 McIntyre J., "Worlds in a Wine Glass: Rethinking the Global and the Local", *Global Food History* vol. 5, n°qui1–2, 26 février 2019, p. 1-4.

become one of the best examples illustrating the connections, symbioses and oppositions at work in the local-global dialectic of food". This special number concerned history and French studies. Following on from collaborations set up during the London meeting, Jacqueline Dutton and Peter Howland co-edited *Terroir and Utopia: Making New Worlds* (2015)[3]. This collection brought together a larger number of researchers and presented a "multidisciplinary and intersectoral perspective" into the way that wine, terroir and utopia come together to "create new worlds, new wines, new links and new people".

In 2018, Julie McIntyre and the *Wine Studies Research Network* became associated with Corinne Marache and Stéphanie Lachaud, from University Bordeaux-Montaigne, to co-organise the second international conference on wine in the humanities and social sciences, this time in France. As anywhere else, in France the world of wine is the focus of study which is at the meeting point of humanities and social sciences, historic periods and fields of analysis (social, cultural, economic or political)[4]. The vine and wine have been the subjects of famous studies which are already fairly old, such as the *Histoire de la vigne et du vin en France, des origines au xixe siècle*[5] *(History of the vine and wine in France from the origins to the 19th century)* by Roger Dion in 1959, in which the author shows how towns, trading networks and demand-side economics have played a determining role in the birth, development, reputation or decline of vineyards. In this economic perspective, in 1975, Henri Enjalbert wrote a reflexive piece *Histoire de la vigne et du vin: l'avènement de la qualité*[6], (*History of the vine and wine: the arrival of quality*) on the factors linked to the arrival of quality viticulture; and in 1988 Marcel Lachiver published *Vins, vignes et vignerons. Histoire du vignoble français (Wines, vines and wine-producers. History of the French vineyard)*[7].

---

3 Dutton J. and Howland P. J. (eds.), *Wine, Terroir and Utopia: Making New Worlds*, London, Routledge, 2019.

4 Argot-Dutard F., Charvet P. and Lavaud S. (eds.), *Voyage aux pays du vin: des origines à nos jours. Histoire, anthologie, dictionnaire*, Paris, Robert Laffont, 2007; Garrier G., *Histoire sociale et culturelle du vin. Les mots de la vigne et du vin*, Paris, Larousse, 1995.

5 Dion R., *Histoire de la vigne et du vin en France, des origines au XIXe siècle*, Paris, Flammarion, 1959.

6 Enjalbert H., "Comment naissent les grands crus de bordeaux, porto, cognac ?", *Annales Économies, Sociétés, Civilisations*, n°3 and 4, octobre-décembre 1953; *Histoire de la vigne et du vin: l'avènement de la qualité*, Paris, Bordas, 1975.

7 Lachiver M., *Vins, vignes et vignerons. Histoire du vignoble français*, Paris, Fayard, 1988.

In these analyses of the conditions giving rise to regional vineyards, the historic geography faculty in Bordeaux contributed to a better knowledge of local vineyards with the publication in 1975 of work carried out by Christian Huetz de Lemps on the geography of trade in Bordeaux at the time of Louis XIV[8] or with monographs like that by René Pijassou on the Médoc in 1980[9].

Carried out over the long-term, these different works reveal the workings of economic intermediation in the world of wine: by the family owners, the actors in the wine trade, the vitivinicole professionals. Following this first generation of geographers, Philippe Roudié renewed geography studies and the history of the vine and wine with an analysis of the land-owning, social and economic forces at work in the Bordeaux vineyard in 1973[10] and then in research started in the CERVIN (Centre d'études et de recherches sur la vigne et le vin/ Centre for study and research on vines and wine) in 1988[11]. More recently, the work done by Raphaël Schirmer has helped to continue and to renew wine geography, particularly in the fields of globalisation, in wine consumption and its place in our societies. The Atlas of the Bordeaux Vineyard which he edited and which should be published shortly is a major contribution to social science studies on wine.

The work done by Bordeaux historians has also helped to complete this research, particularly studies by Paul Butel on Bordeaux wine merchants in 1973[12], and more recently research by Sandrine Lavaud[13], Marguerite Figeac-Monthus[14], Stéphanie

---

8 Huetz de Lemps C., *Géographie du commerce de Bordeaux à la fin du règne de Louis XIV*, Paris-The Hague, Mouton, École des Hautes Études en Sciences Sociales-Centre de Recherche historiques, 1975.

9 Pijassou R., *Le Médoc, un grand vignoble de qualité*, Paris, Tallandier, 1980.

10 Roudié P., *Le vignoble bordelais*, Toulouse, Privat, 1973.

11 Roudié P. and CERVIN, *Vignobles et vignerons du Bordelais*, Paris, Éditions du CNRS, 1988.

12 Butel P., "L'Histoire commerciale bordelaise dans la seconde moitié du XVIIIe siècle", PhD Thesis, 1973; *Les dynasties bordelaises: de Colbert à Chaban,* Paris, Perrin, 1991; *Histoire de l'Atlantique: de l'antiquité à nos jours*, Paris, Perrin, 1997 and in its English version *The Atlantic*, London-New York, Routledge, 1999. More recently, see Gardey P., *Négociants et marchands de Bordeaux: de la guerre d'Amérique à la Restauration (1780-1830)*, Paris, Presses universitaires Paris Sorbonne, 2009.

13 Lavaud S., *Bordeaux et le vin au Moyen Âge*, Bordeaux, Éditions "Sud-Ouest", 2003.

14 Figeac-Monthus M., *Les Lur Saluces d'Yquem de la fin du XVIIIe siècle au milieu du XIXe siècle*, Bordeaux, Fédération historique du Sud-Ouest Mollat, 2000.

Lachaud[15] and Hubert Bonin[16]. Research into wine is therefore dynamic and well established in this university. Another example is a specific collection "Grappes et Millésimes", published by the Bordeaux university press and devoted to publications on vines and wine in which much research is published, such as the work of Sylvaine Fassier-Boulanger[17] or Raphaël Schirmer[18] on Jura wines and on Muscadet.

This research in Bordeaux, at least as far as recent publications are concerned, belongs to the revival of French historiography into themes about wine and vine terroir and territories, with research being carried out in various French vineyards, such as Champagne by Benoît Musset[19], the Languedoc by Geneviève Gavignaud-Fontaine and Gilbert Larguier[20], Cognac[21] and Bourgogne (Burgundy)[22]. With this in mind, the economic dynamics have been carefully studied by Anne Wegener Sleeswijk for her work on the market for French wines in the United Provinces in the 18th century[23] and by Stéphane Le Bras and his thesis on the wine

---

15 Lachaud S., *Le Sauternais moderne. Histoire de la vigne, du vin et des vignerons des années 1650 à la fin de l'Ancien Régime*, Bordeaux, Fédération Historique du Sud-Ouest, 2012.

16 Bonin H., *Les vins de la Gironde dans la compétition mondiale*, forthcoming, 2019. hubertbonin.fr/les-vins-de-gironde-dans-la-competition-mondiale/.

17 Fassier-Boulanger S., *Le vignoble du Jura*, Bordeaux, Presses universitaires de Bordeaux, 2004. See also Fassier-Boulanger S. and Legouy F. (eds.), "Vins, vignes et vignerons en France et dans le monde", *Historiens et géographes*, n° 402 and n° 404, May 2008 and October-November 2008.

18 Schirmer R., *Le Muscadet: histoire et géographie du vignoble nantais*, Bordeaux, Presses Universitaires de Bordeaux, 2010.

19 Musset B., *Vignobles de Champagne et vins mousseux, 1650-1830: histoire d'un mariage de raison*, Paris, Fayard, 2008; Claudine Wolikow and Serge Wolikow, *Champagne! Histoire inattendue*, Éditions de l'Atelier, 2012.

20 Gavignaud-Fontaine G. and Larguier G., *Le vin en Languedoc et en Roussillon. De la tradition aux mondialisations XVIe-XXIe siècle*, Canet, Trabucaire, 2007.

21 MacCullen L., *Le Commerce des eaux-de-vie sous l'Ancien Régime. Une spécialisation régionale charentaise*, Paris, Le Croît vif, 2002.

22 Abric L., *Les grands vins de Bourgogne de 1750 à 1870. Production, commerce, clientèle*, Dijon, éditions de l'Armaçon, 2008. See also, on the Beauce: Béaur G., "Les vignerons beaucerons à la fin de l'Ancien Régime", *La France d'Ancien Régime. Études réunies en l'honneur de Pierre Goubert*, Toulouse, Privat, 1984, p. 35-45.

23 Wegener Sleeswijk A., *Les vins français aux Provinces-Unies au XVIIIe siècle. Négoce, dynamique institutionnelle et la restructuration du marché*, thèse, École des Hautes Etudes en Sciences Sociales, Paris, Universiteit van Amsterdam, 2006.

trading world in the Hérault department in the 20th century[24]. In 2011, also a book was published, edited by Serge Wolikow and Olivier Jacquet, on wine terroirs from the 18th to the 21st century which are seen as territories produced by a historic construction[25]. We should also note the work by Stéphane Le Bras into small vineyards[26]. What all these studies have in common is to imagine the vineyards as a production system with different actors whose level of involvement appears more or less in detail. Several recent colloquia held in Bordeaux defined the foundations for the thinking that was showcased in the Bordeaux *Wine Studies* symposia *L'Univers du vin* in 2012[27], *La construction de la grande propriété viticole en France et en Europe* in 2013[28] and *Ville et vin* in 2017[29]. These different events focussed each time on different networks in the production, marketing and promotion of wine, whether these be owners, workers, investors, merchants, institution, brokers, retail sellers, consumers, etc.

Seeing the importance of *Wine Studies* in France and the rather particular implication of Bordeaux historians and geographers on these topics, it was therefore quite timely to pursue this historiographic revival with an international conference at University Bordeaux Montaigne. The aim of this new scientific meeting lay in a diachronic approach aimed at showing the interlocking of the different scales present in "the world of wine", such as the multi-form networks which cross over and interfere in this environment, from production to consumption. The objective was to study the actors in these networks who, down the years, have been obliged to adapt to local, national and international pressures,

---

24 Le Bras S., *Négoce et négociants en vins dans l'Hérault: pratiques, influences, trajectoires (1900-1970)*, under press, with a geographical perspective widened to all the Languedoc, Presses Universitaires de Rennes and François Rabelais de Tours.

25 Jacquet O. and Wolikow S., *Territoires et terroirs du vin du XVIIIe au XXIe siècles: approche internationale d'une construction historique*, Dijon, Éditions Universitaires de Dijon, 2011.

26 Le Bras S. (ed.), *Les petits vignobles: des territoires en question*, Presses universitaires de Rennes-Presses universitaires François Rabelais de Tours, Rennes-Tours, 2017.

27 Bodinier B., Lachaud S. and Marache C. (eds.), *L'univers du vin: hommes, paysages et territoires*, Caen-Rennes, Association d'Histoire des Sociétés Rurales-Presses Universitaires de Rennes, 2014.

28 Figeac-Monthus M. and Lachaud-Martin S. (eds.), *La construction de la grande propriété viticole en France et en Europe XVIe-XXe siècles*, Bordeaux, Féret, 2015.

29 Colloquium held in Bordeaux in November 2017, directed by Marguerite Figeac-Monthus and Stéphanie Lachaud-Martin, forthcoming publication by Presses universitaires de Bordeaux in 2019.

perspectives and constraints whether these be legal, normative, economic, commercial, social or cultural. The main themes tackled therefore bear on the regulation and the control of wine production, the role of distributors and the different commercial players in the circulation of wine products, the transfer and transmission of knowledge and know-how in the production and marketing of wine, and taking into account consumer expectations according to the type, the quality and the areas where the wine is commercialised.

These lines of questioning have their place in the studies into links between rural production and urban spaces, which have been studied in depth at University Bordeaux Montaigne by Corinne Marache and Philippe Meyzie, during the regional programme Vivalter (2012-2016), "La ville, espace de valorisation des produits du terroir du XVIe siècle à nos jours" (The Town, a space for the appreciation of terroir products from the 16th century to the present day) which was recently published under the title *Les produits de terroir. L'empreinte de la ville (Terroir products. The mark of the town)*, in 2015[30]. The town figures clearly as much as a space as it is an instrument in the valorisation on different scales of agricultural products, by insisting on the play between actors who are complementary. This research programme has been extended by the current programme TERESMA (Produits des terroirs, espaces et marchés/ Products of terroirs, spaces and markets)[31], also co-directed by Corinne Marache and Philippe Meyzie, and it is particularly interested in the actors, the networks and the mechanisms at work in the production, processing, distribution and consumption of products from the terroirs, in the dissemination of know-how, reputation, distinction, etc. How do they get to be known beyond their home terroir, what are their links and how do they fit into the economy of their place of production? Another regional programme, headed by Stéphanie Lachaud, focusses on sweet wines in Aquitaine and particularly on the actors who, at different levels and at different times in the production, processing and distribution of these wines, have contributed to the enhancement of techniques, of reputation and of the specialisation of these terroirs. It is for this reason that the regional programmes TERESMA and Liquoreux d'Aquitaine

30 Marache C. and Meyzie P. (eds.), *Les produits de terroir. L'empreinte de la ville*, Presses Universitaires de Rennes-Presses Universitaires François Rabelais, collection "Tables des Hommes", Rennes, 2015.

31 https://teresma.hypotheses.org/.

(hosted by the research team CEMMC (Centre d'Études des Mondes Moderne et Contemporain/ Centre for the study of the modern and contemporary worlds) have supported this second meeting of the *Wine Studies Research Network*.

In fact, this idea of terroir today constitutes a kind of semantic commonplace, used widely in marketing and communication centred on products and on wine in particular, but where the transposition to other places and other languages poses some difficulties. Recently, in November 2017 for the French version and two years earlier in English, Thomas Parker published an essay on the concept of terroir, showing that it is well and truly a French idea, a sort of cultural mythology and according to him it developed between the Renaissance and the French Revolution[32]. However, the topic of this book is the role of man in the production and marketing of wine. Thomas Parker's remark is all the more interesting since it shows that research into the history of wine is not divided into two, between the "old" and the "new" worlds of wine: on the contrary, a good deal of research is currently focussing on the influences, complementarities and common issues. One example is the thesis by Guyonne Blanchy who has shown how the Mendoza vineyard in Argentina has benefitted from input from the Bordeaux vitivinicole model and from human and economic networks between Europe and South America. Another case is the thesis recently submitted by Mikaël Pierre on the vitivinicole exchanges between France and Australia in the 19th century.

This book therefore proposes an original synthesis on the topic of economic intermediation. In fact, while this theme has already been tackled at other levels of analysis, such as the world of brokerage (with a colloquium organised by Vincent Demon, Matthieu Scherman and Anne Wegener Sleeswijk[33], articles[34] on work carried out on the consuls in the

---

32 Parker T., *Tasting French Terroir: The History of an Idea*, Oakland, University of California Press, 2015; *Le gout du terroir: histoire d'une idée française*, Rennes-Tours, Presses universitaires de Rennes-Presses François-Rabelais, 2017.

33 Demon V., Scherman M. and Wegener Sleeswijk A. (eds.), *Le pouvoir des courtiers: univers marchand et acteurs du courtage en Europe (XIVe-XVIIIe siècles)*, Paris, Éditions rue d'Ulm, 2018.

34 Lachaud-Martin S., "Les courtiers bordelais, intermédiaires de commerce du vin aux XVIIe-XVIIIe siècles", *Revue historique*, 2018, n° 686, p. 321-346.

Mediterranean[35]), it has never been broached through the lens of the vitivinicole world. The comparatist, pluridisciplinary and international dimensions of the views expressed here are thus somewhat new, especially with the perspective over the long-term (17th-21st centuries). The articles brought together here first examine the question of the development and adaptation of markets, concentrating on the merchants, the agents and other prescribers of purchases and taste. Several following articles analyse the role of public and private intermediaries (brokers, cooperatives...) in the production, marketing and consumption of wine. Finally, there are some thoughts on the networks woven in the world of wine, on the consequences and influences of migrants and migration in the vitivinicole world or even the links which exist between wine and identity, and these will throw fresh light on the field of *Wine Studies*, which is still undergoing extensive revision. The selection of the countries studied in this book is not the result of an editorial choice, but of papers we received for the symposium from which it came out. Nevertheless, the areas investigated in Europe (France, Italy, Great Britain, United Provinces), the United States, Australia and South Africa prove to be meaningful. They show the diversity of the vine and wine territories and reveal their specificities, their similarities, their links and their respective influences, in terms of wine production, distribution and consumption.

---

35 Bartolomei A., Calafat G., Grenet M. and Ulbert J. (eds.), *De l'utilité commerciale des consuls. L'institution consulaire et les marchands dans le monde méditerranéen (XVIIe-XXe siècles)*, Rome-Madrid, Publications de l'École française de Rome, 2017.

State of the Field in Wine Studies

Wine as an Instrument of Global History

Kathleen A. Brosnan

An anonymous author once penned, "Water separates the people of the world; wine unites them"[1]. Designed to celebrate the communitarian value of wine, this poetic phrase nonetheless obfuscates an important historical reality. Rather than barriers, oceans and rivers long have served as regional, national, and international highways of commerce. They have connected the world's distant peoples in trade, and, in turn, in interconnected environmental, social, and political transformations. The history of wine is such a story of migration. Waterways provided transport networks for wine, and all that wine entailed – vines and their pests, viticultural and enological knowledge, and consumer preferences. As ships moved *vitis vinifera* from Eurasia to Africa, the Americas, and Australasia, wine functioned as an instrument of ecological imperialism, settler colonialism, and cultural homogenisation.

The international movement of commodities, people, capital, culture and ideas, as well as the dispersion of flora, fauna, and microbes – has occurred for millennia. Trade goods, including living beings, flowed across porous, ever-shifting political borders. Vines and wines were part of this traffic. There is general consensus that by 5500 BCE, farmers in the Caucasus first domesticated the wild Eurasian grapevine, *vitis vinifera sylvestris*, to produce wines which developed a reputation as a luxury drink. Significant shipments of such finished products would wait perhaps another 2500 years until the development of bottle-necked pottery jars facilitated the storage and carriage of wine over long distances. Vine cultivars, however, began to move sooner leading to the development of wine-growing regions. By 2300 BCE, slaves served wine to the royal household in the Assyrian capital of Nimrod according to evidence found

[1] This phrase has been cited since 1971; it may be older.

in the Ur-Nammu Tablets. Elites encouraged experimentation in local wine production in the eastern Mediterranean. Vineyards thrived in Syria and Palestine. From the eastern shore of the Mediterranean, grape cultivation spread gradually westward to Crete, Greece, Italy, France, and the Iberian Peninsula by 600 BCE. By the Middle Ages, wine was France's major export. Transport was key. A premium was placed on vineyards near navigable waterways, which led to the predominance of wine-growing regions in the Loire (via Nantes), the Ile de France (via Rouen), and Gascony (via Bordeaux), as suppliers to northern Europe's prestige markets. After 600 CE, wine-producing and marketing structures slowly solidified. The Mediterranean littoral produced a huge variety of mostly cheap wines from small farms to meet local mass markets. French wine-growing regions regularly shipped their produce to non-producer countries, especially Bordeaux wines (claret) to Britain, and Burgundy wines to Flanders, the Netherlands, and Scandinavia. Climatic change, notably the "Little Ice Age", circa 1300-1850, altered the wine trade. It encouraged the development of sweet wines in the Mediterranean region, especially during its peak in the 1690s when low temperatures opened the door for Portuguese wines. By the eighteenth century, Bordeaux wine exports reached new heights due to increased demands in Britain and a much smaller, but burgeoning market in the newly independent United States[2].

Starting in the late fifteenth century, Spanish and Portuguese travellers had carried viticulture to the Americas via Atlantic Islands such as the Canaries and Madeira. Carried primarily by Jesuits, it reached Mexico by the 1520s; penetrated much of South America by the 1550s; and reached southern California in 1619. In the 1650s, the Protestant Dutch introduced viticulture to South Africa, where it was consolidated after the 1680s by the arrival of French Huguenots. The British introduced vines to Australia in 1788 and New Zealand by 1819[3].

These transportations of *vitis vinifera* beyond Europe and the larger Mediterranean were part of a significantly expanded global trade from 1500 to 1800. Heading to the Americas, ships carried settlers and manufactured goods, as well as livestock and crops with proven monetary

---

2 Johnson H. and Robinson J., *The World Atlas of Wine* 6th ed., London, Michael Beazley, 2007, p. 12-17.

3 *Ibid.*

value. On the return, European nations brought home raw materials such as furs, timber, fish, tobacco, sugar, and precious metals[4]. In addition to those purposely introduced by colonisers, other plants and animals defined as pests joined diseases as passengers in this expansive global trade, invading and altering local environments. Economists generally discuss this trade "in purely economic terms, but it is also a biological phenomenon; indeed, from a long-term perspective it may be *primarily* a biological phenomenon… the Columbian Exchange is arguably the most important event since the death of the dinosaurs"[5].

Despite significant increases in global trade between 1500 and 1800, these oceanic transports accounted for a relatively small share of the European economy and involved limited instances of the economic integration that distinguished later globalisation. It moved high-value-to-volume products. The best French wines might be shipped great distances, but not the ordinary wines from much of Europe yet only those of the "New World". Individual merchants and investors earned wealth from trade but its aggregate economic impact was slight. For example, England was the most successful trading nation, but into the eighteenth century, domestic agriculture was its most important economic activity by every measurement[6]. Nonetheless, global trade and all that it entailed induced profound ecological changes for marginal ecosystems, indigenous human populations, and animal and plant species.

Taking a macroscopic view of European expansion from 900 to 1900, historian Alfred Crosby introduced the concept of ecological imperialism, arguing that the exchange of species was one of the most important elements in the expansion of human settlement. The movement of species was an essential part of the larger pattern of human

---

4 For example, see Mintz S. W., *Sweetness and Power: The Place of Sugar in Modern American History*, New York, Viking, 1985; Norton M., *Sacred Gifts, Profane Pleasures: A History of Tobacco and Chocolate in the Atlantic World*, Ithaca, Cornell University Press, 2008; and Gilbert E. T. and Reynolds J., *Trading Tastes: Commodity and Cultural Exchange to 1750*, Pearson, 2005.

5 Mann, C., *1493: Uncovering the New World Columbus Created*, New York, Vintage, 2012, p. 7; and Crosby A., *The Columbian Exchange: Biological and Cultural Consequences of 1492*, Greenwood, 1973.

6 Priest T., "Globalization", in Brosnan K. A. (eds.), *The Encyclopedia of American Environmental History*, New York, Facts On File, 2011, p. 627; and Marks R. B., *The Origins of the Modern World: A Global and Ecological Narrative from the Fifteenth to the Twenty-First Century*, New York, Rowman & Littlefield, 2007, p. 67-96.

migration. Crosby initially wrote of the Columbian exchange, or the biological exchanges between Europe and the Americas – "the crunching collision of hemispheric ecosystems that began in 1492"[7]. Crosby's later theory of ecological imperialism expands our understanding of the consequences of human expansion across the globe. He contends that regions of dense animal and plant populations, such as Europe and parts of Africa and Asia, produced species that possessed biological advantages because greater competition and increased immunities allowed them to dominate indigenous species when they entered new regions. Ecological imperialism involved the intentional introductions of crops and livestock and the accidental introductions of diseases, pests, and weeds[8]. Therefore, we must recognise that the introduction of European viticulture in the Americas, Africa, or Australasia was never a benign operation. The cultivation of *vitis vinifera* usurped indigenous plants that previously grew in native soils.

When George Yount became the first non-Indian settler in California's Napa Valley in 1838 and introduced cattle, wheat, and wine grapes, he engaged in a form of ecological imperialism. Despite the presence of small groups of Wappo Indians, Yount and the settlers that soon followed him saw the valley as an underdeveloped wilderness, or as a later historian in 1881 described it, a "whole domain [that] lay in its virginity"[9]. The perception was inaccurate. These Indians did not exist in some primitive state of nature, but instead demonstrated a deep understanding of and complex interactions with the local ecosystem. Skilled native Californians crafted weapons to kill small game and deer on occasion. The Wappo shaped their foodscape by pruning, transplanting, and burning. They scattered seeds of preferred plants to increase their yields. Acorns from the Black Oak and Tanbark Oak trees were perhaps the most important food source. Nuts and berries filled out their diet[10]. The introduction

---

7 Cioc M. and Miller C., "Alfred Crosby interview", *Environmental History* 14, July 2009, p. 563.

8 Crosby A. W., *Ecological Imperialism: The Biological Expansion of Europe: 900-1900* 2nd ed., New York, Cambridge University Press, 2004, p. 269-291.

9 Palmer L. L., *History of Napa and Lake Counties, California*, San Francisco, Slocum, Bowen, & Co., 1881, p. 49.

10 Anderson M. K., *Tending the Wild: Native American Knowledge and Management of California's Natural Resources*, Berkeley, University of California Press, 2005, p. 45, 61, 262, 287, 348; Driver H. E., *Wappo Ethnography*, Berkeley, University of California Publications in *American Archaeology and Ethnology* 36 (3) (1936), p. 184;

of market-based crops and livestock supplanted a native-cultivated landscape of indigenous plants and animals in Napa, replicating a process that occurred across the "New World".

Tom Griffiths, Libby Robin, William Cronon, and Thomas Dunlap are among the historians who contend that this ecological component of human migration was more complicated than simple biology[11]. The colonisation of lands on the peripheries involved the sometimes unconscious introduction and sometimes purposeful imposition of culture through the human prioritising of species and physical spaces. Within settler societies, people transported various human attitudes toward nature and toward daily living that helped to promote certain species while contributing to the decline of others. The Jesuits' introduction of *vitis vinifera* across much of the Americas was essential to their religious mission. Migrants also imported legal systems that codified the supposedly proper use of land and water resources. They brought crops, farming practices, and assumptions about cuisine from the Old World. They invested in the land beyond the mere commercial expansion of an empire, attempting to create a home that offered some cultural familiarity. Recognising the unavoidable meshing of ecology and culture inherent in ecological imperialism, in turn, brings us to the theories of settler colonialism that can provide a larger contextualisation for probing the networks and scales of wine.

Settler colonial states include wine-producing nations such as Canada, Australia, New Zealand, South Africa, Argentina, Chile, and the United States. Its scholarly adherents contrast settler colonialism from other systems. Resource extraction (such as mining) and labour exploitation (such as chattel slavery) occurred in these societies, but neither was the

---

Hoffman J., *Trees of Napa Valley*, University of California Cooperative Extension & Master Gardeners of Napa Valley, 2002; *Native American Garden: A Guide to Plants and Their Uses*, Calistoga, Cal., Bothe State Park, n.d., cited in Paula Amen Judah and Lauren Coodley, with the Napa County Historical Society, Charleston, S.C., Arcadia, 2011, p. 11-17; and Beard Y. S., *The Wappo: A Report*, Banning, CA, Malki Museum Press, 1979, p. 52.

11 Griffiths T. and Robin L. (eds.), *Ecology and Empire: Environmental History of Settler Societies*, Seattle, University of Washington Press, 1997; Cronon W., *Changes in the Land: Indians, Colonists, and the Ecology of New England* rev. ed., New York, Hill and Wang, 2003; and Dunlap T., *Nature and the English Diaspora: Environment and History in the United States, Canada, Australia, and New Zealand*, New York, Cambridge University Press, 1999.

principal objective of settler colonial projects. These projects sought land. Their colonists envisioned and attempted to construct "new, permanent, reproductive, and racially exclusive" societies. They had no plans to return to the mother country, nor did these settlers intend to merge with, submit to, or even permanently dominate native peoples[12]. Even when settler societies relied on indigenous labour, the historian Patrick Wolfe observes, settler societies ultimately aimed for the "elimination of the native"[13]. In Napa Valley in the 1830s and 1840s, Yount and other white settlers initially relied on Indian workers. In the end, however, the settlers' ultimately successful goal was to remove the Indians from the valley[14]. The Wappo's numbers in Napa Valley dipped to fewer than 800 in the 1840s, and possibly as few as 200 members in the 1850s as Napa and California's population grew exponentially with the gold rush. With forced relocations, few Wappo remained in their Napa homelands by the end of the nineteenth century; indigenous place names were all that persisted[15].

Settler colonial societies around the globe relied on similar spatial constructs, power structures, and social narratives. They began with the concept of *terra nullius*, or the perception that lands in long-term use by indigenous peoples were empty, underused, or "virgin" as Napa was described. Asserting sovereignty and legal authority, the new arrivals

---

[12] Hernández K. L., *City of Inmates: Conquest, Rebellion, and the Rise of Human Caging in Los Angeles, 1771-1965*, Chapel Hill, University of North Carolina Press, 2017, p. 7; Adas M., "Settler Colony to Global Hegemon: Integrating the Exceptionalist Narrative of the American Experience into World History", *American Historical Review* 106, 5, December 2001, p. 1692-1720; Belich J., *Replenishing the Earth: The Settler Revolution and the Rise of the Anglo World, 1783-1939*, New York, Oxford University Press, 2009; and Hixson W. L., *American Settler Colonialism: A History*, New York Palgrave Macmillan, 2013.

[13] Wolfe P., "Settler Colonialism and the Elimination of the Native", *Journal of Genocide Studies* 8, December 2006, p. 387.

[14] Revere J. W., *A Tour of Duty in California*, New York, C. Francis and Company, 1849, p. 100.

[15] As late as 2010, the self-identified Wappo population was only at 291. U.S. Census, 2010, American Indian and Alaska Native Tribes in the United States and Puerto Rico, found at http://www.census.gov/population/www/cen2010/cph-t/t-6tables/TABLE%20(1).pdf. Also Gudde E. G., *California Place Names: The Origin and Etymology of Current Geographical Names*, revised and expanded by Bright W., 4th edition, Berkeley, University of California Press, 1998, p. 256.

carved indigenous lands into private property[16]. Settlers justified such actions as simple economic improvements, but they also infused their efforts with the rhetoric calling forth larger civilising purposes. Historian Erica Hannickel, who embeds viticulture within horticulture in the United States, argues, "growing grapes was not just a material practice, it was a powerful ideology, set of aesthetics, and ubiquitous discourse of national power"[17]. Viticulture became linked in the American imagination with continental expansion and Manifest Destiny. Historian Julie McIntyre and sociologist John Germov share a similar narrative in telling the history of viticulture in Australia's Hunter Valley and the usurpation of Aboriginal lands. "The answer to the question 'why wine grapes in the Hunter?' was a combination of imperial ideologies and aspirations, and theories about plant cultivation that were not yet formalised into science. First, there was a concentration of early settlers in the Hunter who were influenced by currents of thought about winegrowing as a higher form of cultivation than some other crops; a symbol of respectable, civilised settlement"[18].

Historically, what people ate and drank and how they ate and drank it were intrinsically environmental and intrinsically cultural, based on available local resources but also dictated by rituals and traditions. The importation of *vitis vinifera* constituted forms of ecological imperialism and settler colonialism with all that they entailed. Embodying complex values ranging from religious sanctity to ethnic pride and elitism, wine was part of a material culture carried from home and continuously re-shaped by settlers and their successors in new social milieus and physical environments. Lorenzo Veracini, a leading scholar in settler colonial studies, reminds us, "Settler colonialism makes sense especially if it is understood globally, and that we live in a settler colonial global present"[19].

---

16 "Debates around settler colonial studies have been contentious, especially around intersections between settler colonial racism and identity politics". For further discussion see "Settler Colonialism" Global Social Theory website at https://globalsocialtheory.org/concepts/settler-colonialism/.

17 Hannickel E., *Empire of Vines: Wine Culture in America*, Philadelphia, University of Pennsylvania Press, 2013, p. 14. Hannickel focuses more on the creation and dissemination of viticultural discourses than their impact and reception.

18 McIntyre J. and Germov J., *Hunter Wine: A History*, Sydney, NewSouth, 2018, p. 37.

19 Veracini L., *The Settler Colonial Present*, Palgrave Macmillan, 2015, p. 53.

The global expansion of *vitis vinifera* was part of the tandem, intrinsically interconnected, and ongoing processes of ecological imperialism and settler colonialism. Again, however, these processes began in an era of global trade, not globalisation. This commerce involved limited levels of economic integration regionally or globally and consisted primarily of high-value-to-volume products. Consequently, it included only a limited number of wines. Most vintages lacked the quality or stability to justify the cost of transport over long distances. These limitations on the wine industry continued even as the world became entrenched in the first era of globalisation by the mid-nineteenth century. Globalisation, according to many economic historians, is distinguished from the global trade that preceded it. A contemporary definition describes "the phenomenon as the integration of commodity, capital and labour markets on a global scale". Market integration occurred when commodity prices converged, or when prices for the same commodity in different regional or local markets around the world approached each other. Using this definition, there have been two eras of globalisation. The first lasted until World War I; the second began around 1980[20].

The Industrial Revolution was the key development in the first era of globalisation. Exploitation of coal-powered production boosted trade on a global scale. Fossil fuels radically transformed manufacturing and transportation. Steamships and railroads lowered international transport costs and integrated new regions, new resources, and new workforces into the world economy. Mass trade in basic commodities – not just luxuries or high-value-to-volume products but lower-value-to-volume bulk products such as cotton, wheat, tropical fruits, petroleum – became profitable for the first time. Mass trade led to international price convergences[21]. A mass market for wine did develop in many industrial nations as expanding working class and urban populations demanded cheap wines, but most countries met this demand through their own vineyards. The transportation of grapevines and the exchange of wine expertise and technology continued to be part of global trade, but while

---

20 Priest, "Globalization", p. 627; and Held D., McGrew A., Godblatt D., and Perraton J., *Global Transformations: Politics, Economics, and Culture*, Stanford, CA, Stanford University Press, 1999, p. 153-161.

21 Marks, *Origins of the Modern World*, p. 98-107; and Crosby A. W., *Children of the Sun: A History of Human's Insatiable Appetite for Energy*, New York, W.W. Norton, 2007, p. 65-79.

premium vintages demanded increasingly consistent and high prices across the globe, ordinary wines were not subject to price convergence nor deemed sufficiently valuable to demand long-distance trade[22].

The "new imperialism" that underlay the first era of globalisation also intensified nationalist, imperial, and military competition between European nations, culminating in World War I. During the next two decades, the first global economy disintegrated. Postwar reparations and advanced economies' adherence to the gold standard, among other factors, magnified the Great Depression while protectionism shattered global markets. Commodity price gaps returned to earlier levels[23]. A marked swing toward economic nationalism contributed to World War II. Following the war, restrictions on currency convertibility, along with the fact that trade was generally conducted on a bilateral basis, limited global market integration. During the 1950s and 1960s, cheap and accessible hydrocarbons fuelled surges in production, trade and population in industrialised nations, but decolonisation and the extension of the cold war to the developing places destabilised the international system. A global dollar glut and OPEC's emergence weakened the West's hegemonic leadership in the world economy. These developments ushered in an extended stagnation in the 1970s, but also set precedents for the second global economy. By 1980, the deregulation of financial markets, combined with the spread of high-speed telecommunication links, spurred a dramatic expansion in global financial flows and networks and led to high levels of speculative activity. The market convergences that defined globalisation followed[24]. Before 1980, with the exception of France, most European nations had limited wine export sectors. With few exceptions, viticulture in Australia, Africa, and the Americas was limited to local markets. After 1980, Italy and Spain claimed new market shares. Led by Australia and the United States (albeit primarily California), New World producers adopted more efficient production, distribution, marketing and tourism techniques that enabled them in the 1990s to claim growing market shares in northern Europe, North America, and Southeast and

---

22 On larger global trends in the wine market, see Anderson K., Nelgen S., and Pinalla V., *Global Wine Markets: A Statistical Compendium, 1860 to 2016*, Adelaide, University of Adelaide Press, 2017.

23 Marks, *Origins of the Modern World*, p. 141, 170-172.

24 Crosby, *Children of the Sun*, p. 87-101; Held, et al., *Global Transformations*, p. 425-427; and Marks, *Origins of the Modern World*, p. 174-188.

East Asia. There was increasing price convergence within different wine categories, particularly at the lower end. This growth of the New World wine sales reflected the general acceleration of globalisation[25].

This second era of globalisation prompted historians to consider new approaches, such as transnational history, that emphasised the movement of expertise, technology, and species as people grappled with solutions for different locational realities. Scholars question how well arbitrary political borders explained the ways in which people experienced time and space in the past. Environmental historians ask whether political borders adequately explained the migration of ideas regarding nature or the movement of commodities and biotic entities. Transnational history rejects the nation-state as the sole analytical unit, although it may be one of many analytical units. Instead we might contemplate the dialectical engagement between the local, the national and the global. These are, among other things, matters of spatial scale – created partially through social constructions and partially through environmental conditions. Historical understanding depends on finding the appropriate scales, even while using notional entities such as the New World. The history we write is profoundly shaped by the spatial frame we choose. Historical phenomena look different when interpreted as local, national or global. Moreover, space is dynamic and integrated. Historical phenomena occurred on spatial scales that intersect, interpenetrate, and superimpose themselves. No single scale is sufficient to understand ecological problems or complex production systems such as viticulture[26].

The past few decades have witnessed engaging transnational studies on world commodities, such as salt, sugar, cotton, fish, coffee, and potatoes[27]. Wine is distinguishable from these, however, because it is one

---

25 Also see "Overflow – World's Wine Trade: A Survey", *The Economist*, 24 December 1983, p. 3-18; Rachman G., "The Globe in a Wine Glass", *The Economist*, 18 December 1999, p. 91-92; "Terroir and Technology", *The Economist*, 18 December 1999, p. 92-95; "The Price Puzzle", *The Economist*, 18 December 1999, p. 95-97; and Tabor G. M., *Judgment of Paris: California vs. France and the Historic 1976 Paris Tasting that Revolutionized Wine*, New York, Scribner, 2005, p. 230-241.

26 On spatial scale, see White R., "The Nationalization of Nature", *Journal of American History* 86, December 1999, p. 976-986. For an example of transnational environmental history, see Evans S., *Bound in Twine: The History and Ecology of the Henequen-Wheat Complex for Mexico and the American and Canadian Plains, 1880-1950*, College Station, Texas A&M University Press, 2013.

27 Kurlansky M., *Cod: A Biography of the Fish that Changed the World*, New York, Penguin, 1998 and *Salt: A World History*, New York, Penguin, 2003; Beckert S., *Empire of*

of the few global products identified so clearly by its specific local place of production. Unlike most distilled alcohols, wines were portrayed by many in the industry as natural products that embodied *terroir*. On a national level, different countries' appellation systems allowed consumers to associate the liquid in their glasses with specific places. Every wine-producing country regulated when a grower may use a place name on a label. Some nations such as France, further limited the grape varieties and winemaking methods that may be employed within the given region. International agreements also regulated labels. All internationally traded wines were created from *vitis vinifera* or its hybrids, vines that travelled from Eurasia around the world. Thus, a single bottle of wine embodied the local, the national, and the global.

In an age of globalisation growers and vintners around the world borrowed from each other, utilising expertise and production technology or mimicking marketing patterns such as varietal labelling and tourism schemes. This second era of globalisation, particularly with the availability of air travel and the communication of consumer choices through multiple media, has contributed to a growing homogenisation of taste preferences in wine and other products. In the past, regions around the world developed and drank wines that perhaps reflected their distinctive environments or cultural experiences. For example, for more than a century, well into the 1980s, Canadians who drank wines often imbibed those made from locally grown French hybrids or *vitis labrusca*. Sweetened and fortified to mask musky tones inherent in such grapes, these wines grew out of fashion as Canadians participating in the global marketplace drank more wine generally and began to choose drier imported table wines that became the norm within perhaps five years. These trends led to a cool climate viticultural revolution in British Columbia and the Niagara Peninsula with the substitution of *vitis vinifera* for native grapes and the replacement of tender fruit orchards with vineyards and tourist tasting rooms[28]. In another example, to some French critics, New World wines that relied on varietal labelling and fruit forward palates

---

Cotton: A Global History, New York, Vintage, 2015; Reader J., *Potato: A History of the Propitious Esculent*, New Haven, CT, Yale University Press, 2011; and Pendergrast M., *Uncommon Grounds: The History of Coffee and How It Changed Our World*, New York, Basic Books, 2010.

28 Bramble L., *Niagara's Wine Visionaries: Profiles of the Pioneering Winemakers*, Lorimer, 2014; Schreiner J. M., *The Wines of Canada*, Mitchell Beasley, 2005, chapters 2-4 *passim*.

reflected global homogenisation, particularly in the lower end products. Yet French growers faced their own crisis in declining wine consumption among fellow citizens who choose from a bevy of beverages available in the global marketplace[29].

Mondovino, the well-known 2004 documentary by the American filmmaker Jonathan Nossiter, explored the impact of globalisation on different wine regions across the globe. In some ways, the film revealed the complexities of the wine trade by identifying the important roles played by people other than the growers and viticulturists. In doing so, Nossiter pits noted critics, influential consultants, and powerful publicly traded corporations against supposed traditionalists. The documentary argues that the former group is undermining quality by "enforcing a bland, mass-produced taste on a world of wine drinkers who fancy themselves connoisseurs but basically like what they are told to like"[30]. Doing so erases or obscures the character of the land where the grape is grown. Nossiter, also a sommelier, is a dedicated proponent of the concept of *terroir*, but in its simplistic narrative that "big equals bad", the film, as well as Nossiter's subsequent book, fails to consider important players in the global wine trade, from the Australians who radically shifted market trends in the 1990s to the actual consumers exercising the power of their wallets and the preferences of their palates. It also fails to place wine in the larger economic and ecological context. However, the story is more complicated. Despite the supposed loss of local character bemoaned by viticultural traditionalists and the fact that many consumers focus on the varietal more than the appellation, other buyers, particularly in the premium sector, still emphasised place of production in their purchases[31].

At the Bordeaux conference that led to this volume, one participant inquired about the implications for the wine industry of new tariffs and other forms of economic nationalism that have arisen across the world in the second decade of the twenty-first century. While many

---

29 Anderson, et al., *Global Wine Markets*, p. 470-503; "Overflow", p. 5-6, 9, 11-12, 14; "The Disappearing Drinker," *The Economist*, 18 December 1999, p. 118-119; and "The Brand's the Thing", *The Economist*, 18 December 1999, p. 113-117.

30 Ebert R., *Mondovino* movie review, *Chicago Sun Times*, 12 May 2005, at https://www.rogerebert.com/reviews/mondovino-2005; and *Mondovino*, a film by Jonathan Nossiter (Diaphana Films, 2004).

31 Lechmere A., "Mondovino Reviewed", *Decanter*, 20 October 2004, at https://www.decanter.com/wine-news/mondovino-reviewed-99887/; and Nossiter J., *Liquid Memory: Why Wine Matters*, New York, Farrar, Straus and Giroux, 2009, p. 11-18.

consumers have benefitted from the lower prices associated with market convergences, inequities in both developed and developing nations have emerged that have prompted resistance to globalisation but are too numerous and complicated to elaborate here[32]. If new trade wars emerge, how will this affect wine markets? As a historian, my fallback position is that I can at best offer parables based on the past rather than predictions. If future tariffs target wine exports, history and theories of economic elasticity suggests the most significant impacts would be at the lower end of the market, while products in the premium categories would be less affected because those who can afford luxury items would continue to pursue them. However, it is important to remember that even in the second era of globalisation, the wine market has never been fully free from government oversight. In some nations, regulations and taxes reflect persistent neo-Prohibitionist values and revenue-generating schemes, while winegrowers in other countries benefit from agricultural subsidies that enhance their competitiveness[33]. As the past suggests, winemakers will adjust to their shifting economic and political landscape. Whether those adjustments result in geographically distinctive products or increasing homogenisation, or alternatively take some third path, is unknown.

As scholars, there is perhaps a tendency to embrace the supposed essentiality of cultural heterogeneity just as ecologists have strongly emphasised the importance of biodiversity to planetary health. These processes of cultural homogenisation that continued through ecological imperialism, settler colonialism, and globalisation arguably mirror Crosby's conclusion that "the Columbian exchange was and is simply

32 Friedman T. L., *The Lexus and the Olive Tree: Understanding Globalization* rev. ed. New York, Picador, 2012, 1999; Helleiner E. and Pickel A. (eds.), *Economic Nationalism in a Globalizing World*, Ithaca, Cornell University Press, 2004; and Stiglitz J. E., *Globalization and Its Discontents Revisited: Anti-Globalization in the Era of Trump*, New York, W.W. Norton, 2017.

33 Regarding European Union subsidies, see "Put a Cork in It", *The Economist*, 27 June 1998, p. 87-88. Also see Annual Report, Ontario Liquor Control Board, 2014-2015, at http://www.lcbo.com/content/dam/lcbo/corporate-pages/about/pdf/LCBO_AR14-15-english.pdf; and Pittman D. J., "The New Temperance Movement", *Addiction* 88, February 1993, p. 167-178.

an early phase in the slide toward worldwide biological homogeneity"[34]. Wine, because of its traditional association with specific places of production, allows us to ask complex questions about the implications of these synthetic processes. Wine has involved the replacement of native fauna, colonisers' subjugation of Indigenous peoples and indigenous lands, and hegemonic expressions of culture. Operating on intersecting spatial scales, wines have provided persistent connections to nature through their expression of local character while uniting many consumers and their preferences across the world. As English historian Arnold Toynbee once observed, "Anyone who knows history… must surely know his wines". This essay poses more questions than it answers, but demonstrates that our study of wine can and should expand our understanding of these larger global trends.

[34] Cioc and Miller, "Alfred Crosby", p. 563. Crosby adds, "we will never get there because the world's climates and soils, etc., are heterogeneous, but we are bound to continue at higher and higher speeds in that direction, scattering ecological dislocations in all directions", p. 563-64.

Overview of Current PhD Theses in Wine Studies

Cultivating imperial networks: British colonial wine production at the Cape of Good Hope and South Australia, 1806-1910

Chelsea Davis – George Washington University

This dissertation focuses on the British Empire's colonial wine industries at the Cape of Good Hope and South Australia from 1806-1910. The wine industries in South Africa and Australia are today some of the most well known and profitable in the world, yet their integration into the global market was a slow, stuttering process, one that started on British colonial foundations during the long 19th century. It is about investigating how the wine industries in the British colonies at the Cape of Good Hope and South Australia *needed* to invest in global networks of knowledge, communication, trade, and transport in order to transform into successful global enterprises. In a way, the history of Britain's colonial wine industries is a microcosm of the story of globalisation. The need for an export market and the creation of 'taste' for wine ultimately required making connections to the outside world. This commodity history will be used to argue that a colonial industry can only succeed when it becomes tied to global trade and invests in networks of knowledge. This comparative history will provide more than dollars and cents to understanding colonial wine; it will show how commodities have social lives of their own.

The introduction, sustenance, and management of Britain's colonial wine industries were contingent on the skills of local colonists, the availability of free or forced labour, scientific and cultural exchanges in knowledge, and, above all, the involvement of colonial governments. This project will include five chapters. Chapter 1 will focus on the social aspect of the growers and producers in each colony. Chapter 2 will focus on the labour used in vineyards – at the Cape this was non-white slave (and later marginalised wage) labour, whereas in South Australia it was white European labour. Chapter 3 will address the role of the colonial government in both promoting or discouraging their colonial wine industries. This ranged from the creation of bureaucratic positions seeking to improve the industry, to the later abolishment of preferential duties on colonial goods. Chapter 4 will consider the cultural implications of wine as a 'civilising tool' for the colonies. Chapter 5 will shift its focus to the environment, seeing how the grape vine disease phylloxera impacted the colonial environments and facilitated exchanges in agricultural knowledge. These themes rely on the creation of networks which ultimately allowed Cape and South Australian wine to be integrated into the global market.

"Natural" winemaking in the global hierarchy of values: an ethnography of female winegrowers in Northern and Southern Italy

Clelia Viecelli – University of Southampton

This research project aims at investigating the production and consumption of "natural" wines, through an ethnographic account of the work undertaken by female winegrowers based in two regions of Northern and Southern Italy, Piedmont and Sicily. The current objectives of this ethnographic research on "natural" wines are structured through three main themes.

First, this thesis intends to shed light on the way both global and local forces participate in the process of "natural" winemaking, through an ethnographic account of the work and lives of female "natural" winegrowers in two Italian regions (taking into account their online presence as Facebook users as well). The objective is to explore the artisanal dimension of this production through a focus on the importance of manual work during harvesting and pruning activities.

Then, it enquires into specific conceptions of "nature", "culture" and "tradition" as they unfold in the actions and narratives of these female wine producers. Moreover, as these "natural" winemakers generally prefer to use autochthonous grape varieties and indigenous yeasts, it is necessary to consider how this choice can be evaluated through a *terroir* perspective.

Lastly, it investigates how specific aesthetic evaluations form the basis not only of a discourse on the appreciation of these contesting and contested wines, but also of a more encompassing cosmology for these wine producers. To do so, it is necessary to take into account the sensorial aesthetic of "natural" wines as a point of entry into notions of "joy", "pleasure", and a more general being in the world which reconnects to the women's relationship with nature and their ethical stances as "natural" winegrowers.

Vineyard and vines in Cahors (1650-1850)

Sophie Brenac-Lafon – Université Bordeaux Montaigne

In 1650, vine growing was already well established at Cahors and the villages of the Lot valley, in southwestern France. The study of agrarian structures unveils shifts in the distribution of landed properties during the early modern era. While smallholders used to dominate this society, medium-sized landowners started to take over the region, especially in the countryside, during the 18th century. This evolution led to the extension of areas under vine cultivation and the region turned to wine specialisation. Henceforth, all social groups, rural and urban, became involved in wine production. Public figures took great care of their vineyards by hiring skilled vignerons who gradually became vineyard owners themselves. The development of vine growing since the middle of the 17th century led to the gradual evolution of agricultural practices following the French Revolution and enabled the establishment of a wine society and identity. Vineyard enthusiasm was stimulated by the rise of new outlets via the port of Bordeaux to northern Europe, the Caribbean, North America and the East Indies. The Cahors wine most suited to export trade was made from a varietal originating from Auxerre in Burgundy and later called Malbec. The town of Cahors was located at a strategic position at the beginning of the navigable section of the Lot river which is connected to the Garonne river and Bordeaux. The trade networks established between the Quercynois – the inhabitants of the Quercy, region of Cahors – and the négociants of the Chartrons – a suburb of Bordeaux specialised in the wine trade – were essential for the development of the wine industry of Cahors. Despite a complicated context at the end of the Ancien Régime, the vineyard was maintained and even developed in some areas, covering more than half of Cahors *terroir* in the early 19th century.

Investigating the Cahors wine area leads to questioning the situation of the rural world of villages located in the former vineyard but also the urban society of Cahors. For this vineyard did not only comprise smallholders and suburban landowners, it was integrated into larger trade network involving many different stakeholders.

Ackerman: strategy, innovation and territorial roots of a family business (1811-1914)

Valentin Taveau – Université d'Angers

This thesis is part of a project funded by CIFRE (*Conventions Industrielles de Formation par la Recherche*) in partnership with the Ackerman company and treating the history of the Ackerman-Laurance family and company created at Saumur, Maine-et-Loire, Pays-de-la-Loire, France, in 1811. The objective is to analyse the links between the family life and the company life and show how these two groups of players were established and developed in parallel with internal and external events which impacted the family business. Family life, relations to territories, innovations and commercial policy are at the centre of this research into the history of Ackerman-Laurance.

By marrying Émilie Laurance, daughter of an important négociant of Saumur, Jean-Baptiste Ackerman, native of Brussels, managed to introduce himself into the local bourgeoisie, develop his own business and innovate with the production of champagne-style wines in the Loire valley (vineyards of Tours, Anjou and Saumur). Despite having only a modest and inconsistent wealth during the first half of the 19th century, the family business survived thanks to Louis-Ferdinand's efforts from 1863. He transformed the company into a champagne-style wine house, outward-looking to Britain and its empire but also exporting to many cities around the world. Then, several new French players from diverse geographical and social origins became involved in the administration of the company. However, the development of sparkling wines houses at Saumur, the unfair competition or generalised fraud concerning the origin and quality of the wines were critically thwarted by the Champagne wines syndicate which took legal actions against these practices in the late 19th century. In 1894, the Ackerman-Laurance business became a public limited company, Louis Ferdinand being its majority shareholder. But he included his trading partners and some English wine and spirits traders in the company capital. The *Compagnie Générale des vins mousseux de Saumur* then became closely connected to the British market and the international markets in general, depending on the demand and supply of Saumur sparkling wines, and more especially on the promotion of its brand *Royal*. The beginning of the 20th century was a difficult time for the company and the family. Following Louis Ferdinand's natural death in 1914, the family finally lost control of the company.

"France of the Southern Hemisphere": transferring a European wine model to colonial Australia

Mikaël Pierre – Université Bordeaux Montaigne, France / University of Newcastle, Australia

The development of viticulture in Australia mostly drew on European models to spread both wine production and consumption in the colonial societies. Among these models, France gradually appeared as a specific example due to the reputation of its wines and its cultural practices. This thesis intends to analyse the transfers of skills, technologies, vine grape varietals and experts from various French wine regions – mainly Bordeaux, Burgundy and Champagne due to their reputation abroad, and Languedoc for geographical and climatic considerations – to the Australian colonies of New South Wales, Victoria and South Australia. These three colonies then included the most productive wine regions during the 19th century and the most evident marks of a French influence. These transfers, their causes, means and impacts in Australia and France are investigated from the 1810s, when the first wine tours were undertaken by British colonists in France, up to the First World War which disrupted world trade and scientific and human exchanges, noticeably regarding wine knowledge.

A transnational or trans-imperial perspective allows us to point out the circulation of persons, objects and ideas through national and imperial boundaries and through a ternary logic between France,

Britain and the Australian colonies in a context of globalisation. The objective is to show that these technology and cultural transfers mostly relied on private colonial Australians' initiatives in order to transplant one or several French wine models as a way to develop the colonies economically and culturally. Their goal was to spread the consumption of French-style light wines, as they were considered healthier and of higher quality, among the settlers accustomed to spirit and beer-drinking. Furthermore, it was expected to strengthen the trade with the British motherland to secure economic wealth. These initiatives were sometimes thwarted by different difficulties (geographical conditions, cultural habits, political and economic context) or challenged by the development of direct competition with France, especially on the British market.

PART I

Market Development and Adaptation

Wine Merchants and Wine Producers in France in the 18th Century: Between Trust and Mistrust

Benoît Musset

It is a commonplace to say that there are two ways of extracting profit in trade. Sales to purchasers must, on the one hand, be made at the highest price while purchasing from the producer, on the other hand, must be done at the lowest price possible. The ideal arrangement is nevertheless when there is agreement between the two partners: as Boullay, the Canon of Orleans, said in 1723 "when the sale is at a reasonable price, then the bourgeois and the merchant each stand to gain and both are content, or at least, they should be!"[1]

From the mid-17th century a series of disruptions disturbed trade. Firstly, new patterns of commerce emerged which increased competition. Up until then trading patterns had been relatively stable: Paris consumed the wines made in the Paris / Ile de France region, Flanders bought wines from Burgundy and Champagne and the English took Bordeaux wines; many wine-producing estates benefited from secure incomes, selling their wine to the regions bordering the vines that had no vineyards themselves. During the 17th century, two major interruptions came to unsettle this geography: the incursion of the Dutch in the west (Nantes region, Anjou, Saintonge) and the rise in the attractiveness of Paris which captured several wine-producing areas (around Orleans, Tours, part of Anjou, upper Burgundy, Beaujolais…)[2].

After that, the range of wines expanded with a stronger segmentation in the demand. Wines established differences between themselves, older

---

1 Boullay J., *Manière de bien cultiver la vigne dans le vignoble d'Orléans*, Orléans, Jacques Rouzeau, 1723, p. 618.

2 Lachiver M., *Vins, vignes et vignerons. Histoire du vignoble français*, Paris, Fayard, 1988, in particular p. 253-400.

wines emerged as an entirely different category on offer, sparkling wines appeared at the beginning of the 18th century. Some wines stood out, like those from Burgundy and Champagne, sold throughout France and in all of Europe at very high prices. Aristocratic customers bought wines from Spain, Italy, Greece and Hungary[3]. It is true that quantities were limited with regard to the total amount of wine sold, but the luxury wines sector was something quite new and worked along with the market for ordinary wines. As a result, the distribution networks extended: more middlemen, shippers and information needed to be mobilised.

Lastly, the old system of regulation came to be questioned. These are the principal issues which focussed discussion, the question being to know whether private profit should be regulated by political authority. But, as Thomas Brennan has shown, the question regarding wine was also raised in the 1730s[4]. Everywhere, the old brokerage system, which helped guarantee the origin and a price that it was customary to practice, was questioned and even abandoned.

From that point on, how should one proceed so that "the bourgeois and the merchant each stand to gain"? These disruptions unsettled those involved, even though it took a generation for them to develop, which seems relatively long to us today. We are going to see how relations between producers and merchants were reconfigured in the 18th century. On the surface, they appear to be hateful on account of a merchant mentality which supported dis-honourable merchant practices. The principle of regulating the market was reflected back in those vineyards which were the most integrated into inter-regional wine markets, giving rise to the appearance of powerful merchant-commissioners. However, private but collective devices for regulating the markets were being set up.

---

3 Musset B., "Vins de Champagne et autres 'vins de distinction': le renouvellement de la consommation vinicole des élites en France (1600-1830)", in Demouy P. and Morell M.-H. (eds.), *De la vigne en Champagne au vin de Champagne. De l'âge du Bronze à l'âge industriel*, Dijon, EUD, 2013, p. 161-176. J.-P Poussou has a publication in preparation on Parisian consumption from the 17th century to the 1860s, which will specify the chronology and shed almost definite light on developments from a Parisian point of view. For an initial approach, see Poussou J.-P., "Approches pour une étude de la consommation et du commerce du vin à Paris du début du XVIIe siècle au milieu du XIXe siècle", in Bouneau C. and Figeac M., *Le verre et le vin de la cave à la table du XVIe siècle à nos jours*, Bordeaux, 2007, p. 120-123.

4 Brennan T., *Burgundy to Champagne. The wine trade in early modern France*, The Johns Hopkins University Press, Baltimore & London, 1997, p. 142.

The range of "dis-honourable" practices

The buyers formed coalitions against the sellers, agreeing not to buy anything and to cause the prices to tumble. This practice was denounced by Jean Eon in *Commerce honorable* (Honourable Trade) in 1646. For him this was the typical practice of the Dutch in Nantes. The tactic is simple but fearsome. First of all, "at the beginning they only buy a fairly small quantity of the wines that they need", then they waited for the owners to panic as they worried about their financial situation and ended up selling off their wines because "there are always a great number left to sell"[5].

Brac de la Perrière in the Beaujolais area also bore witness to this practice in the 1750s-1760s. According to him, the Parisian merchants delayed their visit to the wine estates: "instead of making their purchases, according to the old custom, after All Saints Day, at a time when the owners are on the premises, they delayed their buying, after having amused and fatigued the owners with different pretexts". At this point "they made offers but only to wine growers pressed by their own needs, by tax collectors"[6]. Of course, this system worked because nobody made a move and this required a solid, collective discipline on the part of the buyers so that no outsiders came and took all the wines.

The abbot Delachère, at Volnay, also indicated a collective agreement to delay payments in 1770. When the price was announced at 800 *livres* (pounds) for a *queue* (barrel) during the first days of the grape harvest, the buyers agreed between themselves not to take any wine and waited patiently for the producers' costs to rise (storing the wine, paying suppliers of bread during the grape picking). Wine growers came down to 600 pounds and some even knocked the wine down to 400 pounds the following April[7].

The buyers manipulated information to lower the prices through the practice of buying with no price determined. First of all, the buyer identified the wines he wanted; this was a promise of purchase but with

---

5 Eon J., *Le commerce honorable*, Nantes, G. Le Monnier, 1646, p. 90.

6 Brac de La Perrière F., *Le commerce des vins réformés, rectifié et épuré*, Amsterdam and Lyon, Berthoud, 1769, p. 27.

7 Departmental Archives (henceforth AD) in Côte-d'Or, G 4167, 2nd book, f°44; the "*queue*" was 2 barrels of 228 litres.

no price set. This sum was fixed later, in line with the first transactions concluded in the wine estate. Of course, the owner was sure to sell, whatever happened, but he left to price up to the buyer[8]. Then, all that was needed was to discredit the wine to get the price to fall. From that point, the merchants circulated rumours about the poor quality of the wines. Delachère listed the manipulations of merchants and commissioners. In 1749 "the price of wines was 320 pounds on account of tactics by Mirey and commissioners, who from the outset decried them without knowing them"[9]. In 1752, "the merchants took advantage of this weakness to bring down the prices and when their purchases were done they could not help saying that when we had good wine, we didn't know how to sell it"[10]. In 1754, the merchants denigrated that year's wines to shore up the reputation of wines left over from 1753 and sell these at a good price. A new attack was highlighted in 1761 when "some commissioners from Beaune (David junior) wrote after the grape harvest to merchants informing them that the 1761 wines were not good. We have seen the letter. An enormous lie & infinitely damaging to the public & to the commissioners themselves"[11]. Similarly, the merchants easily evoked the threat of a difficult economic situation. In 1745, Delachère denounced the effects of rumour at the time of the War of the Austrian Succession. While this rumour may not have been spread by the commissioners, they still exploited it skilfully: "the fear about the difficulties in transport because of the war did not prevent the merchants from coming to the region to the point where all the bourgeois let their wines be marked with no price"[12]. Finally, they discredited certain vintages so they could snap up the wines more easily. This practice was denounced by Canon Boullay who noted that the merchants "believed that by denigrating the wine from certain places they would obtain it at a better price"[13]. They spread stories about the poor quality, yet all the while finding the wines to be very good.

[8] Musset M., "Le prix de la qualité: les vins de Champagne et de Bourgogne au XVIIIe siècle", *Revue d'histoire moderne et contemporaine*, July-September 2013, 60-3, p. 110-135.

[9] AD Côte-d'Or, G 4167, 2nd book, f°4.

[10] *Ibid.*, 2nd book, f°10.

[11] *Ibid.*, 2nd book, f°27.

[12] *Ibid.*, 1st book, f°36.

[13] Boullay J., *op. cit.*, p. 612.

Another unfair practice consisted in passing off one wine for another. The simplest way was to buy second-rate wines and sell them as quality wines. The great diversity of wines around Bordeaux allowed this trickery, according to the memoir by Canasilles, relayed by Jean Eon in order to denounce the Dutch merchants who used to buy "lesser vintages" and "get the outsider to believe that they were more prestigious wines, selling them at high prices and gaining 50 % on them"[14]. It was also equally tempting to buy wines from one estate and pass them off as coming from another property. In such cases the wine was simply sold under another name. Brac states that the Flemish and Lorraine merchants who came to Burgundy bought Beaujolais wines, known in their home regions as "wines from Mâcon, from the Mâcon region or lower Burgundy" at low prices[15]. We can only deduce that they took advantage of this to sell them on more expensively and thereby acquire comfortable mark-ups for themselves. In quite another region, in 1756, the *subdélégué* (a local official) at La Flèche gave notification about the discredit of wine from Vouvray caused by merchants from Tours who were buying massive quantities of wines in the Loir Valley and passing them off as Vouvray wines. The *subdélégué* saw this as a short-term, suicidal strategy since, in just a few years, so-called Vouvray wine dropped from 180 pounds to 50 pounds for a *pièce* (barrel) while still being sold just as expensively in Paris[16].

Finally, merchants did not hesitate to blend wines to valorise those bought cheaply and make a profit. Blends were made using wines from different origins. According to Brac, this was the main source of the problems for Beaujolais wines. In his opinion, it was widely known that "the Paris wine merchant never buys Beaujolais wines to sell them as such to the consumer"[17]. Merchants only took light wines, pale in colour with the complicity of the wine producers who voluntarily halted the fermentation process so that the wines would not gain too much colour. They blended them with other wines in their cellars in Paris thus harming the reputation of these wines and keeping prices extremely low. According to Boullay, wines from Orleans would only be bought with

---

14 Eon J., *op. cit.*, "Extrait du mémoire des pratiques de commerce des étrangers dans la ville de Bourdeaux n'aguères dressé par le sieur Canasilles", p. 112.

15 Brac de la Perrière F., *op. cit.*, p. 10.

16 AD Indre-et-Loire, C 91, report of the *subdélégué* of La Flèche, 26 August1756.

17 Brac de la Perrière F., *op. cit.*, p. 22.

this purpose in mind and this would have been behind the collapse in the reputation of wines from Orleans in the capital. Wine merchants bought Orleans wine, which were reputedly more tannic (they kept better, and were at maturity after two or three years) in order to blend them with wines from Burgundy: "they still use them these days to pass on their weak wines which have no colour or which have other defects, or they even use them to reinforce the finer and more delicate wines including the most renowned"[18]. This practice, widely noted across the United Provinces in the 18th century, was the driver of a wine economy that was totally different, which made wine a generic product that could be altered according to the customer's wishes[19]. Most wines were sold with no clue as to their origin.

These merchants introduced outside elements to the wines in order to modify them. In Orleans wine producers made "*râpés*" which were wines that were boosted by adding oak chips in the barrels to enhance the tannins. While these wines were made by the winegrowers at the merchants' request – it was not really a question of falsification, strictly speaking – we cannot be sure that the drinker actually knew anything about it. Canon Boullay once more took the opportunity to denounce the merchants' dictatorship which obliged the bourgeois to produce these "*râpés*", which led to production being harmonised so that minor wines were enhanced with oak chips. Logically, the Dutch were once more blamed since "they have introduced into France certain practices of bottling, racking, fortifying and adulterating the wines so that they keep better during transport and they sell them in northern countries", which meant they could change the wines, creating different qualities while still buying anonymous wines cheaply in the vineyards[20]. If these practices were not unfair in their principles insofar as buyer and seller were both aware, they represented a break with the entire regulation system which stipulated that wine must have a clearly identifiable origin and have no substance added to it[21]. However, this regulation system was

---

18 Boullay J., *op. cit.*, p. 567.

19 Sleeswijk Wegener A., "Du nectar et de la godaille: qualité et falsification du vin aux Provinces-Unies, XVIIIe siècle", *Revue d'Histoire Moderne et Contemporaine*, 2004/3, n°51-3, p. 17-43.

20 Eon J., *op. cit.*, p. 90.

21 Any change in the character of a wine is considered as fraud. Although this was never defined by a law, the definition of wine under the Ancien Régime was more or less the same as the 1905 law. While it is accepted that one can add water and diverse

also specifically under attack itself as it benefited a kind of free market, pitting buyers against sellers to the greater advantage of the former.

Merchants-commissioners in a position of strength?

The old regulation system defended the producer in relation to the buyer. In the first place, the identification of wines was controlled by the existence of official gauges and measures. Each wine-producing area had its gauge to such a point that it was almost impossible to cheat in any given vineyard. In Burgundy, the famous Beaune mark allowed the certain identification of wines from the area up until it was abolished in 1752[22]. In Champagne, there were two gauges, one at Reims and one at Epernay which differentiated between the two areas[23]. In the Bordeaux area the wine gauge from the Haut Pays was not the same as that of Bordeaux wines. Tax indexing based on the different gauges in fact made them more inflexible[24].

Also, there were privileges which limited competition in favour of certain producers. Practically every town set up exclusive wine-producing zones through the privileges that they granted to the inhabitants who owned vines. Nearly all towns allowed the bourgeois to bring their wines in without paying taxes or licences. These were supposedly wines for domestic consumption even though the bourgeois could sell them, as they wished. This placed the sellers in a position of strength facing the buyers even though it was always possible to go directly to the wine estate to buy providing one did not pass back through the town, which the road and water transport system made difficult.

---

products at will to one's own wine, any modification of the product at the point of sale is a falsification and a fraud; adding old wine to new wine is an example of this. See the clarification of this in Delamare N., *Traité de la police*, tome 1, Paris, chez Jean-Pierre Cot, 1719, p. 580-583.

22 Délissey J. and Perriaux L., "Les courtiers gourmets de la ville de Beaune. Contribution à l'histoire du commerce du 'vin de Beaune' du XVIe au XVIIIe siècle", in *Annales de Bourgogne*, 34e année, 1962, p. 46-57; Labbé T., "La revendication d'un terroir viticole: la Côte de Beaune à la fin du XVIIIe siècle", *Histoire & Sociétés Rurales*, 2011–1, n°35, p. 117.

23 Musset B., *Vignoble de Champagne et vins mousseux. Histoire d'un mariage de raison, 1650-1830*, Paris, Fayard, 2008, p. 719.

24 It is always possible to decant wine from one barrel to another but that requires a certain kind of logistics.

Moreover, several wine-producing areas were isolated by tax and customs barriers. The case of Paris is typical of this with the 1577 barrier. Parisian wine merchants no longer had the right to buy wine inside a perimeter set more or less twenty leagues outside the city. This measure aimed at protecting bourgeois owners who sold their wines at a higher price in Paris than at the vineyard. This peri-urban wine-producing area was far from being on the decline since it accounted for a quarter of consumption around 1750[25]. The case of Bordeaux is also well known. The wines from the Haut Pays were not allowed into the city before 11 November and neither could they leave before 30 November (decree of 1501). Those destined for England even had to wait until Christmas and while waiting were stocked outside the city[26]. Wines from Gaillac were admitted nonetheless but mainly to be exported or to be mixed with Bordeaux wines when the colour was too light[27]. The Bordeaux market was strictly controlled, limiting manipulation and competition. Similarly, Roger Dion has strongly emphasised the Ingrandes barrier which taxed wines at 21 pounds per *pipe* (barrel) in the 1750s, which is between a quarter and a half of a common wine *pipe*. This meant that the wines from Nantes region and their producers enjoyed real earnings since competition from other wine-growing areas was limited even though the Loire Valley wines managed to provide some competition[28].

Finally, in theory, every sale had to be made through the intermediary of a broker, who is the basic commercial agent in the wine trade. In most towns, his intervention was more or less obligatory. For the purchaser, he guaranteed the provenance of the wine and for the seller he guaranteed the solvability of the buyer. Brokerage represented a true ideal of justice

---

25 Lachiver M., *op. cit.*, p. 316.

26 This exclusion was set up in 1373 and consolidated by different regulations. Lavaud S., "Les vins de Bordeaux au Moyen Age. Entre 'protectionnisme de clocher' et grand commerce", in Le Bras S. (ed.), *Les petits vignobles*, Rennes-Tours, PUR-PUFR, 2017, p. 67-84. See also Loirette F., "Colbert, le privilège de Bordeaux et le commerce des vins du Languedoc dans la seconde moitié du dix-septième siècle", in *Vignobles et vins d'Aquitaine*, Bordeaux, FHSO, 1970, p. 93-116.

27 Larguier G. and Gavignaud-Fontaine G., *Le vin en Languedoc et en Roussillon. De la tradition aux mondialisations, XVIe-XXIe siècle*, Perpignan, Trabucaire, 2007, p. 53-57.

28 Dion R., *Histoire de la vigne et du vin en France des origines au XIXe siècle*, Paris, Chez l'Auteur, 1959, p. 449-455. See Lachiver M., *op. cit.*, p. 131-135, who highlights the high volumes of shipments of wines in the 16th century, based on the works by Jean Tanguy.

in commercial exchange and for a long time was not at all perceived as a form of parasitism. Since the 14th century the institutionalisation of brokerage had been strong, since brokers were public agents (most of the time the payment of their fees was split between the buyers and the sellers). They were incorporated in Auxerre in 1346 (there were 9 of them by 1623) and in Beaune in 1551, where each *courtier-gourmet* (official wine tester) had to keep a register and he was strictly forbidden to act for an absent person – no doubt the proof that the question nevertheless arose. Similarly, he should only sell wines from Beaune: in 1642, Pierre Domino was struck off for having sold wines from the Mâcon area[29]. The spread of this institution to the whole of the kingdom from 1691-1692 seemed to mark the zenith of the institution, imposing *courtiers-jaugeurs* (broker-gaugers) there where there were none[30]. However, this fiscal manœuvre revealed a complex situation. In certain cases, the brokers in a place bought up the job title in order to continue operating while in other cases "free" brokers were obliged to regularise their situation whereas their profession was closer to commerce than to brokerage[31].

Whatever the case, the importance of brokerage should not be overestimated. It seems obvious that brokers have never controlled all trade all the more so since the bourgeois were free to sell their own wines, as well as those that they had bought from other producers. In Bordeaux, most wine producers had bourgeois status as did foreign merchants who bought the wines for export[32]. It is likely that many sales made in the vineyards were made without having recourse to a broker.

This relatively constraining and stable context seemed to be overwhelmed by new commercial actors. In the first third of the 18th century there were many complaints about the tyranny of the broker-commissioners. They were denounced in many vineyards for not respecting anything. In 1727 in Volnay, abbot Delachère noted with dismay "that one is no longer surprised at the vast fortunes which suddenly appear in their hands. Trade is a sure way to become rich when good faith is excluded"[33]. In 1749 he criticised "the sentiments of persons

---

29 Délissey J., Perriaux L., art. cité, p. 53.

30 Brennan T., *op. cit.*, p. 84-90.

31 *Ibid.*, p. 107-110.

32 Lachaud S., "Les courtiers bordelais, intermédiaires de commerce du vin aux XVIIe-XVIIIe siècles", *Revue Historique*, 2018–2, n°686, p. 307.

33 AD Côte-d'Or, G 4167, f°5.

who are so avid and interested"[34]. In the Languedoc area in 1752 the same complaint is noted about broker-commissioners in brandy: "today we are highly dependent on the price proposed by the commissioners"[35]. For Brac also, the enemy is the commissioner, who succeeded the honest broker: "the commissioners of Mâcon had the idea to band together in a group to make themselves masters of all the business"[36].

According to many authors, everything had been better when the buyers were moderate and respected balanced exchanges. In Volnay, when Gombaut died (1744) "there were no longer any others like him to defend the interests of the bourgeois & get the merchants & sellers to see reason"[37]. In the same way, at Roquemaure, in the Languedoc (1752):

> In the past we used to get together after the harvest in the town hall at Roquemaure and, after having weighed up how much the land had cost for cultivation and what had been produced, we fixed a common and reasonable price whereby the buyers and the private citizen could be satisfied.[38]

Brac de la Perrière (1769), also described the olden days:

> The Paris merchants came themselves every year; each commissioner had his merchants. The commissioner did not see himself as just a trading merchant: (…) At the same time, rivalry between merchants caused an advantageous competition; the goods were sold at about the right price, they were sold promptly.[39]

The commissioners therefore seemed to be in a position of strength. In that context of change mentioned in the introduction, it seems that broker-commissioners were the new pivot in the commercial chain. As the result of documentation produced by the creation of *courtiers-jaugeurs* (broker-gaugers). Thomas Brennan has revealed the emergence of these commissioners in the Loire valley, in Champagne and in Burgundy in the 1690s-1700s. At Chablis, in the Yonne department, it was the commissioners who ran the vineyards at the end of the 17th century.

---

34 *Idem*, 2e notebook, f°4.

35 Géraud-Perracha G., *Le commerce des vins et des eaux-de-vie en Languedoc sous l'Ancien Régime*, Montpellier, University of Montpellier, 1955, p. 172.

36 Brac de la Perrière F., *op. cit.*, p. 20.

37 AD Côte-d'Or, G 4167, 1er notebook, f°33.

38 Géraud-Perracha G., *ibid.*, p. 172.

39 Brac de La Perrière F., *op. cit.*, p. 19.

In 1705 a small group of six commissioners were concluding immense deals, buying wines for Parisians with whom they had close links[40]. They were also to be found around Beaune or in the Epernay wine area where the five largest commissioners carried off two-thirds of the shipments[41]. Traditional brokerage was outclassed. In Beaune the institution was abolished in 1752. In Reims brokerage survived but only on the Reims market: twelve modest broker-barrel makers served in turn throughout the year. But most sales were made by mutual agreement with no broker. In Bordeaux, the brokers were agents of the Bordeaux merchants who controlled the trade and who needed middlemen who knew the wines, their reputations and the stocks available[42].

Help from "the invisible hand": between interest, morality and sociability

However, the commercial arm should not be reduced to an opposition between producers and commissioners. In Champagne, the merchants were truly an ill-defined group with very varied interests. It is true that about twenty of them did about half of the shipping, but they were part of a much broader system of actors. Wine producers sold their wines directly to their Parisian and Flemish clients who made the trip to the wine estates personally. This was how the two largest establishments, Abbaye d'Hautvillers and Maison de Pierry, sold up to about half their wines. The outstanding debts of the major producers showed that they did the same thing: they were selling to Parisian merchants[43]. Producers also acted as commissioners in some years. They offered their wines to the commissioners but also wine produced by others, like Bertin du Rocheret, father and son, at Épernay, from the 1700s to the early 1760s. Also, to be taken into account were local brokers who made purchases and helped to set the qualities and the prices. These brokers knew the stocks, tasted the wines, proposed prices and advanced payments: they were the indispensable relays for the major merchant-commissioners who did business with them.

---

40 Brennan T., *op. cit.*, p. 122-127.

41 Musset B., *op. cit.*, p. 482.

42 Lachaud S., art. cit., p. 321-346.

43 Musset B., *op. cit.*, p. 466-468.

Stéphanie Lachaud has described a proliferation in actors in the Sauternes area. These included bourgeois from Bordeaux selling their own wines, buying and selling on others' wines as if it were their own, major wine producers (who were also Bordeaux bourgeois) who made direct sales through their family or friends, country brokers who took wine for commissioners, winegrowers selling to major producers who sold this on under their own name as well as priests and parish clergy who acted as middlemen[44]. All of these actors took part in a collective setting of prices which could not be summarised as the manipulations of some commissioners. Most often, the prices were negotiated collectively. Delachère indirectly reveals the workings of this process in Beaune. Although he complains very often about the manoeuvres of the commissioners, he also reveals the cooperation between estate owners who knew each other, who met up and discussed their wines. A few owners negotiated on behalf of others, who agreed to align their prices. The first price set served as a reference for the rest: it was a coordination mechanism that was simple but efficient. On several occasions, it was a Beaune lawyer, Maitrize, who established the price, and the other prices were indexed on his. Owners agreed to align with each other in a hierarchical system, based on the vintages and on status (nobles /clergy / officers /bourgeois /wine growers …)[45]. This system was thus based on a collective practice that was more less accepted.

In Champagne the setting of prices brought to the fore the group of actors just described. Correspondence from Buiron, the Reims merchant, in the 1760s revealed the mechanisms at work. In the front line, small brokers contributed to the setting of prices; they proposed a price and revised this according to what the new harvest or the evolution of stocks promised. In November 1764 Michel Dravigny, a broker in Bouzy, suggested sampling the wines of five different producers, the price of which was announced at 340 pounds[46]. In August 1765, Louis, from Damery, announced that the wine of the *curé* (priest) "is not going for less than 150 pounds a *queue*" and sent off a trial sample[47]. The producers also acted on the prices. In February 1766, Lacour de Saint-Eulien, a bourgeois from Châlons, proclaimed that his wine from Bouzy was

44 Lachaud S., art. cit., p. 332-334.

45 Musset B., "Le prix de la qualité…", art. cit, p. 131-133.

46 AD Marne, Reims depot, 25 B 89, letter of 26 November 1764.

47 *Ibid.*, letter of 16 August 1765.

priced at 200 pounds but he was offering it at 180 pounds[48]. A few days later, Delavieuville, a bourgeois from Reims, said he would not let his wine go for 300 pounds, because of the rise in prices but only for at least 325 pounds (except for cash payment)[49]. There is nothing to say that the prices were strictly followed but they did form a solid basis for negotiation. Information spread quickly and producers did not wait around for orders from the commissioners in order to negotiate the price of their wines.

This collective closeness created a classification system in several wine-producing areas. Structured classifications began to appear in the 1730s-1750s. A few years ago I showed how these classifications appeared in those areas which were the most integrated into major markets (Paris, London). From the 1730s, the list of vintages and estates with price scales was circulating in the Bordeaux vineyard. As Dewey Markham showed, these were co-constructed by merchants and owners who negotiated the prices and kept up their reputations[50]. Other classifications appeared in Champagne and Burgundy with a scale for the vintages, then the climates, becoming more and more refined; also in Anjou, around Orléans, with two or three classes of wines. These classifications helped to give the market a framework and to facilitate the social task of establishing prices and reputations from one year to the next. These were the result of negotiations between all those involved in trading as all the while they evolved according to the relations of power, reputations and winemaking initiatives by producers[51].

Relations between merchants and producers were based on reciprocal trust which was built up by actions and words. Long considered to be superficial, a short while ago these exchanges became the subject of renewed interest[52]. These practices were common between merchants but

---

48 *Ibid.*, letter of 6 February 1766.

49 *Ibid.*, letter of 27 February 1766.

50 Markham D., *1855. Histoire d'un classement des vins de Bordeaux*, Bordeaux, Féret, 1997, p. 55-104.

51 There are many aids to analysis, very useful to a historian, in Chauvin P.-M., *Le marché des réputations. Une sociologie du monde des vins de Bordeaux*, Bordeaux, Féret, 2010.

52 Bartolomei A., de Oliveira M., Eloire F., Lemercier C. and Sougy N., "L'encastrement des relations entre marchands en France, 1750-1850. Une révolution dans le monde du commerce?", *Annales*, 2017/2, 72e année, p. 425-460.

also between merchants and wine producers. We can take the example of a letter to Buiron in Reims from Dom Bouchez, a monk at Orbais near Épernay, who was engaged in the wine trade: "Rest assured that as long as you trade in wines you have my confidence. I thank you for the two good bottles that you sent me"[53]. Exchanging gifts was important in the relationship between Billecart-Joffrin, a wine producer and broker at Mareuil-sur-Ay, and Loubeau de Saint-Frajou, a Reims merchant in 1767: "my wife wishes me to send you greetings on her behalf, she has made a sausage, and I would like you to accept a piece"[54]. He sent off some fish in October 1767, then two young rabbits and four lapwings in February 1768[55]. This relationship is not just anecdotal since it is testimony to a relation of trust that was kept going by exchanges of presents and services, such as Loubeau's intervention in a question of payment. In the Sauternes area the broker Ladonne sent new year's greetings to the Marquis de Lur Saluces in 1741, announcing that he was sending two red partridges[56].

The relations between merchant-commissioners and producers were steady. In the case of correspondence from Madame Manouvrier of Reims we are a long way from the tyranny of the commissioner. Producers were far from being disarmed when faced with those involved in the wine trade. One of them put her wines on sale and fixed the price; in June 1773 a producer who was a relative sent her samples of his own wine with fixed prices, asking for her advice and whether she would like to be sent some[57]. Others did not hesitate to compete against the merchants, like the priest at Ludes in April 1776 who enquired after her and threatened to sell her wine to someone else with whom he was already in contact[58]. Similarly, producers did not hesitate to undertake legal proceedings: in February 1781, a winegrower from Fleury la Rivière demanded money off her, the seizing of four *pièces* of wine and threatened her with the bailiff[59].

---

53 AD Marne, Reims depot, 25 B 89, letter of 12 August 1764.

54 *Ibid.*, 25 B 72, letter of 15 February 1767.

55 *Ibid.*, letter of 14 February 1768.

56 Lachaud S., *Le Sauternais moderne. Histoire de la vigne, du vin et des vignerons des années 1650 à la fin du XVIIIe siècle*, Bordeaux, Fédération Historique du Sud-Ouest, 2012, p. 331-332.

57 AD Marne, Reims depot, 25 B 117, letter of 22 June 1773.

58 *Ibid.*, letter of 20 April 1776.

59 *Ibid.*, letter of 14 February 1781.

Finally, the producers did not hesitate about enjoying the pleasure of themselves recruiting the buyers, such as the priest at Brimont near Reims in January 1782, who boasted about doing business with a certain Drouet: "a gallant man, honest in trade"[60]. The trade chain also features in a letter from Louis, a producer-merchant-commissioner at Damery near Épernay to the merchant Buiron during the 1763 grape harvest. In it we can perceive a real trading network where information circulated about stocks, quality and anticipations, all contributing to the setting of prices. He first proposes wines at 200 pounds and then announces he will sell them at 250 pounds after the grape harvest. Then he gives news about the first purchases of the new campaign: Chertemps, a large estate owner from a big family of commissioners, had sold 40 *pièces* from 105 to 150 pounds. He ends up asking Buiron to convince a merchant from Cambrai to come to his house before concluding that "at my place he will always get preference but nevertheless at the going price, which is quite normal"[61].

Dis-honourable practices are not just a theoretical point of view. While they undeniably existed in the 18th century, they certainly existed beforehand. It is very difficult to evaluate the breadth of these kinds of "predatory" behaviour which when pushed to the extreme could have led to the collapse of the markets as has been seen in modern finance. However, the markets continued to function, demand kept on growing and exchanges intensified and spread geographically. Basically, it was doubtless the transformations in the wine trade which disoriented the actors the most: exchanges became broader, interactions in credit chains became more complicated (between producers, commissioners, merchants, consumers ...) and the system of public regulation was overwhelmed and challenged.

A regulation system, private but collective and with a strong social tone, began to spread in the 18th century. Of course, each group of actors defended their own interests therein. But social institutions backed up these actors: groups where they all knew each other, practices of civility and friendship, respect for collective, social and cultural norms. With all due respect to Adam Smith, links of friendship and mutual acquaintance

60 *Ibid.*, letter of 31 January1782.

61 *Ibid.*, 25 B 89, letter of 28 September 1763.

had a large part to play in relations between producers and merchants[62]. To repeat and contradict Polanyi, trading relations dis-embedded themselves from political and moral order (the former system of regulation) but only to re-embed in a social and economic order bearing other constraints and limits[63].

---

62 Smith A., *Enquête sur la nature et les causes de la richesse des nations*, Paris, Garnier-Flammarion, [1776] 1991, p. 82.

63 Karl Polanyi's theory of embedding is of great interest in characterising the emergence of economic priorities in political action in the 18th and 19th centuries. But sociologists have shown that the theory of dis-embedding is not adapted to the characterisation of contemporary economic facts. Care must be taken not to "over-socialise" economic acts, nor to "under-socialise" them. See Le Velly R., *Sociologie du marché*, Paris, La Découverte, 2012, p. 58-64.

Phylloxera Crisis and French-Australian Wine Rivalry on the British Market (1882-1914)

Mikaël Pierre

As Australian wine exports to Britain surpassed French exports in the 2000s, one should question the origins of this shift in the world wine trade. Market disruptions in the last quarter of the 19th century were the first signs of a globalised wine industry with the emergence of new producing countries in the Americas, Africa and Oceania. This phenomenon was observable with the appearance of Australia in French wine literature as a potential threat in international markets and especially in Britain, the most prominent world import centre of fine wines[1]. From the 1880s, the phylloxera crisis, the reappearance of protectionist policies in Europe and America and the development of wine growing in California, Chile, Argentina, South Africa and Australia, represented the end of the hegemonic dream of the French wine industry in the world market. Yet, Jules Guyot, who was hired by the imperial government to carry out a general study of the vineyards of the empire in the 1860s, considered that France had no serious competition regarding fine wines and that it would remain the major supplier of the world for centuries to come[2]. Though inaccurate, one must acknowledge that Guyot's prediction occurred before the phylloxera devastations during what is called the "golden age" of wine in France, owing to the growth of urban populations, increasing alcohol consumption and the development of the railroad networks

---

1 Fine wines constitute quality production sold above average prices. They are sometimes made from particular properties which use advanced technics and methods and which brand is famous among connoisseurs like the *grands crus* of Bordeaux.

2 Wolikow S., "La construction des territoires du vin et l'émergence des terroirs. Problématiques et démarches", in Jacquet O. and Wolikow S. (eds.), *Territoires et terroirs du vin du XVIIIe au XXIe siècles: approche internationale d'une construction historique*, Dijon, Éditions universitaires de Dijon, 2011, p. 15.

connecting southern vineyards to Paris and the main French cities[3]. At the same time, the first era of free trade was being established in western and northern Europe from 1860, which dynamised import markets. Increasing domestic and foreign demands enabled an unprecedented extension of the French vineyards.

According to the statistics gathered by Kym Anderson, Signe Nelgen and Vicente Pinilla, France became the first wine supplier of the United Kingdom in the 1880s with nearly 230,000 hectolitres a year, that is a third of total British imports[4]. Despite this success, wine producers and merchants were increasingly concerned about the progress made by new wine-producing countries, and noticeably Australia although this amounted to barely 1 % of British imports. How can one explain French concerns over such a modest competitor? The answer mostly lies in the importance of the British market as the main outlet for French wines abroad – mainly for fine wines but with the establishing of free trade, increasingly for ordinary wines as well. Yet, this market was also targeted by Australian winegrowers who considered the imperial centre as their natural outlet, given that colonial markets were too limited to allow the expansion of local viticulture[5].

James Simpson has pointed out the emergence of a world wine industry from the mid-19th century to the First World War, that is during the first wave of globalisation. But he also specifies that there was no global consumer market for wine at the time and that it only took shape from the 1980s. Markets did not expand as fast as production and were mainly attached to popular consumption in southern Europe[6]. A global consumer market could only be found for fine wines whose production was very limited. But they could be sold all over the world – Northern Europe, the Americas, the European colonies in the Caribbean, Africa, Asia and Oceania. David Hancock has shown how Madeira wine

---

3 Lachiver M., *Vins, vignes et vignerons: Histoire du vignoble français*, Paris, Fayard, 1988, p. 410.

4 Anderson K., Nelgen S. and Pinilla V., *Global Wine Markets, 1860 to 2016: A Statistical Compendium*, Adelaide, The University of Adelaide Press, 2018, p. 536. In the 1880s, 33 % of British wine imports came from France, 25 % from Spain and 18 % from Portugal.

5 McIntyre J., *First Vintage: Wine in Colonial New South Wales*, Sydney, University of New South Wales Press, 2012, p. 102.

6 Simpson J., *Creating Wine: The Emergence of a World Industry, 1840-1914*, Princeton, Princeton University Press, 2011, p. xxxii.

became a popular commodity across the Atlantic, particularly in the United States, revealing transoceanic trade networks between Britain, Madeira and North America[7]. However, competition between wines from the old continent and from the new worlds has not been the object of much attention. This chapter intends to analyse one of the aspects of this phenomenon during the first wave of globalisation. More especially, it aims at highlighting Franco-Australian rivalries on the British market from 1882, year of the international wine exhibition of Bordeaux, during which Australian wines made an impression on judges and experts, and up to the First World War which disrupted global commercial exchange. Indeed, French and Australian wine producers and merchants mainly competed in the United Kingdom, which was then divided between its duty to absorb products from its colonial empire and its desire to deepen economic relations with France. This context was also marked by the shifting of British taste during what Charles Ludington called the "great 19th century wine debate", opposing fortified wine advocates to French-style light wine promoters[8]. The debate also reached Australia whose production mostly consisted of fortified wines. But more and more influential winegrowers advocated the development of a French wine model whose sales were rapidly growing in Britain thanks to lower duties.

Finally, one last critical event was instrumental in motivating Australian winegrowers' commercial ambitions: phylloxera. This tiny insect originally came from North America and started to devastate French vines between the late 1860s in the southern regions and the mid-1890s in the northern vineyards[9]. While French production plummeted, foreign winegrowers attempted to take advantage of this situation by exporting their production to France and its traditional markets in

---

7 Hancock D., *Oceans of Wine: Madeira and the Emergence of American Trade and Taste*, New Haven, Yale University Press, 2009. Hancock also argues that Madeira wine success resulted from distributors' attention to shifting consumers taste and from the logics of luxury or semi-luxury products economy.

8 Ludington C., *The Politics of Wine in Britain: A New Cultural History*, New York, Palgrave Macmillan, 2013, p. 238-239. Fortified wines constitute wines to which a certain quantity of spirit is added, usually brandy. Light wines generally refer to unfortified wines, that is wines with less than 16 % of alcohol.

9 Garrier G., *Le phylloxéra. Une guerre de trente ans 1870-1900*, Paris, Albin Michel, 1989, p. 25-36. For a more recent study of phylloxera and its impact on the worldwide wine industry, see Gale G., *Dying on the Vine: How Phylloxera Transformed Wine*, Berkeley, University of California Press, 2011.

northern Europe. This first benefited Spain before it was hit by the plague as well[10], then Algeria which welcomed many French vignerons ruined by the loss of their vineyards[11]. But, in this context, Australia expected to make the most of the opportunity to replace France in the British market.

Phylloxera crisis and Australian ambitions

Henry Bonnard, New South Wales representative at the international wine exhibition of Bordeaux in 1882[12], described this event as an opportunity for négociants to get an overview of the wines available in the world to fill gaps left by the plummeting French production in the wake of the phylloxera attacks[13]. Australian growers banked on this exhibition to make their own wines known on an international scale, especially through Bordeaux négociants who were renowned for their tasting skills and their transnational trade networks[14]. Victoria's Winegrower Hubert de Castella was very optimistic regarding Australian results during different international exhibitions in the 1870s-1880s and claimed that it "caused a cry of alarm from the French producers, afraid for the future of their mixtures"[15]. De Castella also hoped that French imports of foreign wines would invigorate the Australian wine industry, as it did for Spain and

---

10 Brémond J., "Rioja et la référence à Bordeaux", in Jacquet O. and Wolikow S. (eds.), *Territoires et terroirs du vin du XVIIIe au XXIe siècles: approche internationale d'une construction historique*, Dijon, Éditions universitaires de Dijon, 2011, p. 193.

11 Isnard H., "Vigne et colonisation en Algérie", *Annales de géographie*, vol. 58, no. 311, 1949, p. 214-215.

12 It was the 12th Exhibition organised by the Société Philomathique de Bordeaux. Its objective was to show the city's wealth despite the effects of a serious economic crisis linked to the devastations of the phylloxera and the increasing competition with other port cities like Nantes or Le Havre. See Lozère C., *Bordeaux colonial (1850-1940)*, Bordeaux, Éditions Sud-Ouest, 2007, p. 61-62.

13 Bonnard H., *Report of the Executive Secretary on the Bordeaux International Exhibition of Wines, 1882*, Sydney, Thomas Richards, Government Printer, 1884, p. 4. This motivation was also mentioned in an introductory work to the exhibition which presented the development of viticulture outside of France, see Sempé R., *Étude sur les vins exotiques*, Bordeaux, Féret et Fils, 1882, p. 3-4.

14 *Bordeaux International Wine Exhibition 1882. Report of the Commissioners for the Colony of Victoria*, Melbourne, John Ferries, Government Printer, 1883, p. 4.

15 *The Australian Vigneron and Fruit Growers' Journal (AVFGJ)*, vol. 1, 1 August 1890, p. 57.

Portugal[16]. This was a hope shared by American immigrant H. Mortimer Franklyn in his book focused on the leading industries of Australia. In a chapter entitled "The Vineyard of the World", Franklyn argued that "colossal fortunes will be made by syndicates of French wine-merchants and viticulturists operating in Australia, and discovering in its vineyards mines of wealth far exceeding those which were laid bare by adventurous miners in the early days of the gold-fields"[17].

However, Australian growers quickly turned their attention to direct trade with their British motherland. After visiting Europe, the Australian Wine Company's owner, Walter Pownall, presented these potential benefits to the Board of Viticulture for Victoria in 1889. Pownall's hope was based on the recent progress of Australian viticulture as well as on wine shortages in France subsequent to the spread of phylloxera. He concluded: "France's misfortune is Australia's opportunity"[18]. At the time, Australian newspapers and journals published a series of articles to announce France's inevitable decline on the world wine market and the gap it created for colonial winegrowers[19]. The *South Australian Advertiser* noted:

> Above all, we have no phylloxera to trouble us. The dreaded pest which has devastated the vineyards of Europe has spared all but a few isolated districts on this continent, and with the exercise of reasonable care we may regard ourselves as safe from its attacks. Thus far almost the only effect of the phylloxera on the colonies has been to enlarge the possibilities of an Australian wine trade with Europe by the diminution of European production. The English market has been deluged with inferior brands of doctored wines from the Continent; and consumers, impatient at such treatment, are now turning towards Australia with unwonted eagerness for the supply of a sound and wholesome wine of agreeable flavour and sufficient cheapness. Europe's extremity ought to be Australia's opportunity[20].

---

16 De Castella H., *John Bull's Vineyard*, Melbourne, Sands & McDougall Limited, 1886, p. 102.

17 Franklyn H. M., *A Glance at Australia in 1880: Or Food from the South Showing the Present Condition of Some Leading Industries…*, Melbourne, The Victorian Review Publishing Company Limited, 1881, p. 162.

18 *Journal of the Board of Viticulture for Victoria*, 5 August 1889, p. 118.

19 *The Garden and the Field*, vol. 13, no. 145, June 1887, p. 11; *The Age*, 4 December 1888.

20 *South Australian Advertiser*, 20 January 1886, p. 4.

In Melbourne's newspaper *The Age*, the phylloxera crisis constituted a turning point:

> While our young industry is expanding surely, if but slowly, and has brightening prospects opening up to it, wine production in France shows unmistakable and continuous signs of decadence. The days when France was practically the wine factory for the whole world are gone, it would seem, for ever. The result is due to two causes – the ravage of phylloxera and the growth of competition[21].

However, the Australians were increasingly concerned by the different obstacles they needed to overcome to reach the British market. The Australian Wine Association lobbied for a reduction of duties on wine which then were based on alcohol content[22]. The objective of the British government was to favour the consumption of light wines, considered to be healthier. This system penalised Australian wines as they generally contained more alcohol. Former Victorian Minister of Justice Archibald Michie deplored this situation in which Britain seemed to deal with its own colonies as foreign countries rather than British dependencies[23]. This issue led more and more Australian wine merchants and winegrowers to promote light wine production on the French model through the import of vine stocks, skills and experts from France, a move which eventually alarmed wine professionals in France.

The French view of the Australian wine industry

From the middle of the century, comments on the Australian vineyard became more common in France thanks to French travellers' writings. Most of them complimented the quality of the vineyards they visited – they were generally properties owned by wealthy colonists like James and William Macarthur's Camden Estate, New South Wales, or St. Hubert's Vineyard, Victoria, established by Hubert de Castella[24]. But the 1880s

---

21 *The Age*, 13 January 1890, p. 4.

22 This tax system had been set up by British Chancellor of the Exchequer William Gladstone in 1861-1862. See Simpson J., *Creating Wine: The Emergence of a World Industry, 1840-1914*, Princeton, Princeton University Press, 2011, p. 113-115.

23 *Australian Vignerons and Fruit Growers' Journal*, February 1886, vol. 1, no. 1, p. 7.

24 See for examples, Delessert E., *Voyages dans les deux océans Atlantique et Pacifique*, Paris, A. Franck, 1848, p. 117; Russel-Killough H., *Seize mille lieues à travers l'Asie et l'Océanie. Voyage exécuté pendant les années 1858-1861 par le comte Henry*

were marked by economic disruptions deeply impacting the international wine trade. In France, it put a sudden end to the 1850s-1870s "golden age" of wine and the country became a net importer of wine and feared the loss of its external outlets to foreign competition.

Australia had been perceived as a potential competitor as early as the 1860s, when the *Revue viticole* attempted to alarm Europeans about the progress of viticulture in the Antipodes[25]. Twenty years later, the experts at the Bordeaux international exhibition expressed similar concerns regarding Bonnard's attempts to send for French winegrowers and capitals to New South Wales. For Bonnard, it was only a way to offer a second chance to those who had lost their vineyards with the phylloxera, and it would eventually give Bordeaux wine merchants an opportunity to secure new supply sources to complement the depressed domestic production[26]. On the French side, however, priority was given to the protection of the national industry from new competition, especially as it was already weakened by the vine diseases. Despite underproduction issues, it seemed too great a risk to allow the transfer of technologies and know-how to emulate French wines abroad. Yet, this strategy was adopted by Bordeaux merchants in Rioja, Spain, in the 1880s[27]. Transfers of experts, skills and technologies were also intense between Bordeaux and Mendoza, Argentina[28]. The École nationale d'Agriculture of Montpellier recommended some of its graduate to take positions in Australian public institutions and private companies in the 1890s. But the end of the phylloxera crisis and the reconstitution of the vineyards in France led to a new issue: overproduction. Thus, the new suppliers became competitors.

Russell-Killough, membre de la Société Française de Géographie. Sibérie, Désert de Gobi, Peking, Fleuve Amour, Japon, Australie, Nouvelle-Zélande, Inde, Himalaya... vol. 1, Paris, Hachette et Cie, 1864, p. 334-335; De Beauvoir L., *Voyage autour du monde: Australie, Java, Siam, Canton, Pékin, Yeddo, San Francisco*, Paris, H. Plon, 1869, p. 290-291; Cotteau E., *En Océanie. Voyage autour du monde en 365 jours, 1884-1885*, Paris, Hachette et Cie, 1888, p. 158-184; Michel E., *À travers l'hémisphère sud: Ou mon voyage autour du monde*, Paris, Librairie Victor Palmé, 1888, p. 404-408.

25 Ramel M., "La vigne en Australie", *Revue viticole: Annales de la viticulture et de l'œnologie françaises et étrangères*, 1863, p. 65-66.

26 *The Sydney Mail*, 18 November 1882, p. 880.

27 Brémond J., *op. cit.*, p. 193.

28 Blanchy G., *Le Vignoble argentin de Mendoza et l'influence française (XIXe-XXIe siècle)*, Paris, L'Harmattan, 2014, p. 28-29.

The arrival of French winegrowers in Australia ended up alarming the vice-consul of Melbourne in 1905.

> From a humanitarian and national point of view, I insist on thinking we should seriously try to prevent the emigration, even limited, of our viticulturists to this Australia which was delighted fifteen years ago with the devastation of our vineyards by the phylloxera and whose wines already compete directly with ours[29].

The return of protectionist policies and the strengthening of nationalism on the European continent responded to global economic crises. The French Third Republic, unlike the Second Empire, did not believe in reaching prosperity through trade and cooperation with Britain and opted for the protection and the development of domestic industries. Custom duties were gradually increased in the 1880s and reached their highest point in 1892 with the Jules Méline tariff[30]. This new custom policy increased average taxes on bulk wine imports from 5 % in the 1880s to more than 25 % in the 1890s[31]. Limiting both goods imports and technology exports became a major national issue to avoid the weakening of one of the most productive sectors in France and the symbol of its culture.

Not everybody shared those concerns though. One of the judges at the 1882 Bordeaux exhibition concluded that Australian wines could not yet compete with the wines of France in quantity and in price, and that French vineyards would be reconstituted before the situation changed[32]. Some comments were sometimes disdainful, or even mocking as illustrated by a piece written for this exhibition in which the author stated:

---

29 Letter from M. Maistre, French vice-consul in Melbourne, to the Minister of Foreign Affairs, 11 December 1905, Archives Nationales de France, Pierrefitte-Sur-Seine, Ministère du Commerce, Missions commerciales, XIXe siècle, F/12/7122: Melbourne.

30 Perez Y. A., "1892: l'année où la France est retournée au protectionnisme", *Humanise et Entreprise*, vol. 308, no. 3, 2012.

31 Pinilla V. and Ayuda I., "The Political Economy of the Wine Trade: Spanish Exports and the International Market, 1890-1935", *European Review of Economic History*, vol. 6, 2002, p. 62.

32 Benoist fils C., "L'Australie et ses colonies", *La vigne française: Revue bi-mensuelle des intérêts français et de la défense contre le phylloxéra*, vol. 3, no. 24, 1882, p. 424.

> Despite productions unable to supply the stores of a secondary négociant or Paris consumption for five days; with inadequate methods of production, prices too high and the extreme distance of consumer markets, the Australians expect, with the aid of the phylloxera, to replace our great and old wine countries[33].

In 1890, a treatise on alcoholic beverages attempted to belittle Australian ambitions regarding the world wine industry highlighting a rather modest volume of production[34]. Indeed, the quantity of wine that each country could make was not on the same scale. Only 100,000 hectolitres per annum were produced in all the Australian colonies in the 1880s, against 30 million hectolitres in France then in the middle of the crisis. In the 1900s, Australia could produce twice as much, but the French production had almost doubled as well[35].

However, the two industries had different objectives. France increasingly turned its attention to its booming domestic market, while Australia concentrated its efforts on Britain. The evolution of British wine imports gives a better idea of the reality of the Australian threat as perceived by some French merchants – especially from Bordeaux – who strongly relied on this market. In 1882, year of the exhibition in Bordeaux, Australia merely exported 970 hectolitres to the UK. At the same time, France could sell around 229,000 hectolitres there. This last figure remained steady throughout the 1880s-1890s before gradually decreasing in the 1900s to only 134,000 hectolitres in 1912. This drop was caused by the general decline of British orders and the growing distrust over adulterated French wines[36]. On the contrary, British imports of Australian wines were constantly increasing during this period and reached 44,000 hectolitres in 1912, that is the equivalent of a third of the imports of French wines for that same year[37].

---

33 Sempé R., *op. cit.*, p. 187.

34 Le Sourd P. et al. (eds.), *Traité pratique des vins, cidres, spiritueux et vinaigres*, Paris, G. Masson, 1890, p. 27.

35 Anderson K., Nelgen S. and Pinilla V., *op. cit.*, p. 180. Figures rounded to the nearest thousand.

36 Paul Butel argued that the rising competition of whisky may have impacted wine consumption in Britain as well, see Butel, P., *Les dynasties bordelaises. Splendeur, déclin et renouveau*, Paris, Perrin, 2008, p. 272. Regarding French wines declining reputation see Phillips R., *French Wine. A History*, Oakland, California, University of California Press, 2016, p. 183.

37 Anderson K., Nelgen S. and Pinilla V., *op. cit.*, p. 535.

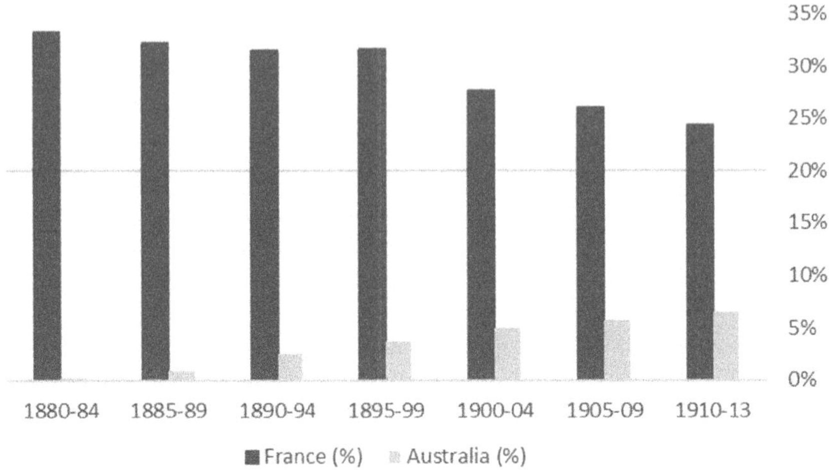

Graph 1: Evolution of British wine imports from France and Australia (1880-1913). Source of data: Anderson K., Nelgen S. and Pinilla V., *Global Wine Markets, 1860 to 2016: A Statistical Compendium*, Adelaide, The University of Adelaide Press, 2018, p. 535

Graph 1 shows a distinct loss of French market shares in Britain to the benefit of Australian exporters from the 1890s to the early 1910s. Thus, it means that British consumers tended to drink less French wine whose reputation had been deteriorated by cases of adulterations and counterfeits, and they increasingly trusted the products of their former colonies. Yet, paradoxically, Australian winegrowers and wine merchants kept using French names to introduce their products into Britain.

French names for Australian wines

Until the 1880s, the use of French names by Australian winegrowers was not questioned though French judges at the universal exhibitions of Paris in 1867 and Vienna in 1873 were discountenanced by some "Hermitages" from Australia. They believed they were wines from the Rhône Valley which had been shipped to the Antipodes before being sent back to Europe[38]. But they remained isolated cases and did not lead

[38] Dunstan D., *Better than Pommard: A History of Wine in Victoria*, Melbourne,

to further disputes. This can be explained by a very favourable economic context for the French wine industry in the 1860s-1870s with growing domestic and foreign outlets. However, the difficulties linked to the phylloxera began to make an impact in different regions of France when the international wine exhibition of Bordeaux was organised in 1882. The shifting French reactions can be found in the different editions of the *Nouveau manuel du sommelier et du marchand de vins* by M. P. Maigne, in which Australian wines are briefly mentioned. In the 1874 edition, the author stated: "In Oceania, only Australia grows vine grapes, and according to the progress made hitherto, the quantity of wine produced will increase significantly. This region will even be able to produce enough wine, not only to supply its domestic market, but also to replace European wines in the Americas"[39]. Ten years later, however, Maigne added in the new edition that Australian winegrowers made wines "burdened with the most pretentious names and generally of very mediocre quality"[40]. This opinion was even more clearly stated by Raymond Sempé who attended the Bordeaux exhibition and who sarcastically denounced the Australian counterfeits in his work:

> One shall now discuss Australian vignerons' detestable habit – especially those from Victoria – of misusing the names of great European wines for their own products! From now on, they can supply wines of Champagne, Madeira, Tokay, Port, Xeres, Sauternes, Rhine, Constance, etc. They own all kinds of growths, with all qualities. They have full confidence and, with almost no equipment and with young vine grapes, they naively claim to be able to produce similar wines to those harvested under different latitudes, on specific soils and made with infinite care[41].

Australian Scholarly Publishing, 1994, p. 54. This mistake echoed the actual practice of the wines so-called "retour des Indes" or "retour de l'Inde" which underwent a return trip to the Americas or India as it was believed it would improve their quality.

39 Maigne P., *Nouveau manuel complet du sommelier et du marchand de vins, contenant des notions succinctes sur les vins rouges, blancs et mousseux*, Paris, Roret, 1874, p. 114-115.

40 Quoted and translated in Phillips R., *op. cit.*, p. 140. According to Phillips, Maigne might have been influenced by the Tahbilk winery in Victoria, renamed "Château Tahbilk" around 1879. This practice impacted several wine properties in Australia and resulted from a trend launched in the Bordeaux district after the 1855 classification celebrating the *grands crus* of the region. The word "château" was then used as a marketing strategy to guarantee the quality of a specific growth and to distinguish it from ordinary wines. See Roudié Ph., *Vignobles et vignerons du Bordelais (1850-1980)*, Bordeaux, Féret, 2013, p. 180-182.

41 Sempé R., *op. cit.*, p. 187.

However, Sempé acknowledged that he admired the Australian colonial society for being highly resourceful and enterprising. In fact, the disdain expressed by some observers toward the Australian wine industry most likely resulted from concerns linked to economic turmoil.

The issue of wine names was not necessarily linked to the concept of terroir or the respect for the product's origin. Bordeaux wine merchants had always practiced the blending of Bordelais wines with wines produced in other regions or even other countries – especially during the phylloxera crisis. The result was then sold in northern Europe as "claret" with no mention of these blends. Among wine merchants and traders, denominations mostly relied on commercial issues and market control. It was a very sensitive question among Bordeaux merchants as they based their economic power on overseas exports, especially to Britain. A thesis submitted to the University of Bordeaux in 1898 denounced practices among Spanish, Californian and Australian winegrowers aiming to deceive consumers. The author, though acknowledging that it constituted an indirect homage to the "superiority" of French wines, strongly urged action against an unfair trade discrediting the products of France on international markets[42]. This issue became particularly critical in the late 1890s as the vine crisis was about to be solved by the generalisation of grafting on American phylloxera-resistant stocks. So much so that the domestic production was growing again. It became thus essential to secure foreign outlets to sell off the surplus.

This discord soured French-Australian relations during international exhibitions for decades, from 1882 in Bordeaux to the Brussels exhibition of 1910 during which Australia decided not to send any samples. It also occurred in a context of tensions regarding the French presence in the South Pacific. On the one hand, the United Kingdom sought appeasement and partnership with France in order to thwart German ambitions on the European continent and overseas. On the other hand, Australia expected the imperial centre to protect British colonies – and the Commonwealth of Australia since the independence of 1901 – against all foreign presence, including the French. In the 1890s, New Hebrides and the penal colony of New Caledonia represented the main cause of tensions between France and the Australian colonies. The establishment

[42] Sempé H., "Régime économique du vin", PhD Thesis, Université de Bordeaux, 1898, p. 236.

Fig. 1: "Australian Burgundy, Rubicon brand", label registered by Messrs. W. and A. Gilbey, Limited, of 173 Oxford Street, London. Source: *The Australian Vigneron and Fruit Growers' Journal*, vol. 6, no. 12, April 1896, p. 413

of an Australian federation independent from the United Kingdom also concerned France regarding the future ambitions of the newly established nation in the southern Pacific[43].

However, some French wine exporters might have hoped that the independence of Australia and the suppression of custom duties between the states of the new federation would increase the domestic demand and limit the quantity of Australian wines available for the British market[44]. Yet, as seen previously, it turned out to be the opposite. British imports of Australian wines did not slowdown with independence and even increased gradually from 1901 to the start of the First World War. This explains the rising concerns and complaints among French wine professionals regarding what was considered counterfeiting during the 1900s.

---

43 Barko I., "The French presence in Sydney and the establishment of the French Chamber of Commerce", *Journal of the Royal Australian Historical Society*, vol. 84, no. 2, 1999, p. 51-52. Regarding the reactions toward the French and the French culture in Australia at the turn of the 20th century, see Bergantz A., "French Connection: The Culture and Politics of Frenchness in Australia, 1890-1914", PhD thesis, Australian National University, 2015.

44 *Revue des vins et liqueurs et des produits alimentaires pour l'exportation*, vol. 25, no. 1, January 1901, p. 121-122.

The 1908 Franco-British exhibition in London celebrated the recently established *Entente cordiale* between France and Britain. This historic event did not prevent French judges and wine professionals from contesting Australian habits of labelling their bottles with French denominations. In their report, the British judges esteemed there was no intention of fraud and simply made a recommendation to Australian growers, arguing it would be more profitable to establish their own names than misusing European regional ones. But this report was far from mandatory and the French judges ended up refusing to taste any Australian wines[45]. The British could not directly act anyway as the Australian colonies had recently acquired their independence. And the Australians were very reluctant to follow this recommendation as they relied on these denominations to indicate the style of wines they produced and distributed to British customers who were accustomed to these names. They also claimed that by adding the adjective "Australian", they could clearly inform the consumers of the origin of the wine, thereby avoiding any confusion. Thus, "Australian Burgundy", "Australian Claret", "Australian Hermitage" or "Australian Champagne" became common designations on the British market to indicate the origin and the style of wine to the customers (see Fig. 1). This solution also allowed them to be distinguished from French wines whose reputation had deteriorated. Australian wine merchants attempted to present their products as a "pure" alternative to adulterated French wines[46].

Australian wine ambitions may have appeared as a pipe dream in the 1880s, but twenty years later, the British trade was clearly shifting to a gradual replacement of French wines by Antipodean wines. This caused growing concerns in France, especially among merchants involved in the wine trade with Britain. Misuses of wine designations became a major issue during international exhibitions as they threatened French market

---

45 Charton C. and Desmoulins A.-M., *Exposition franco-britannique de Londres de 1908*, Paris, Comité français des expositions à l'étranger, 1910, p. 148-154. Goulet E., *Ministère du Commerce et de l'Industrie. Exposition universelle et internationale de Bruxelles, 1910. Section française. Groupe X, classe 60 (vins et eaux-de-vie de vin). Rapport par M. Émile Goulet*, Paris, Comité français des expositions à l'étranger, 1912, p. 100 and 244. Misuses of French denominations also concerned Californian winegrowers who were asked to respect original brands at the Saint Louis exhibition of 1904. See Butel P., *op. cit*, p. 374.

46 *The Australian Vigneron and Fruit Growers' Journal*, 2 February 1891, p. 177.

shares abroad. But the French attempts to counter this phenomenon failed. After the First World War, the Australian wine industry continued its rise and for the first time in 1928, more Australian wines were introduced into Britain than French wines. This was to occur consistently throughout the 1930s[47]. In 1933, Daniel Calvet, a member of one of the wealthiest wine houses in Bordeaux – particularly successful in Britain – deplored the commercial slowdown that impacted this market, pointing to a serious trend for Australian wines[48]. On the eve of the Second World War, France could only export 38,000 hectolitres of wine to Britain against 162,000 from Australia.

The shift started in the 1900s was confirmed during the interwar period due to several causes. First, the context of economic crisis was not favourable to the consumption of expensive French fine wines. Then, the rise of protectionism and custom duties limited Franco-British trade. Finally, the French wine industry increasingly turned its attention to its booming domestic market and neglected the foreign outlets, especially during the period from the 1880s to the 1940s. On the other hand, Australia strengthened its position as wine supplier to its former imperial centre by providing a wide range of wine styles though its total production remained modest. It was not until the 1970s that a real boom finally impacted the wine industry of the Antipodes thanks to a growing domestic market and the development of international markets in the second wave of globalisation[49].

In parallel, the French government tackled the geographical indication (GI) problem head on from 1907 to 1935, setting up the complex system of *Appellations d'Origine Contrôlée* (AOC) defining regions producing quality and typical wines nationwide. This issue was to be sorted out with much more difficulty on the international scale. It was only with the "Agreement between Australia and the European Community on Trade in Wine, and Protocol" signed in 1994 that a solution was finally accepted. It has forbidden the use of European GIs by Australian winegrowers on international markets. The agreement also involved a decrease of non-tariff barriers against the introduction of Australian wines into the European

47 Anderson K., Nelgen S. and Pinilla V., *op. cit.*, p. 180 and 535.

48 Tastet and Lawton, *De l'air du temps. Tome 1: Extraits d'archives: 1900-1944*, Bordeaux, Éditions Confluences, 2007, p. 402.

49 Germov J. and McIntyre J., "The rise of Australia as a wine nation", *The Conversation*, 5 June 2013.

market[50]. Today, the wine rivalry between France and Australia – and more generally between European countries and new wine-producing countries – does not only concern the United Kingdom, but the global market: Europe, North America and Asia, where wine consumption has considerably increased during the second phase of the globalisation from the 1970s to the present day.

---

[50] Stern S., "Wine and Place", in. Harvey M. and Waye V. (eds.), *Global Wine Regulation*, Sydney, Thomson Reuters, 2014, p. 38-40.

'Getting the Favour of the Public' in the Nineteenth-Century Champagne Trade: How Important Was a 'Smart Agent'?

Graham Harding

Between 1860-1862, the British Chancellor of the Exchequer, William Gladstone, substantially reduced duties on unfortified wine and liberalised the licensing laws. His goal was to wean the British public away from the heavily fortified and often adulterated wines characterised by contemporaries as 'black, strong and sweet'[1]. Though his intervention failed to convert the mass of the British population to light wines, it gave an enormous boost to claret and to champagne. Sales of the latter wine rose threefold in less than fifteen years.

This chapter looks at the networks governing the supply and demand of champagne in this period, concentrating on the London agents who represented the French producers in this vital market. It is not a full study of the role of the agents in the nineteenth-century wine trade but focuses on a small number of the most influential and important figures, notably Adolphe Hubinet of the firm of Pommery & Greno who built the Pommery brand from nothing into the most powerful, highly-priced and best-publicised champagne brand of the second half of the century[2].

This expansion of consumption in the 1860s was matched by an increasingly complex market. Before 1850, most champagne was sold by British merchants who received stock direct from a French producer. These merchants were responsible for selling through to customers – mostly private individuals – through their personal 'connection' or

1 Gladstone W., "Financial Statement", 10 February 1860, vol. 156, c. 812-89; *Ridley's Wine and Spirit Trade Circular*, 6 November 1858, p. 10.

2 The only history of Pommery is De Polignac A., *Madame Pommery: le génie et le cœur*, Paris, Stock, 1994.

via the medium of price-focused press advertising. Itinerant 'commis voyageurs' (salesmen on commission) such as those recruited by Jean-Rémy Moët were responsible for finding new customers who would be supplied with stock from France[3]. Most wine bore merchant rather than producer branding[4].

Gladstone's reforms brought new retailers into the market to service the developing middle-class demand for wine. The trade journal, *Ridley's Wine and Spirit Circular*, claimed in a 1908 retrospective that: "[t]he demand was so considerable that all sorts and conditions of shopkeepers rushed into the Trade almost as impetuously as, ten years before, inexperienced youths had flocked to the goldfields of Ballarat"[5].

The retailing of wines for off-premise consumption was dominated by W. & A. Gilbey which grew from a handful of outlets in the late 1850s to over 3,000 by the end of the century[6]. There were no competitors of equal size in the market for on-premise consumption but Gladstone's new licensing structure allowed pastrycooks and confectioners to sell wine for on-premise consumption whilst railway catering was dominated by the firm of Spiers & Pond[7]. The expansion of gentlemen's clubs in London and elsewhere and hotels and restaurants further stimulated the trade[8]. The flood of wine into the market in the 1860s and 1870s was matched by new popular books on which wines to choose, where to buy them,

---

3 For Moët's 'new commercial practice' developed in early nineteenth century, see Musset B., "L'expérimentation d'une nouvelle pratique commerciale: la maison Moët d'Épernay et ses commis voyageurs (1790-1815)", *Entreprises et Histoire*, no. 66, 2012, p. 107-108.

4 *Christie's Sales Catalogue*, 1800-65, records approximately 80 lots of champagne. 60 % were unbranded; 19 % were place-branded (e.g. Sillery), 14 % were merchant-branded and 7 % producer-branded. Of producer brands, Moët, Perrier-Jouët and Ruinart had two mentions each.

5 *Ridley's*, 9 January 1908, p. 52-53.

6 Derived from Gilbey's circulars and price lists. See, for example, "Diageo," 100433/79 of 1865.

7 See Spiers R. G., *Spiers and Pond: Restaurateurs, Cricket Promoters and Hoteliers Extraordinaire*, Tring, R.G. Spiers, 2008.

8 Flanders J., *Consuming Passions: Leisure and Pleasure in Victorian Britain* London, Harper Press, 2006, p. 227-228 for the development of railway hotels. Flanders J., *The Victorian City: Everyday Life in Dickens' London* London, Atlantic Books, 2013, p. 290 for restaurants. Milne-Smith A., "A Flight to Domesticity? Making a Home in the Gentlemen's Clubs of London, 1880-1914", *Journal of British Studies* 45, no. 4, 2006, p. 799-800 for the growth in London's clubland after the 1840s.

how to keep them and where to consume them[9]. Newspaper references to wine increased exponentially. In the decade 1860-1869, there were over ten times as many advertisements for and references to champagne as there had been in 1840-1849[10].

This dramatic increase in the scale and complexity of the networks surrounding the wine market rendered the earlier marketing and distribution model increasingly problematic. The extensive correspondence of Edouard Werlé of Veuve Clicquot Ponsardin illustrates the issues. Until 1860, Werlé, the controlling hand of Veuve Clicquot, had relied on merchants applying to him direct. After conducting credit checks he supplied direct, relying on the reputation of his brand to drive sales[11]. Therefore, Werlé had to negotiate with many individual merchants. Conflicts of interest over pricing and customers were the consequence[12]. Despite his familiarity with the market, he came to the decision to enlist a stock-holding agent for his British trade and chose the London wine merchant, Robert Selby on account of his extensive client base[13]. Whilst he feared that his firm would face hostility from merchants accustomed to dealing direct, he recognised that the increased complexity of the trade meant that, without an agent in place, intermediaries could and would play one merchant off against another to the detriment of Veuve Clicquot[14].

Increasingly entrepreneurial agents came to play a key intermediating and influencing role in the British champagne trade. Using Hubinet's

---

9 The most widely read appear to have been Druitt R., *Report on the Cheap Wines from France, Italy, Austria, Greece, and Hungary*, 2nd ed., London, Henry Renshaw, 1873; Gilbey A., *Treatise on Wines and Spirits of the Principal Producing Countries*, London, W & A Gilbey Ltd, 1869; Vizetelly H., *The Wines of the World Characterized & Classed: With Some Particulars Respecting the Beers of Europe*, London, Ward, Lock, Tyler, 1875; Shaw T. G., *Wine, the Vine, and the Cellar*, 2nd ed., London, Longman, 1864.

10 Analysis of the British Newspaper Archive (BNA) (www.britishnewspaperarchive.co.uk) conducted January 2017. The analysis covered over 600 separate titles.

11 See letter to Robert Votkins, in AMVC,'Lettres particulières d'Édouard Werlé', 23 July 1859.

12 See AMVC, Box 063. K.C.025, H to O for letters to Edouard Werlé from Robert Selby of 19 March 1861 concerning Campbell's of Dublin and 20 and 25 May 1861 concerning Bulloch Lade's underselling.

13 For Selby, see *Liverpool Mail*, 25 June 1853, p. 1 and *Liverpool Mercury*, 13 July 1860, p. 1.

14 AMVC, 'Lettres particulières', 23 July 1859 and 23 September 1859.

extensive correspondence and other sources, I will show the scale and nature of their work in the complex and expanding networks bearing on champagne in Britain[15]. The agents were central intermediaries in three key areas: between the British distributors and retailers and the consumers of champagne, between French producers and the British marketplace generally, and lastly between the influencers and the consumers. In making their interventions, the agents used three key tools: their detailed knowledge of all aspects of the British market, their personal relationships with both trade intermediaries and influencers, and their direct influence over the physical branding of the product.

Sales and distribution

Sales were the primary focus of the agents and their source of remuneration. A key element in the negotiations that preceded the appointment of an agent was the level of commission, which by the 1860s, ranged from 5-10 %[16]. In some cases this sum was required to fund all the costs associated with establishing an office and running a sales organisation; in others, office costs and personal expenses were reimbursed. Hubinet, charged on his appointment in 1859 with establishing the Pommery brand almost from scratch, was an apparently indefatigable traveller covering thousands of miles by train in extensive provincial sales trips and building up strong personal relations with important and influential merchants in every city and major town in Britain[17]. His 1860 contract specified that he should travel for six months per year and his second 1861 tour took in twenty-nine locations in six weeks including Bath, Cambridge, Newcastle, Belfast and Dublin[18]. Hubinet slept on trains and at each new town he would taste samples with important local merchants, ascertain the local taste for champagne

15 For Hubinet's correspondence, see the unpublished 1950s transcriptions in Flocquet A., *Compilation de la correspondance de Hubinet*, Pommery archive, n.d. [1950s].

16 Hubinet initially received 5 % commission excluding office expenses, personal travel and accommodation. See Flocquet, CCH, 30 January 1861 (office expenses); 22 February 1861 (commission); 4 September 1861 (personal expenses).

17 For the development of a close relationship with Robert Little of Liverpool, see CCH, 11 February 1863; 18 March 1863; 2 February 1864; 24 August 1866.

18 See CCH, 16-30 June 1865.

and identify which of the Pommery products might be most suitable, subject to fine-tuning the dosage levels[19]. Further samples would then be sent and discussed by letter before any deal was secured. The process was slow. It took a year of tastings and many samples to convert the influential Liverpool merchant Robert Little[20].

Most trade tastings were competitive. The customer would solicit a range of samples from different houses. Having drawn up a short-list, he would then hold a blind tasting of the contenders in the presence of their agents. The successful house would often be asked to re-submit the wines in a range of different dosages and blends. The customers had to be sure the dosage (or sugar) levels of the wines would suit when delivered some months later[21]. When an order was finally won, it would be relayed back to the principals with details on the *cuvée* and dosage, the bottle size, how the wines were to be corked and wired, what branding was required on the corks, labels and cases, and the timing of the shipment[22]. Each customer had differing requirements and the agent had to ensure these were faithfully executed whilst maintaining brand discipline, such as the use of the shipper rather than the customer name on labels or corks[23]. This process was probably unique to champagne. Other wines such as claret or burgundy could not be customised to taste in this way. For these wines, it is probable that cask samples from one or more merchants would be tasted, assessed for future development and then ordered for later bottling and delivery[24].

This process of competitive tasting enabled the agent to build up detailed knowledge of the changing taste of customers and consumers. It thus provided the agent with the opportunity and the knowledge to influence both the preparation of the wine and the broader strategy of the house. Hubinet took full advantage of this power. As well as persuading his principals to concentrate their sales not on private customers but on

---

19 CCH, 4 March 1861; 11 March 1861; 21 June 1861.

20 The first contact was reported in a letter of 11 February 1863; a sale was finally achieved a year later. See CCH, 2 February 1864.

21 CCH, 23 March 1863: 'taste changes very fast'.

22 See *Aberdeen Journal*, 6 December 1872, p. 7 for a perspective on the differing national tastes.

23 The London merchant, Hamick, required corks branded 'P&G Reims' but no labels. See CCH, 29 April 1863; see also Conrad Reuss to Pol Roger, APR, 6 September 1876.

24 I know of no comparable records of agent or merchant practice for other wine types.

clubs and hotels, he alerted his principals to the growing trend in the 1860s for dry champagne, advised them to restrict the number of *cuvées* (or 'bottlings') on the grounds that a proliferation of different names and qualities weakened the authority of the Pommery brand, and argued successfully for Pommery to pursue a strategy of price maximisation.

The commercial role of agents in the champagne trade extended well beyond their role in generating and negotiating sales. It was their responsibility to check on the creditworthiness and trustworthiness of clients, though they did not normally bear responsibility in the case of failure[25]. Secondly, whilst agents did not set the commercial terms on which wines were vended, they had to enforce these terms. Veuve Clicquot, like Moët & Chandon, set minimum order quantities. Similarly, the houses set distribution strategy but enforcement was entrusted to the agent. Thus, when Moët & Chandon decided in the 1880s to appoint exclusive sub-agents in British cities to maximise distribution and ensure their minimum price levels were not undersold, it was their agency, Simon, Kingscote & Co., who had to execute and defend an unpopular system[26].

Pricing was a key concern for champagne houses and their agents. From the early 1870s onwards, Hubinet argued that Pommery should consistently strive to raise its prices. Towards the end of his life he wrote exultantly in 1890 that Pommery's wine was on restaurant lists at two shillings more than that of its competitors: 'je me suis toujours efforcé d'en arriver là, c'est très important'[27]. His letters gave no reasons for this insistence on high pricing but modern marketing theory agrees that high prices act as a proxy for quality in the minds of consumers[28]. Though Hubinet monitored the economic circumstances of his key customer

---

25 See AMVC, Box 063. K.C.025, H to O, 20-25 May 1861 for Veuve Clicquot commercial strategy and responsibilities.

26 For this controversy, see Harding G., "'Advertisements of Every Kind to Bring Their Brand into Notoriety': Branding and 'Brandolatry' in the Nineteenth-Century Champagne Trade in Britain", *Journal of Wine Economics* 12, no. 4, 2017, p. 383-384.

27 CCH, 10 March 1872; CCH, 24 September 1890. 'I have always striven to get to that point; it's very important.'

28 Vigneron F. and Johnson L. W., "Measuring Perceptions of Brand Luxury", *Journal of Brand Management* 11, no. 6, 2004, p. 489; see also Harding G., "The Establishment of Champagne in Britain, 1860-1914", University of Oxford, 2018, p. 122, 182-183.

groups and recognised when times were hard, he never regretted his insistence that Pommery should be the most expensive wine on the market[29]. Writing to customers in 1879 to justify a price rise during a difficulty period for the British economy, he positioned it as a consequence of Pommery's determination to buy the 'best growths' at the highest prices. He made a similar point in 1889, when, in an extensive profile of Pommery & Greno in the *Illustrated London News,* he claimed that the prices of Pommery's purchases that year were 'the highest ever known [...] a transaction of magnitude never equaled in the trade'[30].

Managing the influencers

A central role for agents was their management of the networks of influence centred on the periodical and daily press, the central Victorian communications medium[31]. Until the 1850s, there is no evidence that producers (or early agents) were involved in advertising[32]. Change began in the late 1850s and early 1860s when the volume of press advertising rose tenfold and the number of brands in the British market increased dramatically[33]. Before 1850, the only commonly advertised brands were Moët and Ruinart, with sporadic mentions of Montebello, Perrier-Jouët and Clicquot. By the end of the 1860s, almost every brand name recognisable to twenty-first century consumers (and dozens more) were being advertised. *Ridley's* listed seventeen 'premium' brands in the early 1870s[34]. With more

---

29 CCH, 15 March 1889. 'Dites carrément que depuis quelques années [...] c'est notre vin qui est coûté au prix le plus élevé.'

30 *Illustrated London News*, 23 November 1889, p. 666.

31 For the contemporary view that the 'newspaper is the fly-wheel by which the motive power of commercial enterprise is sustained', see Mitchell C., *The Newspaper Press Directory*, London, Charles Mitchell, 1859, p. 16.

32 For example, the sole advertisement for Perrier-Jouët was from a Brighton-based importer. See *Brighton Gazette*, 20 December 1849, p. 1.

33 BNA analysis, 27 November 2018, records 21,000 champagne advertisements in the period 1800-1849; 245,000 between 1850-1869, of which nearly 70,000 were published in the 1860s alone. Until the 1830s, brand names were rarely given in advertisements; the focus was on the commune of origin – e.g. Sillery or Ay.

34 The brands listed as premium more than once by *Ridley's* were Ayala, Bollinger, Clicquot, Geisler, Deutz & Gelderman, Goulet, Heidsieck, Irroy, Jules Mumm, Krug, Laurent Perrier, Moët & Chandon, Perrier-Jouët, Pol Roger, Pommery, Roederer and Wachter.

Fig. 1: Derby Day reinforcements', 1878. Source: *Punch*, 8 June 1878, p. 263. Note the preponderance of the Pommery & Greno brand name

brands in the market, successful agents such as Hubinet or Conrad Reuss of Pol Roger needed to fight to assert their own position.

Part of their role was to ensure visibility for the brand's label. Again, Hubinet was prominent, cultivating press contacts to ensure extensive positive coverage of Pommery. The best example was an 1878 cartoon in *Punch*, which showed ranks of champagne bottles lined up as 'Derby Day reinforcements' for thirsty race-goers[35].

As *Ridley's* observed, this was an advertisement of 'no mean merit' which they ascribed to Hubinet's friendship with the editor of the magazine[36]. Hubinet also cultivated valuable relationships with the editor of the *Daily Telegraph*, supplying him with cases of wine and copy for stories praising Pommery. Such contacts made it possible to have stories inserted whenever Pommery supplied the wine for important functions

35 *Punch*, 8 June 1878, p. 263.

36 *Ridley's*, 12 June 1878, p. 181.

such as a dinner given by the Duke of Wellington in 1863 or a Liberal party event laid on for their leader, William Gladstone[37]. Towards the end of his life, Hubinet boasted that 'in London when a champagne is mentioned in theatres or in newspapers, it always is Pommery, *le vin à la mode*'[38]. Analysis of newspaper references in the 1890s confirms Hubinet's assertion[39].

Other agents adopted similar intensive public relations activity. Alfred Simon of Simon, Kingscote, the Moët & Chandon agents[40], wrote to the press whenever the name or reputation of Moët was questioned, hosted 'princely picnics' for customers and distributors and achieved widespread publicity for his pioneering 12,000-mile 1907 tour of Britain by motorcar[41]. In the early twentieth century, his horses raced and won at Epsom (and elsewhere) under the names of 'Moët' and 'Chandon'[42]. In 1895, Simon, Kingscote engaged in an advertising and public relations battle with the equally entrepreneurial Julius Hertz, the London agent for Laurent-Perrier. Advertisements for the latter's 'Sans Sucre' brand in 1894-1895 had claimed that this was the 'only wine permitted by Physicians to those suffering from Gout, Rheumatism and diabetes'[43]. Not only Simon, Kingscote but also Percy Fox, the agent for Lanson, vehemently challenged the medical analyses and endorsements supporting these claims[44]. Hertz then shifted the positioning of Sans Sucre away from a disputed 'lowest sugar' claim towards a broader 'natural champagne' claim and re-took the initiative with a large-scale consumer promotion

---

37 See CCH, 29 April 1863 (Wellington); 24 April 1883 (Gladstone). See letter of 8 March 1891 for another *Daily Telegraph* article on Pommery.

38 CCH, 30 January 1897.

39 BNA, 28 November 2018. Note that classification and OCR errors in this database make such analyses less than wholly reliable.

40 For Moët & Chandon advertising, see *The Times*, 26 September 1905, p. 5. For a more detailed study of Moët & Chandon advertising in this period, see Harding G., "Inventing Tradition and Terroir: The Case of Champagne in the Late Nineteenth Century", in Dutton J. and Howland P. J. (eds.), *Making New Worlds: Wine, Terroir, Utopia*, London, Routledge, 2019.

41 See *Birmingham Daily Post*, 16 April 1886; Moët & Chandon archives, press cuttings 1883-1889, p. 79-80, 89, 91; the *Car*, 1 January 1908, p. 293.

42 For Simon's racehorses, see *Illustrated Sporting and Dramatic News*, 19 June 1909, p. 689.

43 *Globe*, 14 January 1895, p. 4; *London Evening Standard*, 22 November 1894, p. 4.

44 *Ridley's*, 12 March 1895, p. 186.

which offered a total of 'about £6000' worth of prizes in exchange for Sans Sucre corks[45].

Corks (and, later, labels) played an important role in the networks of the champagne trade. The reintroduction of corks in the 1600s and improved glass technology enabled producers to distribute in bottle rather than in cask from the 1730s onwards. This not only lessened the risk of spoilage but made champagne more easily identified than other wines which were mostly decanted before serving. Secondly, the corks were branded with the producer name and thus served as a guarantee of authenticity. As *Ridley's* confirmed in 1881, 'champagne is taken by the consumer on its real or supposed merits, which to him are typified, as a rule, by the brand on the cork'[46]. The introduction of coloured labels in the 1830s further strengthened the social impact of champagne[47].

The label was important for three reasons. Firstly, it attracted consumers. As *Ridley's* noted in 1865, 'tinfoil, pink tissue-paper, and neat but showy labels, have much to do in recommending champagne'; a charge repeated in 1898 with the claim that for a 'large proportion' of consumers, any wine will suffice, 'so long as it is furnished with an attractive label'[48]. Secondly, since champagne was served in bottle, the label showed how much the host had spent[49]. Branded champagnes carried greater status on the table. Lastly, the power of the label was strengthened by its visibility in public prints. Corks might guarantee quality but labels sold the wine. As a merchant complained to *Ridley's* in 1890, 'one can but seldom take up a Comic or Illustrated Journal without seeing a Champagne bottle introduced into the woodcuts with the name of some House conspicuous in the label'[50]. The overall effect was that by the late nineteenth century, there was a clear ladder of brands.

---

45 For the troubled Hertz promotion, see Harding G., "The Establishment of Champagne in Britain, 1860-1914", p. 257-258.

46 *Ridley's*, 12 July 1881, p. 208. See also Feuerheerd H. L., *The Gentleman's Cellar and Butler's Guide*, London, Chatto & Windus, 1899, p. 67. This confirms the cork was a 'direct guarantee' of the wine in the bottle.

47 For the development of label-printing technology, see Davidson J. B., *The Art of the Cigar Label*, Edison, NJ, Wellfleet, 1997, p. 17-19.

48 *Ridley's*, 6 May 1865, p. 7; 12 September 1898, p. 611.

49 For Gilbey's discontinuance of labels for their own brand champagne, see Diageo, 110204/12, 'Note on Champagnes: discontinuance of labels', 28 February 1879.

50 *Ridley's*, 12 September 1890, p. 497.

In 1898 *Ridley's* claimed that 'a vintage champagne has [...] almost as definite a market value as have Railway or industrial shares, which the general run of the public have no difficulty whatever in ascertaining'[51]. Control of the brand collateral such as corks, labels and packaging was central to agents' management of the marketplace.

Managing the marketplace

A vital part of the agents' role was to observe developing trends in customer behaviour, report their insights back to their principals in France and initiate the necessary action. Thus, in 1861, Hubinet argued to his principals that the Pommery name should be given maximum prominence on the label. If, he said, there are several names on the label, 'it confuses them [customers]; a single name sticks better in everyone's mind'[52]. In 1863, he told his principals to brand the corks of a dry wine prepared specially for London with the added term 'UK Extra' to signify that it was drier than the standard 'Sec' wine. Four years later he advised that English customers were now so familiar with the term 'Brut' (signifying a wine with a lower dosage yet) that it should be used on the cork[53].

Powerful agents such as Adolphe Hubinet, Julius Hertz and Alfred Simon were significant contributors to the broader marketing strategies of the brands they represented. Hubinet was central to the Pommery shift from a multiplicity of individual *cuvées* to large bottlings in a consistent house style characterised by finesse, delicacy and elegance[54]. Unless, he wrote in 1871, the house adopted this policy our customers 'could not count on having the same wine twice'[55]. This style should be created via winemaking practices that would enable the house style to be replicated in ever larger *cuvées*[56].

---

51 *Ridley's*, 12 April 1893, p. 217; 12 July 1898, p. 499.

52 CCH, 1 August 1861. 'S'ils observent plusieurs noms sur l'étiquette, ils les confondent; un seul nom se grave mieux dans la mémoire de tout le monde'.

53 CCH, 30 May 1863; 18 December 1867.

54 CCH, 21 October 1865; De Polignac A., *Madame Pommery*, p. 39; offering drier wine than competitors would be a 'specialité plus marquée', he later suggested. See CCH, 30 October 1871.

55 CCH, 12 March 1871. Lacking such a policy, 'nos admirateurs [...] ne peuvent jamais compter boire le même vin deux fois'.

56 CCH, 23 October 1865. '[L]a réputation de délicatesse, d'élégance, que nous avons déjà acquise'.

Agents and intermediaries

Despite the importance of agents in this market, they – and other intermediaries – have received relatively little attention. Frank Trentmann's *Empire of Things* has been praised for its attempts to take in such figures, but his work, whilst highlighting some individuals in the broad sweep of nineteenth- and twentieth-century consumption history, does not allow for detailed study of such figures[57]. The few studies of intermediaries in British commercial life in the nineteenth century have concentrated on the agents of British companies, whether operating in the UK or in overseas territories.

In the commercial context, an agent is one who undertakes negotiations or transactions on behalf of a superior, a principal. The term goes back at least to the 1500s but, as Avner Greif's work on the so-called commercial revolution of the twelfth century has shown, the role is far older[58]. The issue with agents is how to manage the conflict between the requirement for agents to act entrepreneurially and the principal's desire to control the risks that this may present to his capital[59]. Extensive theorisation of this principal-agent problem has mostly focused on job organisation and game theory[60]. Marc Prat argued in 2009 that 'the processes of commercialisation have often been overlooked by economic history studies' and there is a paucity of material on the day to day work of commercial intermediaries such as agents[61]. However, there are exceptions such as Andrew Popp's

57 See, for example, Trentmann F., *Empire of Things: How We Became a World of Consumers, from the Fifteenth Century to the Twenty-First*, London, Penguin Random House, 2016, p. 129-131; see also Chessel M. E., "Des empires aux objets: la fabrique des consommateurs", *Revue d'Histoire Moderne et Contemporaine* 64, no. 1, 2017, p. 167-168.

58 Greif A., "Contract Enforceability and Economic Institutions in Early Trade: The Maghribi Traders' Coalition", *The American Economic Review* 83, no. 3, 1993.

59 Greif A., "Institutions and International Trade: Lessons from the Commercial Revolution", *The American Economic Review* 82, no. 2, 1992, p. 129-130.

60 For job organisation, see, for example, Holmstrom B. and Milgrom P., "Multitask Principal-Agent Analyses: Incentive Contracts, Asset Ownership, and Job Design", *Journal of Law, Economics, & Organization* 7, 1991, p. 24-25 and passim; for game theory, see Clark G., "A Review of Avner Greif's Institutions and the Path to the Modern Economy: Lessons from Medieval Trade", *Journal of Economic Literature* 45, no. 3, 2016, p. 735.

61 Prat M., "Between the Firm and the Market: An International Comparison of the Commercial Structures of the Cotton Industry (1820-1939)", *Business History* 51, no. 2, 2009, p. 182.

studies of John Shaw, the Wolverhampton hardware factor, and Stephen Nicholas' 1983 examination of agency contracts[62]. These studies of the British commercial practice provide useful insight into the general frameworks of commercial life in a range of markets, though the wine trade is not part of their examination.

These studies have suggested that agent-principal relationships are inherently unstable. Nicholas has argued that instability arises from informational asymmetries. Decision problems arise because agents have the market knowledge that principals lack, whilst agents lack the principals' product knowledge. Conflicts therefore arise over levels of stock holding, promotional effort, price optimisation and appropriate service levels[63]. In general, when the cost of monitoring agents outweighs the benefits of local market knowledge the principals will tend to establish fully or majority-owned sales organisations as an integral part of the firm[64]. The wine trade, perhaps because of its emphasis on personal relationships and implicit market knowledge, does not conform to this model[65]. Though there were disputes, these rarely led to frequent changes of agent or to forward integration by the French houses, partly because of the personal links that grew up between principals and agents, and partly because changing to another agent risked relationships already developed in the British market[66].

---

62 Popp A., "Building the Market: John Shaw of Wolverhampton and Commercial Travelling in Early Nineteenth-Century England", *Business History* 49, no. 3, 2007; Popp A. and Holt R., "Entrepreneurship and Being: The Case of the Shaws", *Entrepreneurship & Regional Development* 25, no. 1-2, 2013; Nicholas S., "Agency Contracts, Institutional Modes, and the Transition to Foreign Direct Investment by British Manufacturing Multinationals before 1939", *Journal of Economic History* 43, no. 3, 1983.

63 Nicholas S.,*op. cit.*; see also Musset B., *op. cit.* Musset confirms several of Nicholas' points in his analysis of Jean-Rémy Moët's early experience with travellers.

64 See also Popp A., "Barriers to Innovation in Marketing in the Mid-Nineteenth Century: Merchant-Manufacturer Relationships", *Business History* 44, no. 2, 2002, p. 23, 31-33.

65 Explicit market knowledge is that which is publicly available and contrasts with implicit (or tacit) market knowledge which is often based on personal experience.

66 For the close personal links between agent, principal and customers, see APR, 7 August 1876 (Pol Roger to Conrad Reuss); 9 August 1876 (Reuss to Pol Roger) dealing with family affairs; 9 December 1876 (Pol Roger to Reuss) with hunting together; 14 February 1877 (Pol Roger to Reuss) with condolences over a family bereavement.

The champagne trade challenges the dominant paradigm of principal-agent relationships. The partnerships between Perrier-Jouët and the Boursot family and Moët & Chandon and the Simon family lasted over a century[67]. The success of the French shippers and brand owners working in partnership with long-established agencies in the nineteenth and twentieth centuries demonstrates that forward integration was not an essential component of business success as previous scholars have argued[68]. Indeed, it is possible that forward integration is less a pre-requisite and more a hindrance in the drinks industry, where personal market knowledge and experience are essential to success[69]. Men such as Hubinet were central players in the development and organisation of the champagne trade. Without them, the great brands they represented would not have been so built and so successfully built.

Sources

AMVC. Archives Maison Veuve Clicquot

APR. Archives Pol Roger

CCH. Compilation de la Correspondance de Hubinet (see Flocquet below)

Diageo. Diageo Archives, Menstrie, Scotland

References

Chandler, Alfred D. *Scale and Scope: The Dynamics of Industrial Capitalism.* Cambridge, MA; London: Harvard University Press, 1994.

Chessel, Marie-Emmanuelle. "Des empires aux objets: la fabrique des consommateurs." *Revue d'Histoire Moderne et Contemporaine* 64, no. 1 (2017): 166-174.

Christie's Sales Catalogue, no date.

---

67 Devroey J. P., *Perrier-Jouët: The Essence of Champagne*, Paris, Stock, 1999, p. 59-60.

68 For the US-led paradigm of branding history, see Chandler A. D., *Scale and Scope: The Dynamics of Industrial Capitalism*, Cambridge, Mass; London, Harvard University Press, 1994, p. 169, 267-268.

69 Da Silva Lopes T., *Global Brands: The Evolution of Multinationals in Alcoholic Beverages*, Cambridge, Cambridge University Press, 2007, p. 4-10.

Clark, Gregory. "A Review of Avner Greif's Institutions and the Path to the Modern Economy: Lessons from Medieval Trade." *Journal of Economic Literature* 45, no. 3 (2016): 725-744.

da Silva Lopes, Teresa. *Global Brands: The Evolution of Multinationals in Alcoholic Beverages*. Cambridge: Cambridge University Press, 2007.

Davidson, Joseph B. *The Art of the Cigar Label*. Edison, NJ: Wellfleet, 1997.

de Polignac, Alain. *Madame Pommery: le génie et le coeur*. Paris: Stock, 1994.

Devroey, Jean-Pierre. *Perrier-Jouët: The Essence of Champagne*. Paris: Stock, 1999.

Druitt, Robert. *Report on the Cheap Wines from France, Italy, Austria, Greece, and Hungary*. 2nd ed. London: Henry Renshaw, 1873.

Feuerheerd, H. L. *The Gentleman's Cellar and Butler's Guide*. London: Chatto & Windus, 1899.

Flanders, Judith. *Consuming Passions: Leisure and Pleasure in Victorian Britain*. London: Harper Press, 2006.

Flanders, Judith. *The Victorian City: Everyday Life in Dickens' London*. London: Atlantic Books, 2013.

Flocquet, André. *Compilation de la correspondance de Hubinet*. Pommery Archives, n.d. [1950s].

Gilbey, Alfred. *Treatise on Wines and Spirits of the Principal Producing Countries*. London: W & A Gilbey Ltd, 1869.

Gladstone, William. "Financial Statement", 10 February 1860, vol. 156, c. 812-89.

Greif, Avner. "Contract Enforceability and Economic Institutions in Early Trade: The Maghribi Traders' Coalition." *The American Economic Review* 83, no. 3 (1993): 525-548.

Greif, Avner. "Institutions and International Trade: Lessons from the Commercial Revolution." *The American Economic Review* 82, no. 2 (1992): 128-133.

Harding, Graham. "'Advertisements of Every Kind to Bring Their Brand into Notoriety': Branding and 'Brandolatry' in the Nineteenth-Century Champagne Trade in Britain." *Journal of Wine Economics* 12, no. 4 (2017): 378-385.

Harding, Graham. "The Establishment of Champagne in Britain, 1860-1914." University of Oxford, 2018.

Harding, Graham. "Inventing Tradition and Terroir: The Case of Champagne in the Late Nineteenth Century." In *Making New Worlds: Wine, Terroir, Utopia*, edited by J. Dutton and P. J. Howland. London: Routledge, 2019.

Holmstrom, Bengt, and Paul Milgrom. "Multitask Principal-Agent Analyses: Incentive Contracts, Asset Ownership, and Job Design." *Journal of Law, Economics, & Organization* 7 (1991): 24-52.

Milne-Smith, Amy. "A Flight to Domesticity? Making a Home in the Gentlemen's Clubs of London, 1880-1914." *Journal of British Studies* 45, no. 4 (2006): 796-818.

Mitchell, Charles. *The Newspaper Press Directory*. London: Charles Mitchell, 1859. 1846.

Musset, Benoît. "L'expérimentation d'une nouvelle pratique commerciale: la maison Moët d'Épernay et ses commis voyageurs (1790-1815)." *Entreprises et Histoire*, no. 66 (2012): 103-115.

Nicholas, Stephen. "Agency Contracts, Institutional Modes, and the Transition to Foreign Direct Investment by British Manufacturing Multinationals before 1939." *Journal of Economic History* 43, no. 3 (1983): 675-686.

Popp, Andrew. "Barriers to Innovation in Marketing in the Mid-Nineteenth Century: Merchant-Manufacturer Relationships." *Business History* 44, no. 2 (2002): 19-39.

Popp, Andrew. "Building the Market: John Shaw of Wolverhampton and Commercial Travelling in Early Nineteenth-Century England." *Business History* 49, no. 3 (2007): 321-347.

Popp, Andrew, and Robin Holt. "Entrepreneurship and Being: The Case of the Shaws." *Entrepreneurship & Regional Development* 25, no. 1-2 (2013): 52-68.

Prat, Marc. "Between the Firm and the Market: An International Comparison of the Commercial Structures of the Cotton Industry (1820-1939)." *Business History* 51, no. 2 (2009): 181-201.

Shaw, Thomas Ridley's Wine and Spirit Trade Circular

George. *Wine, the Vine, and the Cellar*. 2nd. ed. London: Longman, 1864.

Spiers, R. G. *Spiers and Pond: Restaurateurs, Cricket Promoters and Hoteliers Extraordinaire*. Tring: R.G. Spiers, 2008.

Trentmann, Frank. *Empire of Things: How We Became a World of Consumers, from the Fifteenth Century to the Twenty-First*. London: Penguin Random House, 2016.

Vigneron, Franck, and Lester W. Johnson. "Measuring Perceptions of Brand Luxury." *Journal of Brand Management* 11, no. 6 (2004): 484-506.

Vizetelly, Henry. *The Wines of the World Characterized & Classed: With Some Particulars Respecting the Beers of Europe*. London: Ward, Lock, Tyler, 1875.

PART II

Intermediaries in the Production, Marketing and Consumption of Wine

Guardians of Trade Secrets: Brokers and Wine Distribution in the United Provinces in the 18th Century

Anne Wegener Sleeswijk

Various 17th and 18th century writers of merchant handbooks have drawn attention to the key position of brokers in Dutch wholesale and intermediate trade[1]. French writer and merchant Jacques Accarias de Sérionne [1768], reports for instance: "Ce sont des agents dont le commerce ne peut se passer, principalement dans les grands entrepôts, tels que Rotterdam et Amsterdam. [...] C'est chez eux qu'on trouve en même temps tous les prix relatifs de chaque article: ils en connaissent l'abondance et la disette sur place, ils sont les dépositaires de la demande, & pour ainsi dire, du secret du commerce"[2]. Accarias' words refer to brokerage in general, but in reality, brokers were particularly active in certain services and in sectors of commerce, where product differentiation was large, such as the wine trade. In the United Provinces, hiring a broker when selling or purchasing wine was not mandatory, but widespread both for locals and foreigners. Wine brokers mediated in various positions within the distribution channel: between wholesalers but also, and probably more often, in semi-retailing between importers and specialised wine merchants and sometimes between wine merchants and retailers. Some

1 Ricard J. P., *Le négoce d'Amsterdam: contenant tout ce que doivent savoir les marchands et banquiers*, Amsterdam, Etienne Lucas, 1722, p. 324-328; Krünitz J. G., *Oeconomische (Oekonomisch-technologische) Encyclopädie*, Berlin, Joachim Pauli, 1781, p. 405-408.

2 "No trade can be conducted without these agents, especially in cities with a warehouse function, such as Rotterdam and Amsterdam. [...] They can provide the relative prices of each item: they know the abundance and the scarcity on the spot, they are the depositories of demand, and so to speak, of all trade secrets". Accarias de Sérionne J., *Le commerce de la Hollande ou tableau du commerce des Hollandois dans les quatre parties du monde*, Amsterdam, Changuion, 1768, II, p. 368.

of them had a wide range of activities: they were not just matchmakers, but also provided all kinds of services and specialised information[3].

Traditionally, brokerage was a municipal office that was supposed to be awarded free of charge by the mayors to the people "most qualified" for the job. In many towns, only male citizens (often Christians as well as Jews) could become a broker. Upon acceptance of their position, brokers had to take an oath, promising to act in the interest of both their clients and the city, to apply the official brokers' rates, to renounce trading on their own account (at least in the product they were brokering), to keep contracts secret and to perform their duties in accordance with local ordinances. Formally, commercial intermediation was the monopoly of the brokers' guild, but Amsterdam and Rotterdam also had numerous illicit brokers, who were more or less tolerated by the authorities[4]. The position of illegal brokers differed in several respects from that of sworn brokers. They were not allowed to organise voluntary auction sales of goods and since they were not under oath, their word was not legally binding. However, they also had a number of advantages compared to official brokers. For instance, they were not required to adhere to the official brokers' rates, which could be highly beneficial in a seasonable trade.

The Dutch wine market was characterised by indirect distribution channels, often involving various interconnected intermediaries between the importer and the consumer. This complexity of trade networks was in part a consequence of tax policy. Urban and provincial authorities levied heavy excise duties on wine, payable by consumers and retailers. In order to control the collection of these taxes, an artificial (and unworkable) distinction between wholesalers, semi-retailers and retailers had been introduced[5].

Unlike wine-producing countries, and especially France, where some in-depth research has been conducted on the history of wine brokerage,

---

3 For an overview: Ogilvie S., *Institutions and European Trade: Merchant Guilds, 1000-1800*, Cambridge, Cambridge University Press, 2011, p. 369-371.

4 Ricard J. P., *op. cit.*, p. 324.

5 Wholesalers were allowed to sell at least one cask of wine per transaction (about 900 liters); semi-retailers could sell quantities of at least 4 stoops at a time (approximately 9, 6 liters) and only retailers were allowed to sell wine by the glass or by the can. Purchase was not bound by legal restrictions. This all applied to Amsterdam: the boundaries between wholesale, intermediate trade and retailing differed from one town to another.

the profession has attracted hardly any attention in the Netherlands[6]. Some studies on Dutch trade history, however, do contain a chapter on brokerage in general[7]. Unfortunately, most of these are, as Velinov has recently pointed out, largely based on regulation, whereas documents reflecting commercial practice have hardly been studied[8]. Historians have moreover exclusively focused on Amsterdam wholesale trade. Transaction cost analysis is the dominant explicative framework.

Instead of compressing the object in a preconceived model, this research on the contrary, makes a case for an empiricist study of the praxis of wine brokerage, based on merchant letters, books and bills. I will investigate why semi-retailers hired wine brokers, even though this was not compulsory. The first section discusses the main features of the Dutch wine market and the organisation of the brokers' profession in the foremost distribution centres: Amsterdam, Rotterdam, Middelburg and the inland port of Dordrecht. The second and third parts examine the circumstances under which specialised wine merchants appealed to a broker. The backgrounds and careers of these intermediaries in trade are also discussed here. Finally, special attention is given to the brokers' role in the provision of information, as this has always been a central aspect of wine brokerage.

---

6 Brennan T., *The Wine Trade in Early Modern France*, Baltimore/London, John Hopkins University Press, 1997; Musset B., "Le courtage des vins de champagne du XVIIe au XIXe siècle", in Lavaud S. (eds.), *Vendre le vin de l'Antiquité à nos jours*, Bordeaux, Féret, 2012, p. 255-265; Lachaud-Martin, S., "Les courtiers bordelais, intermédiaires de commerce du vin aux XVIIe-XVIIIe siècles", *Revue historique*, n°686, 2018, p. 321-346.

7 Gelderblom O., *Cities of Commerce: The Institutional Foundations of International Trade in* the Low Countries, 1250-1650, Princeton University Press, 2013, p. 57-75; Lesger C., *The Rise of the Amsterdam Market and Information Exchange: Merchants, Commercial Expansion and Change in the Spatial Economy of the Low Countries*, c. 1550-1630, New York, Routledge, 2006, p. 224-226; Tielhof M. van, *The "Mother of All Trades": The Baltic Grain Trade in Amsterdam from the Late 16th to the Early 19th century*, Leiden, Brill, 2002, p. 153-156; Boerner L. and Quint D., Medieval matching markets. Economic History Working Papers (241/2016). The London School of Economics and Political Science, London. Online: https://www.econstor.eu/bitstream/10419/43870/1/643936505.pdf.

8 Velinov D., "Parasites ou abeilles? Le rôle des courtiers dans les marchés médiévaux et modernes (Bruges, Anvers, Amsterdam, XIVe-XVIIIe siècle)", in Demont V., Scherman M. and Wegener Sleeswijk A. (eds.), *Le pouvoir des courtiers. Univers marchand et acteurs du courtage en Europe XIVe-XVIIIe s.*, Paris, Éditions rue d'Ulm/Presses de l'ENS, 2018, p. 41, 42.

Brokerage and wine distribution in the United Provinces

In the 18th century, the Dutch wine market had some stable features, but also went through a number of significant changes. In the first half of the century, the United Provinces were the chief market for French wine and conversely French wines had an overwhelming share of the Dutch wine trade. Outside periods of war, the vast majority of Dutch maritime wine imports (70 to 90 % depending on the year) came from France. High tolls were levied at the Rhine, preventing Rhine and Mosel wines from gaining a large market share[9].

Amsterdam and Rotterdam were the main ports for imports of wine in Holland, the former increasingly surpassing the latter. The town of Middelburg in Zeeland, which had dominated maritime wine imports up to the first decades of the 17th century, still played a second-rate role, with a share of approximately 15 %. The former staple of Dordrecht controlled part of the distribution of German wines, a greatly reduced branch of trade.

Over the course of the century, several independent phenomena such as the falling purchasing power of the middle classes and the increasing profitability of Dutch and French West-Indian trade, contributed to a decrease in wine imports in the United Provinces. However, at the same time, the increasingly complex structure of the Dutch wine market may have furthered the need for specialised intermediaries. Around the middle of the century, elite consumer preferences shifted from the sweet white wines of the Garonne Valley and the Bergerac area to the red wines of Médoc, Cahors, Languedoc and Spain. Improvements in conservation techniques encouraged wine aging, and producer names and regional brands became ever better known among regular consumers. Diversification also occurred at the lower end of the market. There was a strong demand for cheap processed wines (for instance from Poitou), softened by the addition of sugar syrup and also for locally produced Ersatz. Small consumers, whose daily drink consisted of beer and tea, attached

---

9 Unless mentioned otherwise, this paragraph is based on: Wegener Sleeswijk A., "Les vins français aux Provinces-Unies au XVIIIe siècle. Négoce, dynamiques institutionnelles et organisation du marché", PhD Thesis, Université d'Amsterdam and EHESS Paris, 2006.

Fig. 1: The Amsterdam brokers' guildhall, built in 1633. Above the door: " 't maekelaers comptoir" ("The brokers' hall"). Above the upper window: "Vryheid is voor geen geld te koop" ("Freedom is not for sale"). © Anne Wegener Sleeswijk, 2019

great importance to drinking "wine" at special occasions: christenings, weddings, funerals and the annual fair.

Given the dominant position of Amsterdam in imports, it seems logical that this city had the largest number of wine brokers. Around 1720, according to Jean-Pierre Ricard, sixty to eighty brokers -both official and illicit- specialised in the wine and brandy trade[10]. However,

10 Ricard J. P., *op. cit.*, 1722, p. 325. For an overview of total numbers of official brokers in Amsterdam in the early modern period: Stuart T., *De Amsterdamsche makelaardij.*

some of them hardly practiced, because they were either too old or combined wine brokerage with other activities. The 1730 official brokers' directory for Amsterdam mentions twenty-three names of professionals who considered the wine and brandy trade as their specialisation[11]. In Rotterdam, the number of official wine brokers was at least eleven in 1735[12]. Eight sworn wine brokers were active in Middelburg in 1648; in 1754 they were only four[13]. In Dordrecht, the number of brokers allowed to mediate in any trade except for grain was set at six in 1726[14]. Newspaper advertisements show that Dordrecht brokers did not specialise and those involved in the wine trade also settled transactions in other goods and services[15].

In all four cities, brokers were required to join the local brokers' guild. Whereas the Middelburg wine brokers formed a separate guild from 1648 onward, with its own ordinance and guild house, the Amsterdam, Rotterdam and Dordrecht wine brokers belonged, to the general brokers' guilds. In other respects, there were also major differences between the four cities. Brokerage rates for wine varied considerably for instance from one city to another. They were the highest in Amsterdam, but hardly ever exceeded 3 % of a wine's value[16].

Bijdrage tot de geschiedenis onzer handelswetgeving, Amsterdam, Spin en Zoon, 1879, p. 160.

11 Demont V. and Wegener Sleeswijk A., "Milieux du courtage à Amsterdam et à Hambourg (fin XVIIe-début XVIIIe siècle)", in Demont V., Scherman M. and Wegener Sleeswijk A. (eds.), *op. cit.*, p. 185, 186.

12 Stadsarchief Rotterdam (from now on SR), 1 Oud Stads Archief (from now on OSA), 2192, Dossier van het geschil tussen wijnkooplieden en makelaars gebracht voor burgemeesteren, 1735.

13 Zeeuws Archief (from now on ZA), 3/68, Ordonnantie voor de makelaars van de wijnen binnen de stad Middelburg in Zeeland, met aanvullingen tot 1723; *Naamwyzer, aantonende alle de namen en woonplaatsen van de Edele achtbare magistraat der stad Middelburg in Zeeland* [...], vol. 8, Middelburg, Callenfels and Taillefert, 1758, p. 27.

14 Regionaal Archief Dordrecht (from now on RAD), 134, 6, Ordonnantie op 't makelaars ambt, 21 Sept. 1726.

15 Advertisements for wine and timber auctions in Dordrecht, *Oprechte Haerlemsche courant*, 11 June 1722; 29 April 1723; *'s Gravenhaegse courant*, 18 April 1725; 27 May 1726. Online: Delpher.

16 SR, 1 OSA, 2192, Dossier van het geschil tussen wijnkooplieden en makelaars, 1735.

Brokers were responsible for two major commercial institutions that held a key position in the provision of commercial information. The Dean and the Council of the Amsterdam brokers' guild were in charge of the publication of the commodity price lists, the *Amsterdamsche Prijscourant*, which had appeared weekly or bi-weekly since 1585[17]. Every week, the Amsterdam wine brokers had to transmit current wholesale prices. They also selected the types of wine to be mentioned, changing the classification several times in the course of the century. Between the end of the 17th and the end of the 18th century, the *Prijscourant* thus mentioned the wholesale prices of sixteen to twenty-eight categories of French wine, three to fourteen Spanish and Portuguese wines and occasionally an Italian wine. German wines were not included as they were imported by wine merchants and generally sold without brokers' intermediation.

In all four cities, brokers also had the privilege of organising voluntary auction sales of merchandise, under the supervision of a city official. Wine was one of the goods most frequently sold. Around 1720, in Amsterdam, about a quarter of all imported wine was sold at the auction. Most sellers were wholesalers; the buyers were mostly wine merchants, distillers and institutions such as trading companies and old people's homes. Only sellers at the auction were obliged to hire a broker, but buyers also often did so. In Amsterdam, Rotterdam and Dordrecht, wine auctions took place in specialised inns, whereas the Middelburg auctions were organised at the wine merchants' guild house[18].

While regulation gives an idea of the contours of the wine brokers' profession, correspondence between wine merchants and their brokers provides more insight into the position of these intermediaries in distribution networks.

Formal representatives and troubleshooters

In January 1750, the Dordrecht wine merchant Matthijs Marshal wrote to his Rotterdam broker, Pieter van Overzee, that he had received in good order, the six hogsheads of new Bergerac wine that the latter had

17 Mc Cusker J. and Gravesteijn C., *The Beginnings of Commercial and Financial Journalism*, Amsterdam, NEHA, 1991, p. 44, 45.

18 *Middelburgsche courant*, 17 Dec. 1776. Online: Delpher.

shipped to him. He also asked him to buy some barrels of a red Bordeaux from the 1748 vintage, preferably of a *cru* that he had previously sampled, provided that the wine was "clean" and not too expensive. Finally, he enquired how his broker valued the latest "vin du Haut-Pays". Had he already tasted these wines? Where they "good and sweet" and at what prices did they sell[19]? Pieter van Overzee was Marshal's regular Rotterdam broker. Purchase orders and information on prices and on the quality of wines formed the main subjects of their correspondence.

Matthijs Marshal was born in Dordrecht in 1705. In spite of his English sounding last name, he was probably of German descent: he spoke and wrote German fluently and belonged to the Lutheran congregation. He learned the wine trade with his father[20]. Only one archival piece has survived for his enterprise, a messy copybook of outgoing correspondence for the period 1745 to 1762, also containing some copies of bills. Marshal was well-to-do: he owned several houses and warehouses in his hometown, and possessed a carriage and a country house near Wieldrecht, where he enjoyed spending the weekend. He belonged to "De Veertigen", the council of representatives of the guilds that compiled the lists from which the Dordrecht aldermen and the town councillors were chosen[21]. By the end of his life, Marshal was appointed Dean of the wine merchants' guild[22].

As a *wijnkoper*, Marshal specialised in semi-retailing. However, like many of his Dordrecht colleagues, he also imported Rhine and Mosel wines on his own account. He had a stable network of suppliers in the German hinterland including merchants and producers from Trier, Trarbach, Bingen-am-Rhein, Mainz and Cologne (Map 1). His German correspondents acted as commission agents, but he also regularly

---

19 The term "Vin du Haut-Pays" was used to refer to all wine from outside the city of Bordeaux jurisdiction. In Holland, this was mainly Bergerac, Cahors and Gaillac wine. RAD, 9 Gerecht van Dordrecht, 1390, Matthijs Marshal Letter copybook (from now on MML), Letter to Pieter van Overzee, Rotterdam, 20 Jan.1750.

20 RAD, 3 Stadsarchieven, 3849, Auction sale of wine, 29 July 1700; 3850, Auction sales of brandy and wine, 16 Oct. 1700; 27 Dec. 1700; 12 and 17 May 1701.

21 RAD, 32 Collectie van eigendomspapieren van huizen en landerijen, 32, 15-1, Akte van transport, 18 april 1769, f. 31; RAD, 9 Gerecht van Dordrecht, 1663, transportakte 27 okt. 1761, f. 130; Frijhoff W., *Geschiedenis van Dordrecht van 1572 tot 1813*, Hilversum, Verloren, 1996, p. 22.

22 RAD, 3 Stadsarchieven, 3520, Lijst houdende een opgave van de toegelaten wijnkopers [...] 1773.

Map 1: Wine supply network of Matthijs Marshal, Dordrecht, 1745-1762. RAD, 9 Gerecht van Dordrecht, 1390, Matthijs Marshal Letter copybook, 1745-1762.

travelled to Germany to purchase wine on the spot. He imported a wide range of German wines: both "modest" Mosel from Wehlen, Bernkastel and Piesport, as well as Rhine wines from Rüdesheim, Bodenheim and even the very best Hochheim, from the vineyards of the Dean of Mainz Cathedral[23]. He also dealt in French and Spanish wines, which he

23 RAD, 1390 MML, Letters to Jean Georg Voith, Mainz, 15 Oct. 1745 and 9 Nov 1745.

purchased from Rotterdam and Amsterdam wholesalers or at the brokers' auction in his hometown[24].

Marshal's clientele was composed of dozens of customers in Dordrecht and other Dutch towns as distant as Leeuwarden and Groningen[25]. Most of them belonged to the local elite, others were military officers. They usually ordered a basket containing 45 bottles (one *anker*) of wine once or several times a year. Marshal also occasionally supplied fellow wine merchants in other cities of the United Provinces with German wine. In 1760, he even made an attempt to export Rhine and Frontignan wine to Batavia, but this proved unsuccessful[26]. The volume of his wine sales is only known for one year: from November 1745 to October 1746 they amounted to approximately 47 thousand litres.

Marshal mainly used brokers in two cases: when he sold Rhine or Mosel wines at the auction in his hometown and when he bought French or Spanish wine in Amsterdam or Rotterdam. As his dealings with Dordrecht brokers have proved to be difficult to document, we will concentrate on his metropolitan brokers.

Between 1745 and 1762, Marshal maintained exclusive and long-term relationships with one Rotterdam broker and one Amsterdam broker. The two men had very different backgrounds. Pieter van Overzee from Rotterdam belonged to a prosperous and influential brokers' clan. He had been active as a broker since at least 1723, but like his father, he focused initially on the timber trade[27]. He started to specialise in wine from the 1730s, probably as a consequence of his marriage, in 1733, to a daughter of Florens Eilbracht, one of the foremost Rotterdam wine brokers[28]. Van Overzee's career is interesting because it shows that in

---

24 For instance: RAD, 3 Stadsarchieven, 3852, Brokers' wine auctions, 22 Aug. 1723 and 22 Aug. 1727.

25 RAD, 1390 MML, Letters to Jacoba Guerre, Leeuwarden, and Johannes Smith, Groningen, 20 Aug. 1746 and 27 June 1748.

26 *Ibid.*, Letters to Willem Welborn, Batavia, 28 March; 30 Oct. 1760 and 19 Sept. 1761.

27 SR, 18 Notarissen Rotterdam, 3856 Gerrit Post, Report of a timber auction, 23 May 1684. Advertisements for timber auctions: *Amsterdamse courant*, 28 Sept. 1723 and 6 April 1726; Advertisements for wine auctions: 's *Gravenhaegse courant*, 23 June 1724; 5 May 1732; *Leydse courant*, 4 Feb. 1733 and 17 May 1734, Online: Delpher.

28 SR, DTB 1-02, 73, Marriage certificate for Elisabeth Eilbracht and Pieter van Overzee, 22 Nov. 1733.

Holland a successful wine broker was not necessarily in the first place a wine expert.

Usually, Van Overzee bought batches of four to eight hogsheads of wine for Marshal. Before carrying out his assignment, the broker would send sample bottles of different producers and vintages. Sometimes, Marshal also travelled to Rotterdam himself (about 18 kilometres from Dordrecht) to taste wines in the company of his broker. It is noteworthy that Marshal even appealed to his metropolitan brokers when purchasing wine with importers he knew quite well himself. He seems to have hired his brokers not in the first place to reduce search costs, nor to enforce contracts. He essentially turned to them because they provided him with a "package" of services. They had barrels cleaned up if necessary, took care of payment and import taxes and acted as shipping agents[29].

From 1748 on, Marshal also employed an Amsterdam broker, Arent van Eldick[30]. At the time, Van Eldick, who seems to have established himself in Amsterdam around 1730, worked as an illicit broker. He only obtained a license in 1758 after a long career[31]. Initially, there was some confusion about his position, as Marshal's German correspondent had presented him as "an Amsterdam wine commissioner"[32]. However, Van Eldick charged a broker's fee and not a commission (a percentage) and acted in every respect as a broker[33]. This confusion is remarkable because it bears witness both to the proliferation of all sorts of middlemen in 18th century trade and to the blurring of boundaries between official and illicit brokerage. Young brokers often worked as illegal brokers before obtaining an office. Moreover, although strictly forbidden, official and illicit wine brokers regularly collaborated.

Attitudes towards illegal brokerage changed considerably in the course of the 18th century. In the 17th century and at the beginning of the 18th century, the Amsterdam city council had enacted many laws to counter this practice[34]. However, from the first decades of the 18th century on,

---

29 RAD, 1390 MML, Letter to Pieter van Overzee, Rotterdam, 12 Feb. 1750.

30 *Ibid.*, Letter to Arent van Eldick, Amsterdam, 21 Nov. 1749.

31 *Lyste der naamen en woonplaatsen van de makelaars [...] der stadt Amsterdam*, 1760, p. 31.

32 RAD, 1390 MML, Letter to Adolf Böcking, Trarbach, 18 Nov. 1749.

33 *Ibid.*, Letter to Arent van Eldick, Amsterdam, 1 Sept. 1751.

34 Stuart T., *De Amsterdamsche makelaardij. Bijdrage tot de geschiedenis onzer handelswetgeving*, Amsterdam, Spin en zoon, 1873, p. 160.

the brokers' guild filed fewer and fewer procedures against the so-called beunhazen[35]. At the same time, illegal brokers increasingly declared themselves as such in public. In 1742, on the occasion of the "personele quotisatie", a one-off tax on income and property, several well-to-do illicit wine brokers such as Wiggert Winter and Justus de Rolder even officially stated "beunhaas" as their profession[36].

Marshal contacted Van Eldick with a special purpose: to get rid of an unsalable lot of wine, which he had exceptionally received as a commission from his correspondent Adolf Böcking from Trarbach in the Palatinate[37]. In September 1748, Böcking had sent Marshal about 30 pieces of old low-quality Mosel wine[38]. At the time of shipment, Marshal had expected a quick sale to the State army, which was stationed close to Dordrecht to fight the War of the Austrian Succession (1740-1748). However, due to all kinds of setbacks, transport took more than two months and when the wine finally arrived in Holland, peace had been signed and most army units had been demobilised[39].

Marshal had first asked a Dordrecht broker to sell the wine at the local auction. The brokers' auction was often successfully used when a quick sale was required, for example because wine started to spoil, or because a merchant needed cash. However, this particular auction became an outright failure: although advertisements were published to announce the sale, not a single potential buyer from outside town showed up. The main part of the wine therefore went unsold and had to be stored again in Marshal's cellar.

A year later, after having incurred substantial costs, Marshal and Böcking at last decided to ship the wine to Amsterdam and charge Van Eldick with its sale[40]. The remaining barrels were sold to four Amsterdam wine merchants, including Jan Bols, a relative of the famous distiller

---

35 SA, 366 Guilds, 1289, Register van de bijloopers, 1682-1723.

36 Oldewelt W., *Kohier van de Personeele quotisatie te Amsterdam over het jaar 1742*, Amsterdam, Genootschap Amstelodamum, 1945, II, p. 251, 267.

37 RAD, 1390 MML, Letter to Arent van Eldick, Amsterdam, 21 Nov. 1749.

38 *Ibid.*, Letter to Adolf Böcking, Trarbach, 17 Sept. 1748.

39 War ended on 18 October 1748 with the signing of the Peace of Aix-la-Chapelle. RAD, 1390 MML, Letters to Adolf Böcking, Trarbach, 22 and 26 Nov.; 6 Dec. 1748.

40 *Ibid.*, Letter to Adolf Böcking, Trarbach, 21 and 27 Nov. 1749; Letter to Arent van Eldick, Amsterdam, 27 Nov. 1749.

Lucas Bols, whose company still survives today[41]. Prices were so low, that it seems likely that the wine was indeed only suitable for distillation.

Marshal's small brokers' network was thus characterised by sustainable personal relationships. His brokers had different backgrounds and may not have been knowledgeable wine experts. In addition to purchasing wine for him, they provided a wide range of other (paid) services, and can best be regarded as all-round metropolitan business agents. They also kept Marshal informed about prices and vintages, a role that appears even more clearly in the brokers' correspondence of the Middelburg wine merchants Van der Poest and Clement.

Information from the brokers' auction

In the third quarter of the 18th century, Andries van der Poest was a considerable Middelburg wine merchant[42]. He had started out in business with his father-in-law and established his own company around 1750[43]. Elected Dean of the wine merchants' guild shortly thereafter, he also held various offices[44]. He was related to the "French" families of Middelburg and for a long time, he was an Elder in the Walloon church[45].

Around 1775 -possibly to secure his old age-, Van der Poest hired Johan Clement as a bookkeeper. The young Clement had studied law

---

41 *Ibid.*, Letters to Arent van Eldick, Amsterdam, 5 and 12 Feb. 1750.

42 The outgoing correspondence and excerpts from accounts have been preserved for this company for the period 1766-1803 including letters to brokers for 1766 to 1793.

43 Extract uit de resolutien ten raade der stad Middelburg in Zeeland, 22 Sept. 1753, in *Ordonnantie voor de aanslagers van de kraan binnen Middelburg*, Middelburg, 1780, p. 77-80. ZA, 87, Verzameling Verheye van Citters, 1111-1824, 12d, Stukken rakende imposten op bier, wijn, brandewijn, azijn [...], Request aan de Staten, van Jan Wybo, met apostille van 27 April 1733. BHIC, 5122.152 Index schepenprotocol Schijndel, 20, 37, Machtiging door Willem Roessing door Jan Wybo burger en koopman te Middelburg, 17 Feb. 1723; Verklaring van Antony van Turnhout inwoner van de stad Helmond, 14 Feb. 1726.

44 *Naamwyzer, aantonende alle de namen en woonplaatsen van de Edele achtbare magistraat der stad Middelburg in Zeeland. Verder alle de hooge en aanzienlijke amptenaren [...]*, Middelburg, Callenfels et Taillefert, 1743, vol.1, p. 4; 1758, vol. 8, p. 27, 1763, vol. 9, p. 23, 106. *Middelburgsche courant*, 7 Feb. 1769. RAZ, 483 J.C.

45 *Ibid.*, 1743, vol. 1, p. 42; 1743; *Ibid.*, 1747, vol. 4, p. 42.

and in addition to being a wine merchant, he also worked as a lawyer. In 1781, Clement became a partner in the company. After the death of Van der Poest in 1783, Clement continued the firm with his widow. Deeply involved in the revolutionary patriot movement, the wine trade however soon became secondary among his activities[46].

Van der Poest and Clement traded in all sorts of wine, but mostly in French wines from Bordeaux, Bergerac and (from the late 1760s onward) Languedoc. Like Marshal, they were not only involved in distribution, but also imported wines themselves. Over the period 1766-1793, they had suppliers in Nantes, Bordeaux, Bayonne, Marseille, Sète and Toulon (Map 2). They purchased German wine, Champagne and Burgundy from colleagues from Liège, Namur, Maastricht and Dordrecht. However, sometimes they also ordered wines from trading houses in Reims and Beaune and occasionally, they imported from Cologne, Frankfurt-am-Main, Düsseldorf and Mainz. In peak years, the volume of their imports was up to about 25,000 litres of wine, which was substantial for a semi-retailer, but modest when compared to wholesalers.

Van der Poest and Clement had a diverse clientele. Customers in Middelburg were numerous but remain largely invisible in the outgoing correspondence. Letters occasionally mention them though, as in 1791, when Clement wrote to a Rotterdam supplier that he needed wine must for Middelburg innkeepers and operators of music halls for the production of *piquette,* as their clients wanted to drink white wine but could not pay much for it[47]. They also supplied the local Chamber of the East India Company with wine. Outside of Middelburg, customers mostly belonged to the Zeeland and Holland urban elite. Just like Marshal, they also had clients in distant cities, such as Arnhem and Maastricht and in the Austrian Netherlands[48]. Occasionally, they even exported French wine to Batavia and Demerara (nowadays Guyana)[49].

---

46 Augustinus van Cauwenberg, J. de, *Omstandig verhaal van het voorgevallene te Middelburg in Zeeland, bij gelegenheid der revolutie in den jaare 1787*, s.n., 1796, p. 102, 103.

47 ZA, 483 J. C. Clement, Letter copybook (from now on JCCL), 85, Letter to Cornelis van der Kun and son, Rotterdam, 13 March 1791.

48 *Ibid.*, Letters to la Veuve Hardy, Maastricht, 10 Oct. 1791 and 28 Oct. 1792.

49 *Ibid.*, Letters to Caspar Schlebusch, Cologne, 9 Dec. 1791; Letters to J.F. Boode, Rio Demerara, 30 Oct. 1786 and 15 Dec. 1791.

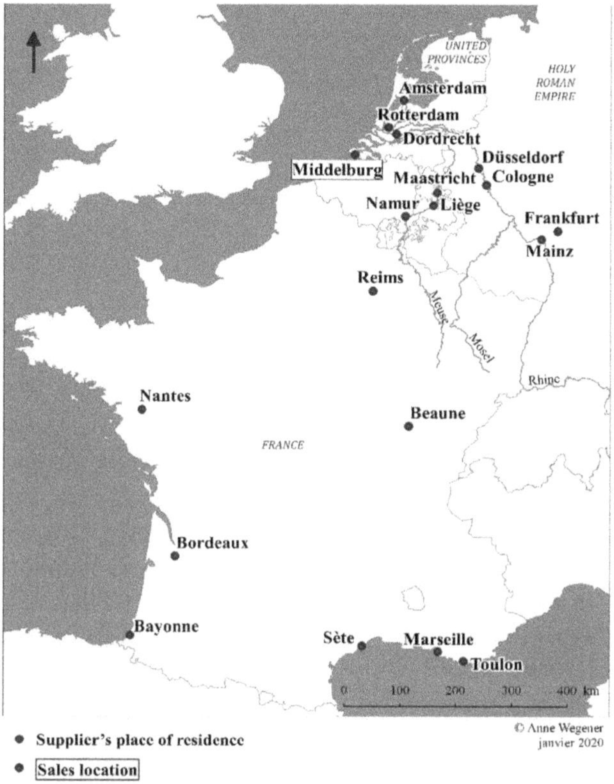

Map 2: Wine supply network of Van der Poest (& Clement), Middelburg, 1766-1793. ZA, 483 J.C. Clement, Letter copybooks, 81-85, 1766-1803

Despite their impressive international network, Van der Poest and Clement also regularly bought wine from Rotterdam and Amsterdam wholesalers. Depending on the political circumstances and the quality of the vintage, this may have involved about half of their annual purchases. Like Marshal, they entrusted their purchase orders in Holland to a small number of regular brokers.

Between 1766 and 1793, the Middelburg merchants subsequently employed three Rotterdam brokers and one broker in Amsterdam (Tab. 1)[50]. Business with Jan van Raalt from Rotterdam remained

50 *Ibid.*, 81-85, 1766-1793.

Tab. 1: Wine brokers hired by Van der Poest and Clement, 1766-1793

Name	Address	
Jan van Raalt	Rotterdam	(at least) 1766-1770
Gerard Verboom	Rotterdam	1771-1775
Jacobus van Overzee	Rotterdam	1775-1789 and 1793
Jan Rademaker	Amsterdam	1768-1778

ZA, 483 J.C. Clement, Letter copybooks, 81-85, 1766-180

occasional[51]. Van Raalt practiced as a broker for nearly thirty years until his death in 1785[52]. Throughout his life, he collaborated intensively with his brother Nicolaas, a wine merchant who lived near him at Wijnhaven[53]. Cooperation between brokers and relatives who were wine merchants or wholesalers was common and allowed brokers to circumvent the strict regulations that forbade private trade to brokers.

Van der Poest regularly hired Gerard Verboom from 1771 to 1775. Their relationship was often tense, the merchant needing to remind his broker repeatedly, that his letters had remained unanswered or that he was late in executing his modest purchase orders[54]. In the 1760s to 1780s, Verboom regularly sold huge quantities of wine at the Rotterdam auction, up to two hundred casks at a time, on behalf of the main "French" wine importers of Rotterdam, such as Jouhanneau, Laregnère and Cornelis Balguerie[55]. It seems that Verboom largely focused on the Rotterdam bulk trade at the expense of provincial wine merchants such as Van der Poest.

A serious crisis of confidence arose in 1773, on the occasion of a purchase order of six hogsheads of five year-old red Cahors wine, for which the choice had been based on test bottles that Verboom had sent to Middelburg. On delivery, the wine turned out to be totally different than

---

51 *Ibid.*, 82, Letter to Jan van Raalt, 10 Dec. 1766.

52 Advertisements for wine auctions, *Leydse courant*, 23 July 1755; *Rotterdamse courant*, 27 oct. 1785. Online: Delpher.

53 SR, DTB 1-02, 25, 26, 32, Christening of Jan van Raalt, 2 March, 1732; Christening of Nicolaas van Raalt, 19 Sept. 1734; Christening of Jacobus Adrianus van Raalt, 3 Oct. 1764. Ad for a wine auction, *Rotterdamse courant*, 7 Apr. 1796. Online: Delpher.

54 ZA, 483 JCCL, 83, Letter to Cornelis van der Kun, Rotterdam, 11 Apr. 1775.

55 Advertisements for wine auctions, *Leydse courant*, 26 Oct. 1767; 21 Feb. 1783; 23 Nov. 1785.

the sample. Van der Poest hence blamed his broker, for not having tasted the wine himself, supposing that he certainly would have noticed that at least half of it was of the latest vintage, and not even from Cahors[56]! In accordance with breach of contract law, Van der Poest then sent the wine back to Rotterdam at the broker's expense. This affair shows that wine brokers were not always as sincere and committed as they had promised when taking the oath.

Between 1775 and 1793, Van der Poest and Clement employed Jacobus van Overzee as a broker, a son of Pieter van Overzee, who had worked for Marshal some twenty years earlier. In the course of the 18th century, brokers' dynasties seem to have become increasingly widespread[57]. Van der Poest used this broker as a matchmaker, as an informant and as a networker asking him for instance to put him into contact with "a good house in Mannheim"[58].

Until 1778, Jan Rademaker from Amsterdam was the broker with whom Van der Poest corresponded most. Rademaker was the son of a painter, but there had been several brokers in his family[59]. By the time he dealt with the Middelburg firm, he had become one of Amsterdam's most active wine brokers. In the printed *Directory of Brokers*, he systematically indicated wine brokerage as his specialisation[60]. However, throughout his career, he was also involved in other trades and brokered for instance at auctions of ships and real estate[61]. While some successful wine brokers specialised, others on the contrary seem to have prospered thanks to diversification.

Van der Poest mainly ordered Spanish and rare French wines from Rademaker. This involved, for instance, Benicarlo used for adding colour

---

56 ZA, 483 JCCL, 83, Letters to Gerard Verboom, Rotterdam, 17 Jan. 1773 and 27 Feb. 1773.

57 For 52 Amsterdam wine brokers appointed in the period 1698-1791, I have been able to trace the father's profession. 14 were sons of wine merchants; 9 were sons of wholesalers or "commissioners" and 20 were brokers' sons. Stads Archief Amsterdam (from now on SA), 5033 Burgemeesters, Civil deeds, 4-29.

58 ZA, 483 JCCL, 83, Letters to Jacobus van Overzee, Rotterdam, 24 Jan. 1778; 24 May 1779.

59 SA, 5033 Burgemeesters, Civil deeds for Dirk Rademaker and Jan Rademaker 4, 8 Feb. 1676, p. 149; 19, 7 Nov. 1741, p. 766.

60 *Lyste der naamen en woonplaatsen van de makelaars [...] der stad Amsterdam*, 1765, p. 10; 1773, p. 7.

61 *De Maandelykse Nederlandsche Mercurius*, nr. 1, 4 Oct. 1756, p. 148, 149; nr. 9, 15 Dec. 1760, p. 234; nr. 27, 4 Sept. and 16 Oct. 1769, p. 117, 172, 174.

and tannin to French wines, Rota "tint" imported from Cadix, fortified "sack" wines from Malaga and the Canary Islands, sweet white wines of the Pedro Ximénez grape variety and red Burgundy from Mâcon[62]. Spanish wines were seldom directly imported to the small harbour of Middelburg but were sought after by the Zealand Chamber of the VOC, for the Company's ship victuals and for the wine supplies of the trading posts in the East Indies[63].

Just like Marshal's brokers, Rademaker performed diverse tasks, but he seems to have been more of a "connoisseur". On several occasions, he carried out wine assessments, as in 1777, when he assessed a batch of damaged Côteaux nantais Muscadet wines that had been recently unloaded from a ship involved in an accident at sea. Van der Poest needed the evaluation to decide whether he should sell the wine at auction in Amsterdam, or if it was worth having it shipped to Middelburg[64].

The exchange of information about wine tastings, prices and other merchants' dealings played a central role in the correspondence with Rademaker. Letters were often detailed, mentioning producer brands and parishes for wine-producing regions in France (Médoc, Graves, Bergerac, Béarn). The Middelburg merchants gathered most of their information at the local brokers' auction. In 1769, Van der Poest informed Rademaker for instance: "Yesterday evening the La Guere brand from Bordeaux was sold at the auction for 30 Flemish pounds. The wine was pretty good for this vintage. As for the Bordeaux red wines, the Médoc of the parish of St Estèphe satisfies me most[65]". Van der Poest regularly tasted wines for sale at the auctions for other merchants, as wine brokers usually organised public tastings on the eve of the sale. On this occasion, he took notes, indicating types of wine, producer brands, names of sellers and buyers and quality appreciations.

---

62 ZA, 483 JCCL, 82 and 83, Letters to Jan Rademaker, Amsterdam, 18 July 1768; 22 Dec. 1769; 31 March 1770 and 20 Feb. 1775.

63 *Ibid.*, Letters to Jan Rademaker, Amsterdam, 11 April 1770; 16 April 1773; 23 April 1773; 5 Oct. 1774.

64 *Ibid.*, Letter to Jan Rademaker, Amsterdam, 21 Sept. 1777.

65 "Gisteren avond is van de Bordeaux van 't merk van La Guere tot L30 int bekken verkogt. Dezelve was nogal redelijk na 't gewas. De roode Bordeaux vinde integendeel nog het beste te voldoen principaal de Medocq en daar uyt van de parochie van St Estephe". ZA, 483 JCCL, 81, Letter to Jan Rademaker, Amsterdam, 13 Jan. 1769.

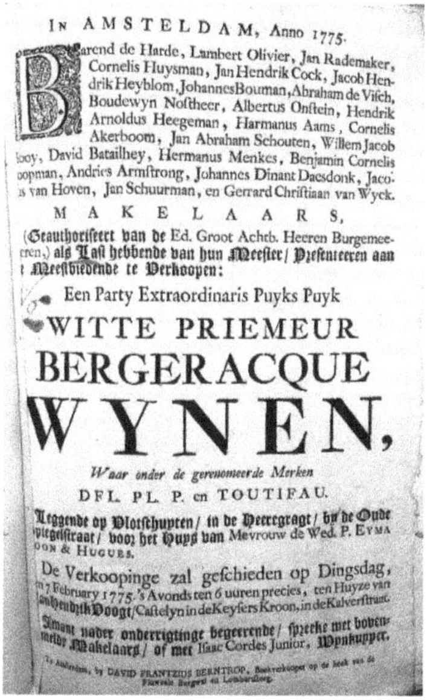

In Amsterdam, in the year 1775.

Barend de Harde, Lambert Olivier, Jan Rademaker and twenty other

BROKERS,

With permission of the honorable gentlemen mayors, as representatives their master, intend to sell to the highest bidder:

A lot of excellent extraordinary

WHITE BERGERAC

PRIMEUR WINE

including the renowned brands

DFL. PL. P. and Toutifau.

Displayed on barges at Heerengragt close to Oude Spiegelstraat in front of the house of the Widow P. Eyma son & Hugues.

Fig. 2: Advertisement for a sale at the Amsterdam brokers' auction of a batch of new Bergerac white wine, 1775. Source: Stadsarchief Amsterdam, 5069 Burgemeesters, Register van verkopingen door makelaars, 73, 7 Feb. 1775

Prior to the auctions, wine brokers typically placed advertisements in newspapers and had posters printed to announce the sale (Figure 2). Through these ads, which mentioned factual as well as subjective information, wine knowledge also reached a larger number of people.

However, the brokers' auction was not a transparent market. Brokers shared private information with befriended clients and frequently colluded. In 1735, for example, Marshal's Rotterdam broker, Pieter van Overzee and his father-in-law Florens Eilbracht were involved in a major scandal. They were accused of forming a bidding ring to keep prices low. Evidence brought against them was blatant, but they were maintained in office, as they had strong personal ties with members of the urban government[66]. Wine brokers and their auctions were indeed not just cost saving and trade facilitating devices.

[66] SR, 1 OSA, 2192, Dossier van het geschil tussen wijnkooplieden en makelaars, 1735.

Official and illicit wine brokers occupied an important place in 18th century wine distribution in the United Provinces. Wine brokers were employed by wholesalers who were often of foreign origin and who were not allowed to sell in semi-retail for fiscal reasons. Specialised wine merchants also often hired brokers. Close investigation into the affairs of two of these semi-retailers, Matthijs Marshal from Dordrecht and Van der Poest & Clement from Middelburg, reveals that wine brokers commonly acted as their general metropolitan business agents. They were at the same time informants, consultants, problem solvers, network builders, legal representatives and matchmakers.

Many Amsterdam and Rotterdam wine brokers no doubt got only a small part of their income from the modest fee they received for their mediation between individual sellers and buyers. They also earned from the organisation of auctions, the storage and handling of wines and from their mediation in insurance and payments and they combined wine brokerage with other (trade) activities.

Unlike their colleagues in wine-producing countries, Dutch wine brokers were not always wine experts. Some of them were more specialised than others, depending on their training and on the possibility of collaboration with relatives involved in the wine trade. The degree of specialisation also differed from one city to another, urban regulation explaining for example the absence of specialised wine brokers in Dordrecht.

Dutch wine brokers constituted an exceptionally heterogeneous group. They had different social backgrounds, though many came from families involved in wine trade or in brokerage. The scale of their activities varied greatly. Some brokers mainly worked for wholesalers while others chiefly carried out purchase orders for semi-retailers.

The brokers' auctions largely contributed to the supply of information on prices, the quality of wines and the activity in trade. The brokers' privilege regarding the organisation of commercial auctions also allowed them to control part of the market. The study of wine brokers' correspondence indeed reveals that practice was sometimes at odds with the model of the neutral mediator in charge of a public service under the supervision of local authorities that emerges from ordinances. For most brokers, however, sincerity and loyalty to their clients were the guiding principles in their business and this undoubtedly largely explains the sustainability of their relationships.

A New Wine for the International Market: Italian Public Institutions' Initiatives to Support the Oenological Sector (1870-1910)

Luciano Maffi, Paolo Tedeschi and Manuel Vaquero Piñeiro

From the 1870s to the First World War, central, provincial and municipal Italian public administrations promoted the modernisation of Italian viticulture and winemaking, as well as the internationalisation of Italian wines. They played a fundamental role in: (a) the transmission and transfer of knowledge and information about the production system (vine growing and winemaking); (b) the control of the final product (to improve its quality and avoid alterations); (c) the distribution of Italian wines on the international market, giving wine producers all the information about customers' tastes and the potential demand concerning Italian wines. During the period analysed, the initiatives of the State, the Provinces and the Municipalities in favour of the creation and the distribution of a new national wine adapted to the international market were numerous: they helped the creation of a national oenology which was able to face an increasingly globalised wine market.

These public institutions in particular financed the creation of: agrarian councils ('comizi agrari') which supported studies aimed at the development of agriculture (obviously including viticulture); agricultural schools training new qualified farmers as well as new winemakers; experimental agrarian stations ('stazioni agrarie sperimentali') conducting scientific experiments in the primary sector; itinerant agricultural chairs ('cattedre ambulanti di agricoltura') whose agronomists explained, in the villages, the new efficient production systems, including new methods of viticulture and winemaking. This policy was accompanied by the dissemination of agricultural almanacs and agricultural journals: the aim was evidently the improvement of the production and productivity of the Italian primary sector[1].

These initiatives also guaranteed considerable help for the oenological sector: even if they were not able to make up for the existing backwardness when compared with other countries (in particular France), the integration between public and private initiatives favoured the improvement of the Italian wine sector. Specialised schools for the vocational training of future winemakers were in fact created: their courses allowed new oenological technicians to easily find a job in the wineries (as well as in the agronomic institutions previously indicated) where they suggested new methods to improve the wine growing and winemaking.

The public contribution to the improvement of the Italian wine sector also involved the promulgation of laws favouring the creation of social wineries ('cantine sociali') and deposits for the agrarian machines (16 wineries were created between 1870 and 1873). The first ones were cooperative wineries which included wine producers: they assisted them during the winemaking (to improve the quality of the final product) and the marketing (to reduce distribution costs related to the sale). The second ones were organised by the Italian government: they rented the

---

1 A wide bibliography exists about the creation and distribution in Italy of agrarian councils, agricultural schools, experimental agrarian stations and itinerant agricultural chairs. See, among others, Stringher V., *L'istruzione agraria in Italia*, Rome, Unione Cooperativa Editrice, 1901; Zaninelli S. (eds.) *Le conoscenze agrarie e la loro diffusione in Italia nell'Ottocento*, Turin, Giappichelli, 1990; Musella L., "La politica della 'continuità'. L'azione del Ministero di Agricoltura in Italia tra il 1878 e il 1897", in *L'agricoltura in Europa e la nascita della 'questione agraria' (1880-1914)*, *Annali dell'Istituto Alcide Cervi*, 1992/93, p. 231-240; Fumi G., "L'amministrazione dell'agricoltura in Italia negli anni dell'unificazione (1860-1867)", in Carera A., Taccolini M. and Canetta R. (eds.), *Temi e questioni di storia economica e sociale in età moderna e contemporanea. Studi in onore di Sergio Zaninelli*, Milano, Vita & Pensiero, 1999, p. 379-424; Bidolli A.P., Soldani S., *L'istruzione agraria (1861-1928)*, Rome, Ministero per i beni e le attività culturali, 2001; Pazzagli R., *Il sapere dell'agricoltura: istruzione, cultura, economia nell'Italia dell'Ottocento*, Milan, FrancoAngeli, 2008; Vaquero Piñeiro M., "Readings for farmers: Agrarian almanacs in Italy (eighteenth-twentieth centuries)", *The Agricultural History Review*, 63, 2, 2015, p. 243-264; Idem, "'Empirici' e 'istruiti'. Fattori e periti agrari in Italia tra XIXe XXe secolo", in Ferrari M., Fumi G. and Morandi M. (eds.), *Formare alle professioni. I saperi della cascina*, Milan, FrancoAngeli, 2016, p. 84-104; Locatelli A. M., Tedeschi P., "Les milieux agronomiques européens et la formation d'un modèle agricole italien au XIXe siècle", in *La fabrique transnationale de la 'science nationale' en Italie (1839-fin des années 1920)*, *Mélanges de l'École Française – Italie et Méditerranée modernes et contemporaines (MEFRIM)*, 2018, 130-2, p. 299-309.

machines for the winemaking process (such as pumps, presses, boilers, etc.) and this reduced the production costs of the grape must[2].

Finally, the Italian state financed the creation of free warehouses ('magazzini or depositi franchi' which exported Italian wine at reduced customs tariffs to some European countries) and especially oenotechnical stations ('stazioni enotecniche') which were set up in the main European cities with the aim of promoting the export of Italian wines. Their managers played a fundamental role in giving Italian wines a precise identity on the market, even if different wines were produced according to the terroir of production. The Italian oenotechnical stations in America were important for both Italian and local viticulture: the presence of Italian emigrants in fact favoured the sale of Italian wines, but it also contributed to the progressive improvement of local wine production. In the case of the Californian oenological sector, emigrants brought their know-how, and the exchanges of information favoured the arrival of new techniques and tools in Italy; in the case of Argentina, migrants developed the local oenological sector and Italian schools for winemakers gradually became a model and a real point of reference. The activity of free warehouses and, moreover, of the oenotechnical stations clearly showed that the role of the Italian state as an agent of innovation in the nineteenth century was not limited to investments in professional education that sought to improve the winemaking and the average quality of Italian wine[3].

---

2 About the 'cantine sociali' see those existing in Lombardy and Umbria: Vaquero Piñeiro M., *Storia regionale della vite e del vino in Italia. Umbria*, Perugia, Volumnia, 2012, p. 164; Maffi L., *Storia di un territorio rurale. Vigne e vini nell'Oltrepò Pavese*, Milan, FrancoAngeli, 2010, p. 121-143; Tedeschi P., "Il rinnovamento colturale. Aspetti della viticoltura bresciana fra Ottocento e Novecento", in Archetti G. (ed.), *La civiltà del vino: fonti, temi e produzioni vitivinicole dal medioevo al Novecento*, Brescia, Centro culturale artistico di Franciacorta e del Sebino, 2003, p. 809. About the deposits for agrarian machines which were organised by the Italian government in the agricultural schools, agrarian councils and agrarian stations see *Depositi governativi di macchine agrarie*, Rome, Tip. Eredi Botta, 1883; Musella L., "La politica della 'continuità' ", p. 236-238.

3 The concept that 'the role of the [Italian] State as agent of transformation in the nineteenth century was limited to investment in professional education' is on the contrary indicated by Federico G., Martinelli P., "Italy to 1938", in Anderson K. and Pinilla V. (eds.), *Wine Globalization. A New Comparative History*, Cambridge, CUP, 2018, p. 141.

The aim of renewing the wine sector

From its birth, the Kingdom of Italy intended to modify agrarian education: a commission was created in 1861 to improve the link between the theory and the practice in the new schools of Agriculture. The commission actually did nothing, but it offered the elites the opportunity to highlight the economic and social centrality of agriculture in the construction of the new state: the landowners sought to impose a model of economic development based on the primary sector. So they had to improve the quantity and quality of agricultural products which, in many cases, were neither able to guarantee the self-sufficiency of the population nor to be competitive on the international market. To realise this aim, it was clear that it was not possible to leave the dissemination of agronomic knowledge to the agrarian councils, the municipalities and the institutions dedicated to the assistance of the peasants. The state had to be more involved because it needed a more qualified rural workforce who had knowledge about the latest technical innovations and who were allowed to modernise the primary sector. In this context the Forest School of Vallombrosa was founded in 1867 and it was followed by the agricultural colleges of Milan and Portici (1871-1872) and then by new agricultural schools and experimental agrarian stations.

One of the most important and widespread crops, the vine, clearly symbolised the need to improve agronomic knowledge and to innovate the productive system. The backwardness of the Italian wine sector was highlighted during the international exhibition of 1862 in London: compared to their more refined French counterparts, Italian wines were of a lower, if not poor, quality[4]. While food and beverage markets were gaining ground in the globalisation of the world economy, Italian wines were not ready to seize the opportunities offered by the progressive globalisation of trade and taste: the Italian wine sector needed a radical change to become competitive and especially to build new productive and distributive structures favouring the production and distribution of new high-quality Italian wines[5].

---

4 See Bertone di Sambuy, E. B., "Sull'industria dei vini in Italia", in *Relazioni dei commissari speciali*, Turin, Dalmazzo, 1865, vol. 3., p. 19-21.

5 About the international market of agrarian products during the nineteenth century and the progressive globalisation of the taste see Federico G., "Oltre frontiera: l'Italia nel mercato agricolo internazionale", in Bevilacqua P. (ed.), *Storia dell'agricoltura italiana in età contemporanea*, vol. III, *Mercati e istituzioni*, Venise, Marsilio,

Italian viticulturists produced millions of hectolitres of wine, but they had to create new wines which were adapted to the taste of more sophisticated world consumers[6]. In 1863, a state oenotechnical commission was created and some private wineries were set up in many Italian towns: they had to promote the production and marketing of high-quality wines. The formation of a ministerial committee to evaluate the wines to be sent to the Vienna International Exposition of 1873 was another important step and an absolute novelty for Italian oenology: this committee aimed at correcting the errors made in previous exhibitions and preventing Italian winemakers participating in new ones without adequate preparation[7].

In order to produce new competitive Italian wines on the international market, it was also necessary to organise initiatives exclusively dedicated to the wine sector and to finance the renovation of cellars and winemaking techniques. The main goal was obviously to reduce the gap between French and Italian oenology: the first had modern productive structures and a

---

1991, p. 189-222; Rowley A. and Ribaut J. C., *Le vin. Une histoire du goût*, Paris, Gallimard, 2003; Nützenadel A., "A Green International? Food Markets and Transnational Politics, c. 1850-1914", in Nützenadel, A. and Trentmann, F. (eds.), *Food and Globalization. Consumption, Markets and Politics in the Modern World*, New York, Berg, 2008, p. 153-171; Magagnoli S., "La globalizzazione del gusto. Esposizioni universali e prodotti alimentari", *Quaderni storici*, 40-1/2, 2015, p. 41-49; Teughels N., Scholliers P., *A Taste of Progress. Food at International and World Exhibitions in the Nineteenth and Twentieth Centuries*, London, Ashgate, 2015. About the wine international market see Simpson J., *Creating Wine. The Emergence of a World Industry 1840-1914*, Princeton. PUP, 2011; Anderson K. and Pinilla V. (eds.), *Wine Globalization*.

6 About the Italian oenological sector during the years 1860-1910 see, among others, Cova A., "Problemi tecnici ed economici della produzione di vino in Italia tra Otto e Novecento", in *Il vino nell'economia e nella società italiana medioevale e moderna*, Florence, Accademia economico-agraria dei Georgofili, 1988, p. 319-337; Ciuffoletti Z., *Alla ricerca del "vino perfetto". Il Chianti del barone di Brolio. Ricasoli e il Risorgimento vitivinicolo italiano*, Florence, Olschki, 2009; Kovatz S., "The Geography of Quality Wine in United Italy Areas and Producers", in Ceccarelli G., Grandi A. and Magagnoli S. (eds.), *Typicality in History. Tradition, Innovation and Terroir*, Bruxelles, Peter Lang, 2013, p. 305-321. See also the contributions concerning Italian wine in Conca S., Le Bras S., Tedeschi P. and Vaquero Piñeiro M. (eds.), *A History of Wine in Europe, 19th to 20th Centuries*, vol I, *Winegrowing and Regional Features*, vol. II, *Markets, Trade and Regulation of Quality*, London, Palgrave Macmillan, 2019.

7 See Bertone di Sambuy E. B., "Vini italiani", in *Relazioni dei giurati italiani sulla Esposizione universale di Vienna del 1873*, Milan, Regia Stamperia, 1873, vol. 5, group 4; Boschiero G, "Industria dei vini in Italia", *ibid.*

commercial network that was well developed and oriented to export; the second had to be renewed to fully enjoy its rich and varied ampelographic heritage[8]. The Italian wine sector in fact had to move from a production system primarily intended for domestic consumption to production on a large-scale and export-oriented. This implied that the quality of wines produced increased, allowing sales abroad in bottles and not only in barrels, as was customary for wine for blending. The supply chain had to be renewed (from winemakers to merchants) as well as structures (cellars) and productive techniques. So public institutions financed all the initiatives promoting the wider spread of ampelographic knowledge in the countryside and the improvement of the wine quality. They also pushed winemakers to give their wine a modern image and a taste that met the requirements of foreign consumers: so they gave information about the characteristics of this potential demand and advised about better advertising campaigns to increase customers. The best winemakers, who obviously already had the money for investments, took advantage of this information and these suggestions and progressively became the first real entrepreneurs in the Italian wine sector[9].

Italian public institutions' initiatives

The search for more modern production techniques to produce higher quality wines and the study of new methods to promote their marketing were entrusted to schools and experimental stations (which were dedicated to viticulture and oenology), experimental wineries, free warehouses and oenotechnical stations. The main differences among

---

8 About the French viticulture during the nineteenth century there is a large bibliography. See, among others, Phillips R., *French Wine. A History*, Oakland, University of California Press, 2016; Dion R., *Histoire de la vigne et du vin en France des origines au XIXe siècle*, Paris, CNRS, 2010; Guy K. M., *When Champagne Became French: Wine and the Making of National Identity*, Baltimore, Johns Hopkins University Press, 2003; Lachiver M., *Vins, vignes et vignerons. Histoire du vignoble français*, Paris, Fayard, 1988.

9 Among the first Italian wine entrepreneurs it is possible to indicate: Laborel-Melini and Ruffino (in Tuscany); Luigi Bosca & Figli, Fontanafredda, Francesco Cinzano and Carlo Gancia (in Piedmont); Antonio Manzi and Amedeo Berner, (in Campania); Duca di Salaparuta (in Sicily); Conti Giorgi di Vistarino and Domenico Mazza (in Lombardy); Principe Sebastiano Apostolico Orsini Ducas and Giuseppe Pavoncelli (in Apulia).

these initiatives which were financed by the public institutions concerned their respective purposes and locations: the first two, located in Italy, sought to develop wines of better quality; the others, located abroad, had to promote the distribution of Italian wines on the international market.

The schools and oenological experimental stations trained expert winemakers who used their new ampelographic knowledge and new productive methods in their vineyards making them more productive. Moreover, they carried out experiments to improve the winemaking process as well as to protect vineyards against parasites. These young people, who were graduates of the new oenological schools, were essential players in transforming wineries which previously had met only local consumption; they were progressively changed into capital-intensive companies operating also on the international market. However, for these transformations financing (also private) was necessary and, at the same time, public institutions had to maintain the social equilibrium in the countryside, that is they had to reassure the big landowners that, despite this technological modernisation, new oenologists remained subordinate employees. Also, although there were sometimes very harsh discussions about the usefulness of viticulture and oenology courses and about the actual possibility for Italian farms to guarantee a job for all new skilled peasant workers, lots of agrarian schools and experimental agricultural stations dedicated to the oenological sector have been opened since the 1870s in Alba, Asti and Gattinara (Piedmont), Conegliano (Veneto), and Avellino (Campania). They trained new technicians who had a practical and rational approach to viticulture and wine production: they created future oenologists (winegrowers and winemakers) who have been able to transform traditional cellars into wineries offering modern winemaking techniques[10]. In addition, some teachers of oenological schools published a new journal dedicated to viticulture and winemaking and organised international exhibitions of "oenological tools and machines" or "filters for the grape must": they helped to promote better knowledge about technological innovations in the wine sector and, at the same time, to promote Italian products abroad[11].

---

10 Stringher V., *L'istruzione agraria*, p. 65-69, 83.

11 The journal was *Annali di viticoltura ed enologia italiana*, founded in Milan in 1872 and then published in Conegliano since 1877 as *Rivista di viticoltura ed enologia italiana*. It became in 1877 *Nuova rassegna di viticoltura ed enologia della Regia scuola di Conegliano*. On the oenological exhibitions featuring award-winning competitions

Using local grapes, the new experimental wineries ('cantine sperimentali') had to produce, wines of good quality with a taste which remained stable over time allowing sales in markets far from the production sites[12]. These modern wineries also had laboratories where the wines brought by the private producers and the consortia were analysed: the results of their experiences were added and mixed with those carried out by the experimental stations in oenology. Faced with the phylloxera crisis, they were responsible for teaching the grafting of American vines resistant to aphids into local vines: in Velletri (Lazio), in the lands surrounding the laboratories, a nursery of American vines was also created.

Moreover, free warehouses were created in several European towns: they had the right to import Italian wines taking advantage of favourable tariff conditions. They were managed by local merchants who signed a contract with the Italian state to promote the sale of Italian wines. At the beginning of the 1880s, these warehouses met the hostility of the other importers of Italian wines because they had had a virtual monopoly. In the following years the situation changed because these merchants gradually become intermediaries between Italian producers and local distributors. The latter in fact had access to a wide range of wines previously not available on foreign markets and they were able to offer their customers new Italian wines at more competitive prices. The largest free warehouses were in Lucerne (managed by the Businger brothers) and especially in Germany, where Daube Donner and Kinen (headquartered in Frankfurt) also managed those of Berlin, Hamburg and Munich and imported, between 1888 and 1890, 30,000 hectolitres of Italian wine worth more than two million Italian liras[13].

---

organised by the oenological schools see, among others, *Concorsi internazionali di macchine agricole. Apparecchi e macchine enologiche (Conegliano, 1881)*, Rome, Tip. Eredi Botta, 1883; *Concorso internazionale di filtri per mosti e vini tenuto in Avellino presso la R. Scuola di viticoltura ed enologia nell'ottobre 1892. Relazione di Livio Sostegni*, Avellino, Maggi, 1893. Please note that all these books were published as "Annals of Agriculture" by the Ministry of Agriculture, Industry and Trade.

12 Stringher V., *L'istruzione agraria*, p. 157-158.

13 See *Annuario generale per la viticoltura e la enologia*, vol. I, Rome, Circolo enofilo italiano, 1892, p. 498. Concerning the Italian export of wine at the end of the nineteenth century see Anderson K., Nelgen S. and Pinilla V. (eds.), *Global Wine Markets, 1860 to 2016: A Statistical Compendium*, Adelaide, University of Adelaide Press, 2017, p. 232.

The oenotechnical stations were established in many relevant towns in Europe (such as Budapest, Bern, Zurich, Paris, London, Berlin and Munich) and in the Americas (Buenos Aires and New York). They provided Italian wine producers with technical and commercial support to open up new markets: they knew foreign markets better and chose the most suitable wines for export, those matching the tastes of foreign customers. Moreover, they indicated and defined the types, quality and specific characteristics of Italian wines for export. Furthermore, led by wine experts, they were also responsible for collecting information on legislation in the foreign markets, the eating habits and preferences of local customers, the prices and distribution channels of wine and the prospects of the local wine market. Their main goal was always the promotion of Italian wine in foreign stores and restaurants.

The directors of the oenotechnical stations were not directly involved in sales, but they had to put themselves at the service of people who, for a fee, analysed the wines. Indeed, among the main obstacles to overcome were the lack of confidence of buyers (wholesalers or mere customers), and the frauds, as tampering and counterfeiting were able to destroy the reputation of the best Italian wines on the markets. The certificates issued by the oenotechnical stations included an analysis of the characteristics of the wines, starting with the control of the degree of alcohol. All casks and bottles had to be stamped and tagged to confirm that their contents had been checked. These measures were clearly intended to certify that the wine was safe and actually came from its place of origin: the certified wines had to be flawless and coherent (that is well structured, harmonious and balanced during a visual, olfactory and taste analysis) and above all have a constant quality over time which generated customer loyalty.

The role of the directors of the oenotechnical stations was fundamental in codifying the organoleptic characteristics of the "good typical Italian wine". For example, to be accepted outside Italy, Chianti wine had be clear and light with a ruby colour and a frank taste: finally it had to be sold in a bottle, the typical 'fiasco' (so when it was available in bulk, as sometimes happened, its origin was not guaranteed).

The Italian oenotechnical stations in New York and Buenos Aires

The oenotechnical stations located on the American continent were particularly important: they sought to take advantage of the presence of Italian emigrants who guaranteed a sure demand and they also helped producers to distribute Italian wines in other migrant communities. In addition, they observed the practices of local producers and sent to Italy relevant information for the renewal of Italian viticulture. Furthermore, they helped Italian peasants (in particular the viticulturists) who had to emigrate: they in fact organised training courses in viticulture and winemaking to improve their ampelographic knowledge. So the most important oenotechnical stations were located in New York and Buenos Aires, that is in great countries with large wine markets and a lot of Italian migrants[14].

New York

The wine station in New York played a key role in defining the characteristics of Italian wine and through regular information, gave Italian public authorities and winemakers the opportunity, to know better the wine sector in a country where the principles of modern industry were applied to winemaking. For the Italian viticulture of the late nineteenth century, which remained attached to artisanal production, there was also another real challenge: it was in fact necessary to help the Italian migrants

---

14 About the Italian viticulturists and the diffusion of Italian wine in the Americas see: Florence J. W., *Legacy of a Village. The Italian Swiss Colony Winery and People of Asti*, California, Raymond Court Press, 1999; Cinotto S., *Soft Soil, Black Grapes. The Birth of Italian Wine Making in California*, New York, New York University Press, 2012; Calderone G., "Il progetto delle colonie agricole negli Stati Uniti della grande emigrazione", *Altreitalie*, gennaio-giugno, 2013, p. 31-56; Vaquero Piñeiro M., Maffi L., "The Diffusion of Italian Wine in the United States (1861-1914)", *Rivar. Revista Iberoamericana de viticultura, agroindustria e ruralidad*, 15 (5), 2018, p. 176-196; Zanoni E., *Migrant Marketplaces. Food and Italians in North and South America*, Urbana, University of Illinois, 2018. See also Baily S., *Immigrants in the Land Promise. Italians in Buenos Aires and New York City, 1870-1914*, Ithaca-London, Cornell University Press, 1999; Choate M. L., *Emigrant Nation. The Making of Italy Abroad*, Cambridge, Harvard University Press, 2008; Cinotto S., *The Italian American Table. Food, Family and Community in New York City*, Chicago and Springfield, University of Illinois Press, 2013.

who could potentially become competitors but who also favoured the distribution and consumption of the best Italian wines[15].

The New York Wine Station was entrusted to Guido Rossati in 1895. This former representative of the Italian Government had been responsible for the promotion of Italian wines in London, and his mission had been to get the characteristics of Italian wines in England better known by consumers. In the United States, he devoted himself to publishing articles on Italian wines in the local press and he was also the author of a vast study on grape growing and wine production in the United States[16]. In this volume, the result of an expedition across the country, he provided relevant information on the viticulture of each state of the USA, emphasising the environmental characteristics and the quality of the railway and maritime infrastructures which he considered fundamental to the increase of exports. He dedicated particular attention to the development of viticulture in the California districts of Sacramento, Napa, Sonoma, Santa Clara, Livermore, San Joaquin and Los Angeles. He also verified the entrepreneurial activities carried out by Italian migrants, such as the Italian-Swiss colony of Asti: they made an essential contribution to the development of the USA wine industry and the Italian-Swiss colony in particular was responsible for the introduction in California, of Italian red wines such as Barbera, Nebbiolo, Muscat, Bonarda and Refosco which were sold under the name Crabb's Black Burgundy.

Rossati's works show that the role played by the Italian state in favour of the process of the internationalisation of the Italian wine industry cannot be underestimated. Rossati indicated that environmental conditions made California an ideal region for the production of large quantities of ordinary wine: he also underlined the superior technological capability of American wine producers. Their mechanical industry designed and built new machines carrying large quantities of

---

15 About the wine sector in USA see, among others, Pinney T, *A History of Wine in American: from the Beginnings to Prohibition*, Berkeley, University California Press, 1989; Walker L., *The Wines of the Napa Valley*, London, Mitchell Beazley, 2005; Hannickel E., *Empire of Vines: Wine Culture in America*, Philadelphia, University of Pennsylvania Press, 2013.

16 See Rossati G., *Relazione di un viaggio d'istruzione negli Stati Uniti d'America*, Rome, Tip. Nazionale di G. Bertero, 1900; Idem, *Descriptive Account of the Wine Industry of Italy*, Rome, Società generale dei viticoltori italiani, 1888.

grapes: at the same time, the automation of some procedures allowed considerable labour saving and reduced the cost of the winemaking. In Rossati's opinion, Italian viticulture had to follow the example of Californian winemakers, so Italian ones needed to obtain new information through magazines and specialised publications or, better yet, they had to organise study trips to observe the new Californian facilities that made wine production easier and more efficient, in terms of saving time and manufacturing costs. Rossati' s book was illustrated with important photographic material showing the machines and buildings of the Californian wineries: he thought that these represented a model to follow for the Italian producers and his photos showed the state-of-the-art of Californian winemaking, with a greater emphasis on storage operations, on the rational disposal of vineyards and on new grape must processing facilities.

For the most enterprising winemakers, each news arriving from the United States was a point of reference and represented a constant stimulus for innovation. Rossati thought that the press was important for the success of the Californian viticulture, both for the feature articles and for the announcements allowing a wide dissemination of information. The publications dealing with the problems of the wine industry were distinguished by significant drawings, documented articles as well as the originality and modernity of their pages (fonts used, images presented etc.). Rossati underlined that in Italy too, the oenological sector had newspapers and specialised magazines: it was necessary to revitalise them by copying the Californian ones. The same suggestions were given to newspapers which were printed in San Francisco in Italian and addressed to migrants: they were more relevant because they allowed migrants to receive information overcoming the linguistic barriers (that is, the use of English in main important American magazines and journals concerning wine growing and winemaking). Rossati considered that California offered Italian migrants all the best conditions to practise a more innovative viticulture. Their good results obviously increased the competition in the US wine market which, in the early twentieth century, continued to grow and consumers demanded that Italian winemakers (producing in Italy or in California) to increase the quality of their products.

Finally, for the new oenologists graduated from new Italian agricultural schools, the growing American viticulture also offered excellent professional possibilities: it was obviously necessary to study the English language which was not learned at the oenological school. They had strong plant breeding skills, but limited knowledge about the machinery turning traditional wineries into modern and efficient ones. Even the simple use of steam engines in fact represented an absolute innovation for most Italian oenologists: they sometimes accepted a job in a mechanical factory where they could improve, but most of them found a job in the best Californian wineries and helped them to improve the quality of their wine.

Buenos Aires

The oenotechnical station established in Buenos Aires ran from 1888 until the beginning of the 1920s. Its first director, Pompeo Trentin, was a graduate of the Conegliano School of Oenology and he was the author of several books on the wine trade. Before becoming director in Buenos Aires, he met with many winemakers in Italy and he collected information on the different varieties of Italian wines, so, when he arrived in Argentina, he had the essential information concerning the quality of products which were adapted to export. He was intensely active promoting the diffusion of ampelographic studies and he also studied the viticulture of South America. In particular, he wrote a detailed report during his trip to Argentina and Chile: his analysis was accompanied by drawings and it gave detailed information about vineyards, grapes, wines, cultivation systems, winemaking techniques and markets. Besides this, he sent the Italian authorities systematic reports on prices, money, operators, the specialised press, legislation and strategies to increase the visibility of Italian wines. His rich observations, regularly included in the 'Bollettino di Notizie Agrarie' and other publications of the Ministry of Agriculture, represented a fundamental source for all people interested in the development of Italian wine export: his work as director allowed Italian wines to adapt to the negative effects of the financial crisis involving Argentina during the 1890s ('Baring Crisis')[17].

Trentin considered that the Argentine wine market had very favourable characteristics for Italian wines with some particular characteristics such

---

[17] See Trentin P., *Manuale del negoziante di vini italiani nell'Argentina*. Buenos Aires, Tip. Elzeviriana, 1895; Idem, *Piccola enografia italiana in rapporto con la esportazione*, Florence, G. Barbéra, 1903. About the Baring crisis and its effects on the consumption of European wines in Argentina see Mitchener K. J., Marc D. W, "The Baring Crisis and the Great Latin American Meltdown of the 1890s", *The Journal of Economic History*, 68 (2), 2008, p. 462-500.

as low alcohol content, ruby colour and fresh aroma, not too acid. To produce them, he explained that Italian winemakers had to mix different types of wine until the right balance was found and the new wine had uniform characteristics. To promote them, in 1896, he organised the first exhibition of Italian wines in Buenos Aires and encouraged the adoption of new commercial strategies adapted to the expensive transoceanic sales[18]. He did not want exported Italian wine to solely depend on the "nostalgia factor", that is on migrants drinking Italian wines to feel themselves closer to relatives and friends in Italy. He thought that the reference to the food of the native country was important for the popular classes, but also that these links were less strong at a higher and internationalised social level: so he considered it very relevant to make Italian wines safe from the point of view of health and, at the same time, pleasant and engaging for foreign customers.

Trentin and his successor Tommaso Chiaramonte (who published a book giving advice to exporters of Italian wines to Argentina[19]) evidently symbolised the relevant changes concerning the wine sector. Their mission was to encourage the internationalisation of Italian wines and to favour more modern and competitive marketing: their books gave important information about the practice of the wine trade and advertising techniques as well as the role of intermediaries in the international markets.

Trentin also underlined the role played by Italian migrants in favour of the birth of an efficient wine industry in Argentina. Indeed, Italian migrants found ideal conditions there to put their ampelographic knowledge into practice. In 1896, the Escuela Nacional de Vitivinicoltura of Mendoza copied the model of the Italian schools in order to train

---

18 On the evolution of the wine sector in Argentina see: Simpson J., "Factor Endowments, Markets and Vertical Integration. The Development of Commercial Wine Production in Argentina, Australia and California, c. 1870-1914", *Revista de Historia Económica. Journal of Iberian and Latin American Economic History*, 29 (1), 2011, p. 39-66; Barrio de Villanueva P., "El empresariado vitivinícola de la provincia de Mendoza (Argentina) a principios del siglo XX", *Historia agraria*, 45, 2008, p. 81-111; Stein S., María Mateu A. M., "Argentina", in Anderson K. and Pinilla V. (eds.), *Wine Globalization*, p. 291-322; Vaquero Piñeiro M., "Italian Wine in Argentina (1861-1914): Market, State Intervention and Wineries", *Storia Economica* (forthcoming).

19 See Chiaromonte T., *Il commercio dei vini nella Repubblica Argentina nel decennio 1895-1904. Istruzioni e consigli agli esportatori italiani*, Roma, Tip. Nazionale Bertero e C., 1906.

the technicians necessary for the formation of a national wine sector. In 1903, 27 out of 34 wineries operating in Mendoza were linked to Italian migrants. At the end of the nineteenth century, the Argentine wine sector recorded a great increase: it produced a large amount of wine and required Italian producers to adopt new sale strategies favouring medium and high-quality wines. New Italian migrants' wineries in Argentina in fact increased the competition in the local wine market and obliged Italian winemakers to further improve the quality of their product.

The policy of Italian public institutions for the modernisation of the oenological sector began in the 1870s. In the context of the progressive globalisation of agricultural markets, the renewal of viticulture and winemaking methods became fundamental to make Italian wines competitive in order to improve the trade balance but also to serve the national prestige. Taking advantage of the demand provided by the millions of emigrants, Italian public institutions promoted a wide dissemination of 'made in Italy' product positioning. For wine, this meant the improvement of sales on the international market by a new, abundant, varied and high-quality production. This 'obliged' Italian public institutions to found new oenological schools (to train qualified wine technicians), to supply public deposits with new machines (to achieve better winemaking), the participation and also the organisation of international wine exhibitions (to promote Italian wines), and the opening, in the main European and American towns, of free warehouses and oenotechnical stations favouring the import of Italian wines. The integration between public and private initiatives favoured the improvement of the average quality of Italian wines and, moreover, allowed the best winemakers, who became the first real entrepreneurs in the Italian wine sector, the possibility of increasing their sales in the international market.

Behind the Italian wine trade, which between the end of the nineteenth century and the beginning of the twentieth century experienced a first phase of internationalisation, there were also important actions by many personalities, such as the directors of the oenotechnical stations, in particular in the Americas. They observed the wine markets and gave relevant information about the characteristics of the products which were able to conquer wine consumers: so they pushed Italian winemakers to create high-quality wines with a clear and recognisable identity. At the same time they helped Italian migrants to develop their wineries in their new countries and, by the related increase in competition, obliged Italian wine to further improve its quality.

Wine Cooperatives in Alsace: Standing Out at Any Cost for a Sale?

Sylvaine Boulanger

The Alsace vineyards are known for their varietal wines which is an exception in France: this situation is both a strength and a weakness for Alsace winegrowers. It is a strength because reference to the grape varietal is known all over the world and it makes sense for international buyers just like any allusion to the colour of the wine. But this can also be a weak point, in particular for Rieslings, because competition with German wines is very strong: some producers therefore feel that their wines would be better valued with references to the terroir. On the national market, varietal wines are a weakness in a country where reference to the locality, to the agronomic terroir where it is produced and to know-how is, to follow Jean-Claude Hinnewinkel speaking of agronomy and the socio-terroir[1], a crucial element for the consumer.

For twenty years, the actors in the Alsace vineyards have been improving the quality of their wines thanks to more rigorous work in the vines and in the cellar, and they have been looking, in a rather dispersed manner, to valorise the localities in an effort to stand out individually in this wine-producing area of over 15,000 hectares. Among these actors are wine cooperatives or cooperative wineries. According to the Comité Interprofessionnel des Vins d'Alsace (CIVA), in 2015, 41 % of Alsace wines were marketed by 11 wine cooperatives (known as SICAs – *société d'intérêt collectif agricole*[2]) who vinify their members' harvest and bottle

---

1 Hinnewinkel J.-C., *Les terroirs viticoles, origines et devenirs*, Bordeaux, Féret, 2004.

2 "The SICA (*société d'intérêt collectif agricole*) is a kind of company which takes the form of a cooperative, as defined in the law dated 10 September 1947. A company of collective agricultural interest or SICA is not be confused with a *société coopérative agricole* (agricultural cooperative). A SICA can be either a

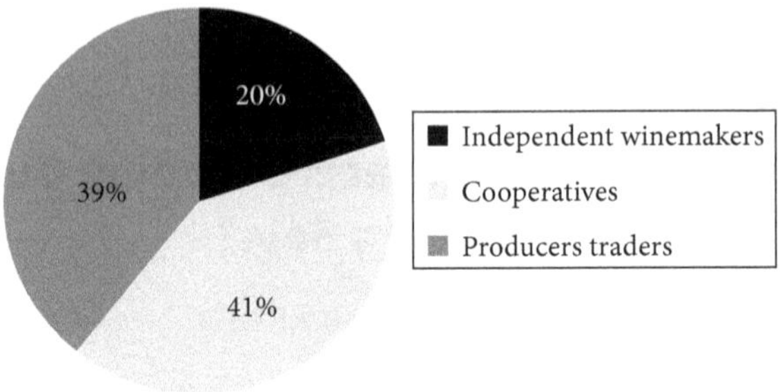

Fig. 1: The marketing of Alsace wines (% of bottles sold). Source of data: CIVA, 2017

it for sale; 39 % was sold by producer-traders who, besides their own harvest, buy grapes from small producers to vinify, age the wine and sell it in bottles; and 20 % was marketed by independent winegrowers who make wine themselves and sell it in their own bottles (Fig. 1). The cooperatives or wineries are therefore key players in the marketing of bottles but also in terms of quantity and 48 % of wine growers are cooperative members.

The eleven Alsace cooperatives are to be found in all corners of the wine-producing area, with a concentration in the centre which receives the most tourists, between Ribeauvillé and Eguisheim (Map 1). They bring together over 22,000 producers over an area of nearly 6,000 hectares, which is 40 % of the Alsace area planted with wine grape varieties. The development in the cooperative structures goes back to after the Second World War, mainly to the decade between 1950-1960. However, over the past ten years, cooperatives have experienced a movement of concentration, mainly for economic reasons.

What are the cooperatives doing to raise the quality of Alsace wines which "are still searching for recognition" (*Le Monde*, 20 June 2018)? How are they trying to respond to the wishes of consumers who want to drink good wine but also want to share in a particular experience that

civil or a commercial undertaking. It is made up of members from different professional branches and its aim is nevertheless to protect the interests of farmers, as a priority". https://droit-finances.commentcamarche.com/faq/24024-societe-d-interet-collectif-agricole-ou-sica-definition.

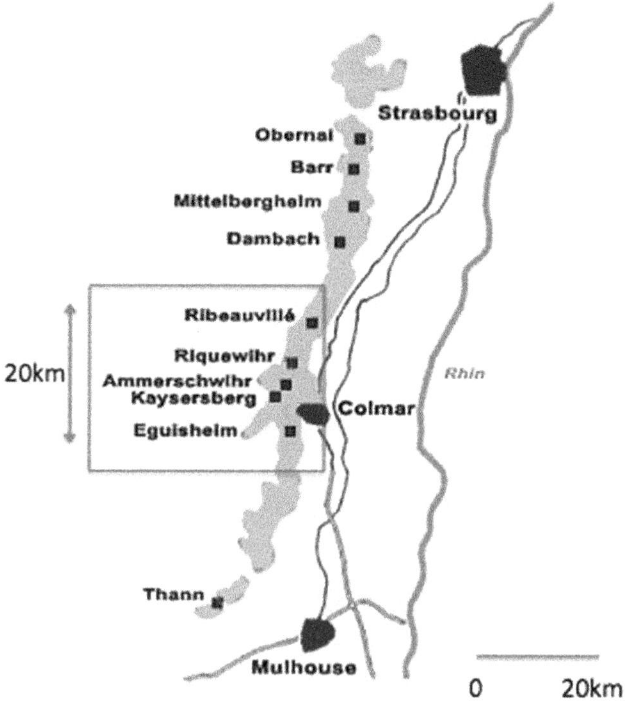

Map 1: Zone where cooperatives are concentrated in the central Alsace vineyard, between Ribeauvillé and Eguisheim. Source: http://www.terroirs-france.com/vin/alsace_carte.htm

is unique within the winery? How are they adapting to national and international economic competition?

The spirit of this article is the continuation of the work carried out by Raphaël Schirmer in 2009, *Les coopératives vinicoles entre marques et terroirs*[3], (Wine cooperatives: between brand names and terroirs) and it focusses on the Alsace wine-producing area. After ten years studying the

3 Schirmer R., "Les coopératives vinicoles entre marques et terroirs" in Durbiano C. and Moustier P. (eds.), *Les Terroirs: caractérisation, développement territorial et gouvernance*, Proceedings of an international colloquium on terroirs, Aix-en-Provence, 9-12 May 2007, May 2007, Aix-en-Provence, Publications de l'Université de Provence (PUP), p. 85-90, 2007. <halshs-00400598>

way independent wine growers function, over the past two years we have turned to cooperatives and the valorisation of their wines. This work is based on thirteen semi-structured interviews carried out with six chairs or directors of cooperatives, actors in those environments or involved in the marketing of the wines. First of all, we must highlight the phenomenon which is the concentration of these vitivinicole organisations and the move upmarket of the products, before moving on to show the way in which the cooperatives are trying to respond to changes in consumer patterns.

Ever more concentration in the cooperative world

Three types of structures coexist

There are two major structures which coexist alongside seven medium size wineries and two smaller ones (Fig. 2 and Tab. 1). These are the result of mergers and purchases which have multiplied over the past thirty years: this is the case of the wineries at Bestheim and Wolfberger, which each have between 400 and 500 members. These wineries are above all brand names. The slogan of the Bestheim winery states this clearly: "Many histories, many wine producers, one single dream, a unique brand". The history of this cooperative winery in fact goes back to 1765 when the Heim family wine merchant business was founded in Westhalten. Gradually, Maison Heim joined forces with the Westhalten

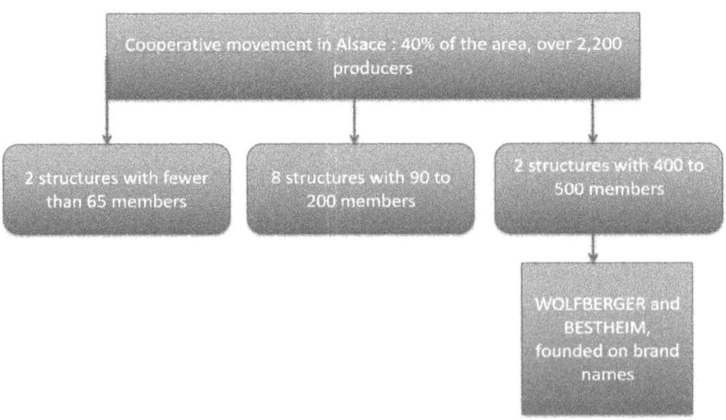

Fig. 2: Structure of the Alsace wine producing cooperative movement.

Tab. 1: Alsace Wineries in 2018 (chronological classification)

	Start Date	Area in Hectares	Number of members
Bestheim winery at Bennwihr	1765	1380	480
Ribeauvillé winery	1895	230	40
Wolfberger winery at Eguisheim	1902	1350	450
Cleebourg winery at Pfaffenheim	1946	191	195
Jean Geiler winery at Ingersheim	1926	390	175
Beblenheim winery	1952	430	180
Roi Dagobert winery at Traenheim	1952	900	250
Hunawhir winery	1954	200	110
Turckheim winery	1955	280	170
Orschwiller-Kintzheim-Les Faîtières winery	1957	140	64
Vieil–Armand winery at Wuenheim	1958	140	90

winery and then with that at Bennwihr and the brand "BESTHEIM" was created in 1997. Then in 2011 the winery at Bestheim merged with the one at Obernai: it sold 15 million bottles in 2014, exported 30 % of its production in over 20 countries with a turnover of 38-40 million euros. In 2015, the Bestheim winery then successfully merged with the prestigious winery at Kientzheim-Kaysersberg which although it only had 60 members producing wine over 160 hectares of vines was selling 1.5 million bottles a year before the merger, including 15 % grands crus. Thus, Bestheim has been able to acquire a bulk wine activity, get premises to vinify small volumes and above all have access to Grands Crus – Schlossberg, Zinnkoepflé, Mambourg – to ensure a quality upgrade for its products, like its competitor Wolfberger. This winery is located at Eguisheim (Haut-Rhin / Upper Rhine) and is a major player in French cooperatives thanks to daring policies. The first winery, located to the south of the Eguisheim vineyard, was set up in 1902 when Alsace was German and when vineyards were recovering after the phylloxera epidemic. At that period, the main role of the winery was to sell wines brought in by cooperative members; it did not do any vinification itself. In 1952 the winery acquired its own vinification equipment and obliged its members to bring in all their harvest. Then under the influence of certain dynamic personalities, in 1976 it joined the cooperative at Dambach-la-Ville, thereby founding the Wolfberger group. In 1979 they acquired the Jacobert distillery and in 1983 the Willm firm, in 1985 the winery at Wuenheim and in 1989 the Jux vineyard at Colmar. The group anticipated the fashion for sparkling wines and in 1992 built a special unit to produce these. The strength of Wolfberger in comparison with other Alsace cooperatives lies in capital investments (in 2011 the group invested 7 million euros in its bottling unit and 5 million in storage), the production of wines of different qualities to meet different markets (60 % of sales are done with major supermarket chains), the accent placed on sparkling wines and owning 15 of the 51 grands crus in the wine-producing area, including the Pfersigberg hillside. In 2017 the winery sold 13 million bottles (including crémant / sparkling wine) with a turnover of 58 million euros.

Other cooperative regroupings between small and middle size structures have taken place for financial reasons and in the search for broader economic impact. In 2010 an important merger took place between the Turckheim Winery and the Cave du Roi Dagobert (Traenheim) Winery through the Union Alsace Alliance GIE (groupment d'intérêt économique / economic interest group). This now brings together the wineries at Turckheim for still wines and the Roi Dagobert for sparkling wines and an investment of 7,2 million euros has been made in a production unit for crémants in response to customer demand.

As for smaller cooperatives they have between 90 and 250 members, except for the most famous, Ribeauvillé which has only 40 members and the one at Faîtières (64 members). These are structures which constantly need to find the means to stand firm in the presence of the two large groups. Some of them, including Ribeauvillé, put the accent on the quality of their wines, or even on their excellence in order to stand out (part 2).

Successful adaptation to sustainable viticulture

The actors in the Alsace vineyards have been aware of sustainable agriculture for twenty years, undoubtedly influenced by their German neighbours. Independent winemakers were the first to adopt this approach. Both small and large cooperative structures then progressively drew up a charter or a document of reciprocal commitments encouraging sustainable viticulture. The forerunner regarding these commitments was the small Dagobert winery to the north of the region. Already in 1999 its members were offered guidelines for best growing practices including the

LE VITICULTEUR S'ENGAGE A	*LA CAVE S'ENGAGE A*
LA REGLEMENTATION	
► Respecter les différents cahiers des charges de l'appellation à savoir : - AOC Alsace, - AOC Alsace Grand Cru, - AOC Crémant d'Alsace. ► Respecter la réglementation. ► Respecter le contrat d'adhésion en vigueur.	► Transmettre le cahier des charges des différentes appellations, ainsi que les évolutions et les modifications. ► Transmettre les textes réglementaires, les évolutions ainsi que les modifications.
LES CONDITIONS DE PRODUCTION AVANT PLANTATION	
► Lors d'un arrachage, transmettre les éléments à la cave. ► Prendre en compte les impacts environnementaux lors des aménagements fonciers à grande échelle. ► Réaliser une analyse de sol avant plantation et lorsque cela est nécessaire (lors de problèmes suite à une observation, ...). ► Conformément à la directive nitrate, réaliser une analyse de sol par exploitation et par an, pour les exploitations de plus de 3 ha. ► La mise en place d'un enherbement temporaire est conseillé.	► Conseiller le viticulteur sur les différentes options possibles lors d'une replantation (cépage, porte-greffe). ► Discuter avec l'adhérent sur la réalisation d'une analyse de sol (par rapport aux analyses déjà effectuées). ► Conseiller une fumure de fond adaptée aux besoins et sur le couvert végétal à implanter.
LA FERTILISATION D'ENTRETIEN	
► Raisonner la fertilisation. ► Enregistrer le prévisionnel et le réel des apports (valeurs, ...) dans le cahier d'enregistrement et motiver l'apport (suite analyse de sol, observations, ...). Exigences HVE n° 8, 10,11 et 12 ► La fertilisation azotée doit être ajustée en fonction du couvert végétal et ne doit pas dépasser 50 Unités d'Azote/an. ► Ne pas utiliser de boues de stations d'épurations (industrielles et/ou urbaines). ► Stocker les engrais et les effluents d'élevage de manière à éviter toute contamination ou toute fuite dans le milieu naturel et notamment dans les zones sensibles. Exigence HVE n°7	► Conseiller sur le choix de la fumure et l'utilité (suite à une visite, discussion, etc...).

Fig. 3: Extract from the reciprocal commitments at the Turckheim winery. Source: Reciprocal Commitments Charter, Turckheim winery, January 2017

growing of grass in the vineyards, getting rid of acaricides, reducing inputs by 20 %, reducing the use of insecticides by 60 % and the use of copper by 50 %, the reuse and recycling of viti-vinicole by-products and waste via specific outlets. The wineries then followed this movement. Since 2015 all the members of the Beblenheim winery have adopted sustainable methods. The Wolfberger group set up an internal charter which is more rigorous than the AOC decree and has adopted an *Agriconfiance* (agri-trust) attitude for all its members such as at the Dagobert and Turckheim wineries where virtually all the plots have grass between the row of vines. The winegrowers at the Turckheim winery have decided to change their practices: they have given up using neonicotinoid insecticides, they have planted hedges, sown wild flower meadows. (Fig. 3).

However, while sustainable practices are widespread, the spread of organic wines is not a priority for most of the cooperatives.

But organic wines in a secondary role

The wineries are not very interested in producing organic wine. When such wine is in fact produced it is for publicity reasons, in particular for the Wolfberger group, which advertises that it has 10 winegrowers engaged in the production of organic wine, which represents about 4 % of the cooperative's vineyard area (53 hectares). Even though the consumer might not buy it, it is reassuring to see it in the catalogue. Paradoxically, even though organic wines are not a big presence in the wineries this is because the client who is a real lover of organic wines prefers to visit the individual producer for this kind of production, feeling that for such products a collective structure is not suitable.

At the Turckheim winery, 10 % of members' vineyards are cultivated organically and this is the highest proportion among all the wineries. This is because the cooperative directors have a deep desire to develop this kind of cultivation in order to meet customer demand as well as to show that cooperatives are capable of upgrading their range of wines, since organic products are synonymous with high standards. The winery thus proposes a selection of seven organic wines which correspond to seven Alsace varietals: sylvaner, pinot blanc, riesling, muscat, pinot gris, gewürztraminer and pinot noir. Similarly, the winery at Ribeauvillé has seven organic wines. However the cooperatives at Bestheim and Beblenheim have no organic wine for sale, and are fully aware of this position. They have made other economic choices based on brand names.

From different strategies to a single goal: finding new consumers in order to survive

Varietal wines, terroir wines and brand names: different means to conquer new markets

Alsace wines meet a national demand first of all: in 2017[4], 74 % of all bottles were sold in France. International sales correspond to 21 % of bottles sold, which is about 20 % of sales, not including crémants. Now, cooperatives are seeking to increase sales on both the national and the international markets. They are adopting and combining different strategies, blending varietals and/or terroirs in order to capture a wider clientele.

4 Source: CIVA.

First assert the physical terroir

The Jean Geiler winery at Ingersheim in effect highlights "terroir wines, from specific localities; plots particularly renowned for the quality of their soil and their exposure to the sun"[5]. As for the Turckheim cooperative, since 2004 it has laid emphasis on the terroir itself with the aid of glass vases holding samples of the rocks and soils where the vines grow and it has created a "terroirs" range of wines. These wineries illustrate the way in which the notion of *agro-terroir* has been deployed for reasons which are widely common to all French vineyards. The idea that Alsace has been generously endowed by "nature", in this case the soil conditions and/or the topography, is supposed to spontaneously convince the buyer. In the winery, there is also an aesthetic effort made to highlight the quality of the soils (Fig. 4).

Fig. 4: Pinot blanc, marls and limestone: terroir and showcasing of the soil varieties in the Turckheim winery. Photo: S. Boulanger, August 2018

[5] https://www.geiler.fr/fr/18-terroirs-specialites-vins-alsace.

Presenting wines by the varietals, the element which is the core identity of Alsace wines

The traditional presentation of wines is still the one which mentions the different varietals before classing them (Beblenheim and Hunawhir wineries, (Fig. 5). In order to refine this presentation by varietal and respond to a demand for localisation and the individualisation of wines, the wine producers often associate the varietals and a locality.

As for crémant, it is always discussed differently, especially as it is the wine which drives Alsace wine sales: it represents a quarter of the

CEPAGE SYLVANER		
AOC ALSACE	2016	Médaille d'Or Mâcon concours 2017
AOC ALSACE	2015	Vieilles Vignes (+ de 30 ans d'âge)
CEPAGE PINOT BLANC		
AOC ALSACE	2016	Tradition
AOC ALSACE	2016	Médaille d'or Paris concours 2017
AOC ALSACE	2016	Vieilles Vignes (+ de 30 ans d'âge)
AOC ALSACE	2016	Cuvée des Hospices de Strasbourg
CEPAGE RIESLING		
AOC ALSACE	2016	Tradition
AOC ALSACE	2016	Médaille d'Argent Paris concours 2017
AOC ALSACE	2015	Kleinfels
AOC ALSACE	**2016**	**Cuvée Mathilde**
AOC ALSACE	2015	Vieilles Vignes (+ de 30 ans d'âge)
AOC ALSACE	2015	Cuvée des Hospices de Strasbourg
AOC ALSACE	2011	Vendanges Tardives
AOC ALSACE	2010	Vendanges Tardives
AOC ALSACE	2009	Vendanges Tardives
AOC ALSACE	2005	Sélections de Grains Nobles
AOC ALSACE GRAND CRU	2014	Sonnenglanz
AOC ALSACE GRAND CRU	2014	Schoenenbourg
CEPAGE MUSCAT		
AOC ALSACE	2016	Réserve Particulière
CEPAGE PINOT GRIS		
AOC ALSACE	2016	Tradition
AOC ALSACE	2016	Médaille d'Or Paris concours 2017

Fig. 5: The traditional presentation of Alsace wines, by varietal, linked to the specific character of the vineyard. Source: taken from the Beblenheim winery catalogue, August 2018

production of Alsace wines (35 million bottles in 2015 of which 21 % is exported). This appellation was created in 1976 and since 1980 has undergone a spectacular development, ahead of *clairette de Die* and *Blanquette de Limoux* and rivals champagne at times of celebration. For the cooperative members, there are two different strategies side by side: Crémant is placed first in the catalogue (Hunawhir, Fig. 6), or completely the opposite, it is placed last, after the varietal wines (Beblenheim).

	VINS
CREMANT D'ALSACE – 75 cl	
1	Calixte Brut Méthode traditionnelle
1	Calixte Brut Rosé
1	Calixte Brut Chardonnay
1	Calixte Brut Blanc de Noirs
1	Calixte Millésime 2013 Elevé en fûts de chêne
CHASSELAS – 75 cl	
1	Chasselas 2016
1	Chasselas 2015 Elevé en fûts de chêne
EDELZWICKER – 75 cl	
1	Edelzwicker
SYLVANER – 75 cl	
1	Sylvaner Vielles Vignes 2016
PINOT BLANC – 75 cl	
1	Pinot Blanc Réserve 2017
1	Pinot Blanc Vieilles Vignes 2016
PINOT NOIR – 75 CL	
0	Pinot Noir Réserve 2016
0	Pinot Noir 2016 Cuvée « 8 » Elevé en barrique
0	Pinot Noir Rosé 2017

Fig. 6: Crémant d'Alsace and edelzwicker highlighted in the catalogue: a deliberate choice. Source: taken from the Hunawhir winery catalogue, August 2018

One might ask questions about the featuring of edelzwicker: why is it still present in the catalogues, sometimes even in a good position (3rd place for the Hunawhir winery) when it is a product that might symbolise the opposite of quality? Edelzwicker is sold in 1 litre bottles and in fact is a white wine made from the leftovers after harvesting chasselas, sylvaner, riesling and gewurztraminer grapes. For some wine producers, consumers and lovers of great wines, this wine should no longer be produced because it harms the image of quality which the whole vineyard is striving to achieve. It just means that the wine leftover in the vats can be sold off. However, others argue that this wine should survive in the name of tradition and because it is used almost daily in Alsace cooking. The cooperative heads answer frankly that there is high demand for this wine, on a daily basis for aperitifs (kir) and picnics so they continue to produce it despite the image that this might convey.

Presenting the wines in ranges

Other cooperatives have preferred to present their wines both by varietals and by ranges with advantageous adjectives. The winery at Cleebourg proposes six ranges of wine: "Prestige", "Vins primes", "Cuvées spéciales", "Lieux-dits", "Les vendanges tardives et sélections de grains nobles" and "Les Crémants d'Alsace". This type of classification helps the less knowledgeable wine lover to find the product that will suit him or her because really knowing varietals and the characteristics is not easy at first. However, such a classification does not highlight the desire to be different from one's competitors nor the underlining of a real move upmarket, unlike what is done at the cooperative in Ribeauvillé where there are nine lines. These show rather more originality and more rigour: the ranges are as follows: Collection (7 varietals), Lieux dits et villages, Grands crus, Clos de Zahnacker (property of the Ribeauvillé Cooperative since 1965), Crémant, Vieilles vignes, Bio, Vendanges tardives, Sélection de grains nobles.

Other choices can be totally different again, deliberately ignoring the presentation of varietals (the foundation of Alsace identity) in order to highlight the cooperative brand. This is how Bestheim works, with a pared-down catalogue as far as presentation goes: it puts the sparkling wines first, then Alsace wines and under this heading it has three lines: Classic, Lieux-dits et terroirs, Grands crus.

"Inventing" new products to widen the range and to build upon a brand

The Ribeauvillé winery has the most diversified offer among all the cooperatives. Firstly, it is the only winery to stock kosher wines with eleven products from all varietals including a crémant. This offer, where sales are more or less symbolic, is to do with identity and is a reminder of the presence of a strong Jewish community in Alsace since the year 1000. Since summer 2018 the winery has also had a new brand on sale, called "*Made in Alsace*" (Fig. 7). It is a blended dry, white wine and the logo is a stork, which reinforces the regional identity and seeks to increase the international market which is sensitive to brand identities. The question of identity is also a strong point for the Beblenheim winery which bought the Pierre Sparr company and brand name in 2009. This firm was a wine producer and wine merchant at Sigolsheim which was undermined by differences between shareholders and found itself

Fig. 7: Creation of the "Made in Alsace" brand, Ribeauvillé winery, in response to international demand for a brand name.
Source: Photo: S. Boulanger, August 2018

bankrupt despite sales of over two million bottles and a turnover of six million euros. The Beblenheim cooperative had a dual aim: upstream, the winery acquired the 30 hectares belonging to Pierre Sparr as well as a further 150 hectares included in different contracts. This reinforced the cooperative's production capacity. Downstream, the winery opened up new exporting possibilities, in particular to North America, Asia (particularly Japan) and Scandinavia. On the national scale, the Pierre Sparr brand was already present in Alsace restaurants and this brought new regional opportunities for the Beblenheim winery. A family name is reassuring.

Some wineries, (Beblenheim, Bestheim) have developed a new product designed for celebrations and as an aperitif: crémant ICE or ICE crémant to be drunk on the rocks. This is about adapting a product (crémant) to new ways of wine consumption (informally, quick aperitifs) and creating new desires.

Standing out by using original bottle designs

The move upmarket of products sold by the cooperatives has been made with the help of marketing techniques. The wineries take on artists to dress some of the bottles in order to change the image that buyers might have of cooperatives and to contest the idea that the wines they produce could be second class. The *Cousu Main* crémant (2018) from the Turckheim winery, where the bottle was designed by William Arlotti, co-founder of *Fashion Post*, tries to highlight the know-how associated with the idea of terroir.

Give the visitor an experience and associate gastronomy and culture

The wineries try to stand out from one another while still wanting to stay linked to the idea of quality, culture and the move upmarket. Ribeauvillé displays its difference through cultural exhibitions by local artists throughout the year. The *En tournée* exhibition (October 2018-January 2019) followed one named the *Cri des Bacchantes*. Within the winery, a room is set aside for pictures, engravings, photographs and sculptures, when there is a temporary exhibition. The cooperative also proposes a visit to its Vine and Viticulture Museum during the summer period, as well as guided tours around the vineyard or the organisation of a meal where the food and wines are in harmony. These efforts towards the well-being of tourists who visit the cellars are also part of the move upmarket, in particular the use of soft lighting which is supposed to create an intimate atmosphere and favour the presentation of the wines.

As for the Turckheim cooperative, they have chosen to ally wines and popular culture by showing reproductions of famous cinema posters (Charlie Chaplin), while the winery at Bestheim focusses on a legend, encouraging people to dream, while keeping an eye on marketing. The legend tells how, in fact, the inhabitants of the village of Bennwihr were nicknamed "Moon hunters", in recognition of their audacity and their ambition. So, the winery has referenced this since 1990 through its "Rayon de Lune"(Moonbeam) vintage where the wines, of all varietals, are in blue bottles.

Alsace wineries are developing economic strategies which are based on both tradition and innovation. They are sometimes torn between the valorisation of their wines through the varietals and/or the terroir, and this bears witness to the recurring questions that Alsace wine producers ask themselves, whether they are independent or in a cooperative. Therefore, the dialogue between the professions needs to be strengthened. In fact, there are tensions between independent winemakers, co-operators and traders to valorise the role of varietal wines, to develop terror wines on the other hand and even to set up new appellations to support the hierarchy of Alsace wines, though the national institute for appellations wants to limit this.

Moreover, at world level, the wine trade is mainly based on three elements: colour, brand name and varietal. While Alsace is well known for its white wines it is struggling to establish brand names (which is why several cooperatives have started doing this) and above all it is meeting sharp competition for its Rieslings, especially from Germany, South Africa and Australia. This explains why, seeing that the home market is the main outlet for Alsace wines, some people wish to develop terroir wines which are much sought after by the French.

Intermediation and the Making of Cirò Marina Wine Markets in Calabria (Italy)

Vincent Fournier

Wines from Calabria are not well known nor are they sought on the international scale. But there is an exception: the town of Cirò Marina where the Cirò DOC wine is produced. There are eleven other *Denominazione di Origine Controlatta* (DOC) in Calabria, but their production is small in comparison with what we find in Cirò Marina. This town is responsible for 75 % of all the DOC wine produced in Calabria. In addition, no other *Denominazione di origine controllatta* in Calabria possesses as much recognition on foreign markets. Mostly exported to Germany and Switzerland, the Cirò wine can also be found in Great Britain, Japan, the United States and Canada. In that respect, on the scale of Calabria, the Cirò wine seems unique. We can wonder how such a place has emerged as a leading wine producing and exporting region. The aim of this chapter is to understand how the commercial networks for this wine were formed historically and who the makers and intermediaries were.

If by definition an intermediary is a person situated between two places or two realities, we can challenge the assumption regarding the existence of such a figure in the wine trade. Through the analysis of the historical development of the different markets for the wine of Cirò, the focus of this paper will be on identifying the categories of individuals involved in the wine trade and on investigating their roles as intermediaries. I will begin by describing the local and regional markets, which provide an explanation for the specialisation of the wine production as early as the 18th century. Next, I will present the formation of a bulk wine market toward the north of Italy and in France. Finally, I will analyse in more detail the formation of contemporary markets, influenced by the introduction of laws regulating the production and commercialisation of wine. At each of these stages, I will focus on identifying the intermediaries, their origins, their roles and their influence.

The information presented here come from a one-year ethnographic research project conducted in Cirò Marina in 2000-2001 and from subsequent shorter stays in 2004, to gather complementary data, and in 2016 and 2019 to observe the evolution of the local context. There are about fifteen wineries responsible for the commercialisation of the local wine on the national and foreign markets. This small number allowed me to carry out interviews in all of them. I conducted more than fifty semi-directed interviews in Italian, translated into French during the transcription process. They were with winery owners or directors, small grape growers and different people related to the wine business such as civil servants, teachers and sales agents. In the interviews with winery owners and directors, I led them to talk about the specific history of their winery, addressing the evolution of the production and the commercialisation, and identifying with them their initial markets, tracing the appearance of new ones and the evolution of each market. This chapter is mainly based on these interviews and as such, subscribes to an oral history approach. It is also based on some archival works conducted at the *Archivio di Stato di Napoli*, where I studied the *Catasto Onciario*.

The local and regional markets

The agrarian history of Calabria is characterised by the pre-eminence of large properties (*latifondi*) and extensive grain production and livestock farming for exportation[1]. This situation predominated especially in the plains area surrounding the city of Crotone, thirty kilometres south of Cirò. These zones of extensive production were then almost deprived of wine production[2]. As such, they offered a commercial outlet that in fact fostered the wine specialisation in Cirò. In a book published in 1849, Giovan-Francesco Pugliese, a local dignitary involved in the public

---

1 Bevilacqua P., "Uomini, terre, economie", in Bevilacqua P. and Placanica A. (eds.), *Storia d'Italia, Le regioni dall'Unità a oggi, La Calabria*, Turin, Giulio Einaudi editore, 1985. Calabria A., *The Cost of Empire, The Finances of the Kingdom of Naples in the Time of Spanish Rule*, Cambridge, Cambridge University Press, 1991.

2 Caridi G., *Il latifondo calabrese nel Settecento*, Reggio Calabria, Falzea editori, 2000 (1990). Petrusewicz M., *Latifondo, Economia morale e vita materiale in una periferia dell'Ottocento*, Venice, Saggi Marsilio, 1989.

administration of the town, compiled an overview of the economic and agrarian conditions of his time. Using the data of the Catasto Provisorio, gathered from 1810 onward, Pugliese states that the total area under viticulture in Cirò covered 464 hectares[3]. Without indicating his sources, Pugliese also provides information regarding the quantities of wine produced during the decade 1837-1846. The average annual production of wine was 30,000 barrels[4]. With a population of 4156 inhabitants in 1837[5], this would mean that the annual consumption of wine would have reached 315 litres per capita, which is hardly imaginable. In fact, while a portion of the wine produced served the local needs, another part was commercialised.

Pugliese gives us interesting information on this topic. According to him, despite bad winemaking techniques, the wine from Cirò could last longer than one produced in surrounding villages and could be kept for almost two years, which made it sought after in August and September, when people started to run out of wine. In that respect, in the course of the year, the price of the barrel would increase, as the quantities would decrease. But the people preferred to drink cheap, young wine and each year, after the harvest, the price would drop. Pugliese states nonetheless that this wine "can age well and travel by sea, making it an esteemed and preferred wine at the table of the greats of the capital [Naples]"[6]. On that matter, François Lenormant[7], a French scholar travelling in Calabria in 1879 praised the wine from Cirò, outlining how it was appreciated and sought after regionally:

> [We see] the burgeoning and animated town of Cirò, under which a vast vineyard produces *the most estimated wine in Calabria* [our emphasis]. This wine is warm and generous. Even in the current state, produced with the most imperfect methods, it is of a remarkable quality, can be preserved and improved with age. It would deserve to be taken care of more seriously, and its winemaking improved. Produced better, with greater attention and better

---

3 Pugliese G.-F., *Descrizione ed istorica narrazione, dell'origine, e vicende politico-economiche di Cirò, in provincia di Calabria Ultra 2,* 2 volumes, Cosenza, Edizioni Brenner, 1983 (1849), vol. 1, p. 47.

4 This wine barrel contains about 44 litres.

5 *Ibid.*, v. 2, p. 107.

6 *Ibid.*, v.1, p. 22, *free translation by the author.*

7 Specialist of the Antiquity and professor at the Bibliothèque Nationale, François Lenormant undertake different travels in Southern Italy between 1879 and 1883.

techniques, it could quickly gain a reputation at the European level and instead of, as today, only been sought in the rest of Calabria, would become the object of an extensive export[8].

Regarding these markets, Pugliese states that when he was young: "The Tarantini[9] were continually coming to buy wine. But with the wine, they also took thousands of grafts and started to cultivate their own vineyards"[10]. Also, "the city of Crotone, where we find a military garrison of 800 men, consumes a large volume of it"[11]. Finally, Pugliese provides the records of the local maritime customs office for the years 1843 to 1846. These records indicate the quantities of goods that officially came in and out of Cirò by sea, the number of ships, their provenance and their destination. Surprisingly, there is no mention of wine, except for two shipments in 1846. This seems to indicate that the wine of Cirò was not exported by sea on a regular basis. The wine trade was then regional and conducted by land. On this point, the *Catasto Onciario*[12] indicates the presence of twenty-two bullock cart drivers and nine mule drivers from a total of 780 households. The bullock cart drivers were in charge of transporting goods in the lowlands, while the mule drivers were in charge of transporting goods through mountain trails. The *Catasto Onciario* also shows that the number of bullock carts and mule drivers were more numerous in Cirò than in the other seven surrounding towns of the Marchesato[13].

The early markets for the wine of Cirò were then formed mainly by the surrounding communities, the mountain ones and the lowland towns situated in the grain dominated plain of the Marchesato di Crotone. In this regard, Cirò occupied a forefront position, as defined by Roger

8 Lenormant F., *La Grande-Grèce. Paysages et histoire, 2 tomes*, Paris, A. Lévy, 1881, t.1, p. 375. *Free translation by the author.*

9 The inhabitants of Tarento in Puglia.

10 Pugliese, *Descrizione ed istorica narrazione, op. cit.*, vol.1, p. 60.

11 *Ibid.*

12 The *Catasto Onciario* consists in a survey of households and land properties of most town and cities of the kingdom of Naples and compiled between 1741 and 1788. For a complete analysis, see Fournier V., "Le développement de l'industrie vitivinicole et les représentations du vin à Cirò en Calabre. Une anthropologie du particulier", thèse de doctorat, Montréal, Université de Montréal, 2005.

13 Caridi G., *Il latifondo calabrese nel Settecento, op. cit.* Caridi comparative analysis also indicates that the total acreage under grape production in Cirò in 1754 (350 hectares) surpass the vineyards acreage of these seven towns put together (255 hectares).

Dion[14], in relation to the plains of the Marchesato where large sized properties stockbreeding and grain production predominated alongside the pauperisation of the peasant population[15]. It is actually this specific situation that explains the wine production specialisation in Cirò at that time. The stories and statements I heard during my interviews tended to support this assumption:

> Pasquale R.[16]: At that time (1920s), my grandfather carried his wine himself on carts around the region, more precisely in the area of the Crotonese. Crotone has never produced any grapes or wine. But it has always been a big city with a great population who consumed the production from Cirò. And the area of Cirò developed precisely because these other areas of Calabria were producing other crops. This mass of people was getting its wine here, in Cirò, the nearest wine producing town.

Before the building of the railway at the end of the 19th century, the improvement of roadways in the 1930s, and the introduction of trucks and automobiles, distances were an obstacle for the transportation of goods over long distances.

> Giovanni F.: Before the completion of the railway, the wine trade was carried on carts drawn by oxen, and on which two large barrels were fixed. People came from outside with these carts and carried the wine away. It was people from outside who came here, and not people from here who were going outside. In the mountains, there were only trails. In Cirò, there were people who were moving wine on the backs of animals. Mule drivers who conveyed it to the surrounding villages mainly carried out this trade.

These stories, like others, stress how part of this trade was taken over by people from outside the area. At that time, small winegrowers would do their own vinification and they would sell it to these outsiders. Others told me how it was their grandfathers who took their wine themselves to the nearby villages. Both cases seem possible. In these villages, the wine was sold in specific places called *cantina* (basement/cellars) specialised in wine retailing and where people would go to buy wine. People would

---

14 Dion R., *Histoire de la vigne et du vin en France des origines au XIXe siècle*, Paris, Flammarion, 1959.

15 Arlacchi P., *Mafia, Peasants and Great Estates, Society in Traditional Calabria*, Cambridge, Cambridge University Press, 1983. Piseli F. et Arrighi G., "Parentela, clientela e communità", in Bevilacqua P. and Placanica A. (eds.), *Storia d'Italia, Le regioni dall'Unità a oggi, La Calabria*, Turin, Giulio Einaudi editore, 1985.

16 All people names are pseudonyms.

also gather there to drink while playing cards. But no food was served. These initial markets explain the wine specialisation at this early time and from them other markets would emerge, following the completion of the railway, for instance.

The bulk wine market to the north

The railway between Tarento and Reggio di Calabria on the Ionian coast was completed in 1875. With the train, it was now possible for the producers from Cirò to send their wine afar, not only to Crotone, but also elsewhere in Italy, following the unification of the country in 1861. The railway enabled the development of new markets for the wine, especially toward the north of Italy and France. The southern regions of Italy began to export large quantities of bulk wine with a high level of alcohol, firstly used to meet the demand caused by the phylloxera crisis, and then used as blending wine to fortify some wines from France and Piedmont. It was merchants from the north who were coming to the south to buy the wine from the producers.

In the absence of any written records, it is impossible to know the quantity of wine and the percentage of the local production that was commercialised in this way. But this market surely contributed to the growth in production and in 1929, the total acreage of vineyards reached 1636 hectares[17], which represented an increase of 1172 hectares since 1810[18]. During the interviews, the people told me that during the 1950s, almost half of the local production was exported by train to the north. Unfortunately, no source provides any information that would allow us to check these claims and to know precisely the volumes of wine exported. And so, beside the "traditional" regional markets for the wine of Cirò, a long-distance trade by train started to develop.

This trade by train led to the appearance of the first local traders (*negozianti*), and then to the first wineries. These wineries were established around the railway, near the train station: "When the railway was built, the wineries moved from Cirò to the train station. Then, small winegrowers started to bring their wine to these wineries, and then their grapes", Giovanni F. told me. And he continued: "In 1953, we [his

17 *Catasto Agrario* of 1929.

18 Pugliese, *Descrizione ed istorica narrazione, op. cit.*, v. 1, p. 47.

family] were producing only bulk wine. But we were selling it abroad, in Piedmont, but always in bulk by tank car, with large barrels. A tank car was composed of two large barrels of 70 hectolitres. So, a tank car had a capacity of about 150 hectolitres". From this time on, the wine trade slowly started to slip out of the hands of the small winegrowers. They stopped selling wine by themselves and began to bring it to the new local traders. These traders, who were more able to meet the demand of the foreign buyers, started to play an intermediary role between the plethora of small winegrowers and the traders from abroad. A couple of these traders became quite rich, drawing the attention of the large landowner to this activity. A group of nine of them joined together and formed a private cooperative called the Cirovin in 1955.

The bulk wine market dominated local production and remained important until the 1970s. As Nicodemo P. recounted: "Between 1970 and 1975, my grandfather's wine was entirely bought by French traders who were buying it as a blending wine". But starting in the 1970s, this market started to shrink rapidly mainly because of the introduction in 1963 of Italian legislation regulating wine production and commercialisation.

The diaspora markets

The bulk wine trade stimulated the local production. But the wine exported in this way remained anonymous, because it was used as a blending wine. Simultaneously, another market for the wine of Cirò, under its own name, started to emerge. Throughout the 20th century, many people emigrated from Calabria and went to Argentina, Brazil, Canada and the United States, and then to Germany and Switzerland[19]. Some of these immigrants were specialised in the wine trade aimed at these diasporas. As Espedito C. told me: "The brother of my father went to work in Brazil for a while and was importing our wine until around 1953. Over there, there were many immigrants from Calabria who wanted our wine". Other persons showed me old correspondences with relatives who had emigrated and in which they wrote that they wanted to import the wine from Cirò to America during the 1950s. But the main markets to emerge around the immigrants occurred in northern

---

19 Carchedi F. and Vitiello M., *L'emigrazione dalla Calabria. Percorsi migratori, consistenze numericheed effetti sociali*, Todi, Tau Editrice, 2014.

Italy, in Germany and in Switzerland. All the producers in the present wineries told me how these markets formed because of the immigrants and how, even today, they are the main markets for the Cirò wine outside of Calabria.

Since the wine of Cirò was already known at the regional level, it was favoured by traders. Some of these traders were from different places in Calabria, and some were from Cirò. It was the case of Vittorio S. who emigrated to Milan in 1950. He first worked in a plant, until the delivery of a residence permit. Then, he started considering other options and decided, a bit spontaneously he said, to import wine from Cirò: "With a truck and wooden barrels, carrying fewer than a hundred quintals per trip, I was the first to import the wine of Cirò by truck to the north"[20]. In Milan, Vittorio S. bottled the wine himself before selling it. Or people came to his warehouse with jugs to buy the wine in bulk. He also started to sell to a supermarket and to some restaurants. He pursued this activity until the end of the 1960s. But in 1969, he had to stop, because the introduction of the DOC Cirò would not allow him to bottle the wine from Cirò in Milan and to sell it as such. He went back to Cirò and opened a grower-merchant winery, producing wine with grapes bought from the small growers.

The introduction and effects of the DOC Cirò

The introduction of the DOC Cirò dates from 1969, only six years after the establishment of the 1963 Italian laws regulating wine production. This early procuration testifies to the dynamism of a group of local producers of the time, the aforementioned Cirovin, but also to the reputation that the wine from Cirò already had. The producers were eager to possess such an instrument to help them in their commercialisation endeavour. But as an external element, the DOC turned out to be in itself an element of intermediation between the local setting and the exterior. The introduction of the DOC Cirò must be seen as the transposition to the local reality of a specific cultural understanding of wine production. Because of their involvement in the wine trade, local winery owners and

[20] Most producers told me in this manner that they had been the first to export their wine to the north.

directors became intermediaries through whom this specific manner of understanding wine came to be implemented locally.

First, following the criteria fixed in the regulation, for the creation of the DOC Cirò the producers needed to decideon the constituent that locally defined the wine of Cirò. They reduced the Cirò wine to a sole grape variety, the*Gaglippo*, although until then different grape varieties had been cultivated and could be used[21]. During my stays, this was then criticised and new grape varieties were introduced in the regulation Cirò DOC in 2005.

Second, the DOC was linked to technical requirements aimed at guaranteeing a level of quality for the consumers. Producers had to follow production rules and be subject to different controls in the vineyards and in the cellars. The effect of this was, thirdly, to make wine production and commercialisation more complicated and difficult and it pushed many small winegrowers out of winemaking activity. Following the introduction of the DOC, the bottle became the main medium for wine retail, predominantly an exterior market exigency. This new way of working turned out to be an overwhelming task for most peasants who were not able to make the monetary investments necessary for this transformation.

Lastly, following the legal requirements regarding wine production, instead of buying wine from small growers, the local traders started to buy the grapes from them to vinify it themselves. These transformations drove the majority of the plethora of small winegrowers to give up winemaking and to devote themselves solely to grape production. From this time on, the local wine industry started to become concentrated in the hands of a few producers who had the means to adapt to these transformations.

The contemporary intermediaries

At the present time, there are about fifteen wineries in Cirò Marina which commercialise their wine on the national and international markets. Beside these, about thirty small wineries have opened recently, but with small production and limited to the local market. Otherwise, there is one public cooperative that is open to all grape growers interested

21 For example, Pugliese indicates eight white grapes varieties and ten red ones, *Descrizione ed istorica narrazione, op. cit.*, vol. 1, p. 59.

in it. There are also some private cooperatives. Often these have formed around a few family groups who are the descendants of the ancient families of landowners, like the aforementioned Cirovin. They opened with state funding from the Italian government aimed at developing the southern regions of Italy, for instance the *Cassa del Mezzogiorno* (Fund for the South). The number of members, initially limited, tends to increase through inheritance and now reaches between fifteen and thirty persons. Finally, there are the private wineries. Initially these were grower-merchant wineries, producing wine with grapes bought from the small growers. The owners come from families of small or medium-sized landowners, families of shopkeepers and some descendants of the great landowners. It is in this category that recently many new wineries have opened with the help of recent funding from the European community. Some of them, with better funding and more ambitions, have managed to reach national and international markets. Others have managed to gain some recognition through the natural wine philosophy and the associated niche market. But most of them are almost artisanal and produce a wine of varying quality. All these wineries differ in size, production capacity and market size. Some produce between two and five million bottles of wine, while others produce between 75,000 and 200,000, and the new ones even fewer. Some wineries are present on the international markets, through representative agents, while other are limited to the regional market of Calabria, or even the local market of Cirò Marina, and do not have any agents.

Besides these wineries, there are about 1,500 small grape growers, descending from families of small landowners and of *braccianti* (agricultural day labourers). As seen before, they don't produce wine, except for their own domestic needs. They sell their grapes to some grower-merchant wineries, take it to the public cooperative or sell to buyers who come from different places in Calabria. There is indeed a regional market for the grapes from Cirò aimed at people who still produce their own wine at home. Since the wine of Cirò has a long-standing reputation in Calabria, the local grapes are sought after. There are intermediaries coming from different places in Calabria who are specialists in this trade. The grape growers feel marginalised from the wine trade, because they only produce grapes and don't commercialise their wine.

As we have seen before, following the introduction of the DOC Cirò, the wine had to be produced and bottled locally. It simply was not possible to export the wine in bulk by truck anymore. This forced a reorganisation of the trade channels and of the ways of working. The task fell on the local producers to export their wine to different markets themselves. During my research, it was revealed that the commercialisation process was considered as important as it is difficult. As the director of a private cooperative told me: "Wine commercialisation is the most important, but also the most demanding part of the whole process". Commercialisation now passes through the search for representative agents. The owner of a prominent private winery explained to me how they had managed to build their markets:

> Giovanni G.: First, we have sought to conquer the regional market. I was filling the trunk of my car with wine samples and going to meet potential agents. My trip was fifteen days long. I started with the northern part of the Ionian coast, after that, the southern part, and then Reggio. Then, we did the same with the Tyrrhenian coast, and also up to Salerno and Naples. After having made the "presentation", the representative agents came. Following that, I did the same thing with the rest of Italy and, finally, abroad. With my car trunk full of samples, I went to meet wine shops. Like this, in each country, I found a national representative agent: in Switzerland, in Germany, in Great Britain… For Germany, it was more complicated, because it's a big market. First, we created different zones with different representative agents. I was going there, taking the telephone books, spending entire days in public phones, carrying samples to traders, and so on. It has been the most difficult market to build, but also the one that now gives us great satisfaction and with which we now do half of our turnover. We have more representative agents in Germany than in Italy! We have one super-representative and about fifteen sub-representatives.

We can see in this narrative the endeavour made by this producer to build a network of representative agents. In this way, the producer himself becomes an intermediary between the local and the foreign markets. He plays an active role in the constitution of these networks where the representative agents are actually simply his first clients. The representative agent himself is normally from the place where he represents a wine and about which he possesses certain knowledge. For example, he may have a certain idea of the customers' tastes and preferences and will agree to represent certain producers if he believes their wines have a chance on his market. His task then is to search for potential buyers: restaurants, specialised wine stores and supermarkets. As stated by Stefano C. the director of a private cooperative: "The representative agent plays an extremely important role in the development of new markets. He is the agent who will work to find new markets for the product he's representing. And he will also try to find products for which he thinks there could be a demand on the markets where he works". It is the representative agent who possesses the knowledge of the markets where he works who will have, an interest in a specific wine or not. It is also through the representative agent that a producer will know the reception given by the customers to his wine. In this way, the agent also plays a role of intermediation. This can influence the perceptions and ideas each producer has about their own wine. But the producers are not passive agents in this process. They themselves play an active role of intermediation, because of their involvement in the wine trade.

In this regard, to export to foreign markets, producers judged that they needed to improve the quality of their wine. According to them, the question of quality has emerged as a market necessity. This preoccupation caused by their desire to be able to export to these markets led to another type of intermediation. In order to reach a higher level of quality, producers turned themselves toward the use of new imported technologies and of consultants. As stated by Michele C. the director of a private winery: "everybody cools their grape must. People have new equipment at the forefront of technology. In recent years, there has been a boom in new equipment. And now everybody has an oenologist". By being submitted to new requirements coming from abroad and by adapting through the use of technologies and knowledge also coming from abroad, producers again were occupying an intermediary role between the local reality and the outside world.

The consultation of winemakers plays an important intermediation role too. As Stefano C. explained to me: "In the past, wine was made in a traditional manner. But today, all the wineries have an oenologist who chooses who will be the technician in charge of the winery, what grapes will be used, who decides the whole strategy, in the vineyards and in the cellar to produce this kind or that kind of wine". The choice of hiring a winemaker was in some cases incidental to their reputation for this can serve to attract the attention of consumers and international wine journalists. But the producers were aware of and are concerned by the foreign aspect of the consultants and how they could affect the typicality of their wine. In this regard, Antonio M., a young oenologist and member of a family owned private cooperative, told me they had chosen their consultant oenologist by looking at the other wines he had made elsewhere in Italy and they thought their specificity has been preserved. Or there is the example of another director who explained to me that their oenologist had been working in Cirò for so long, and where he had started his consulting career that, even if he was from outside (from Puglia), he was able to preserve the local character of the wine and, among the foreigners, he was the best suited to do so.

By being actively involved in the pursuit of outside markets, by being influenced by the exigencies of these markets and, finally, by being influenced by modern winemaking knowledge, technologies and non-local oenologist consultants, the producers themselves play a role of intermediation between the local setting and the outside world. This became obvious during my research through the local presence of a discrepancy regarding the definition of the quality of the wine. The local population in general, including the grape growers, defined the quality of the wine differently than the winery owners. For the population, a good wine was a strong wine, which is a wine with a high level of alcohol. Also, a good wine was a product considered *genuino*. Many people, producing their own wine, for instance grape growers, told me how it was free of: "all the processing the wineries submit their wine to". For this reason, they believe their wine was more "pure", "less transformed" and, consequently, of a better quality than the one produced by the wineries. For them, winery wines were perceived as part of the agri-food business.

Conversely, the winery owners' discourses made references to the DOC regulation and to the demands of the international market. They defined the quality of the wine as any wine enthusiast or wine journalist would do, which is in terms of terroir expression, grape specificity, balance and structure and, finally, by asserting the visual, olfactory and gustative aspects. This distinctive way of conceiving the quality of the wine, and congruent with the international standards of wine appreciation, shows the intermediary position of these producers between the local setting and the national and international markets:

> Stefano C.: We sell wine. They, on the contrary, they drink something which in many cases, is a cousin of wine. Even if the acidity is too high, they will drink it. To produce at home your wine means drinking it four or five months following the harvest. We make a product that can reach four or five years of age. That's the difference. They say that the wineries do "other things". But these "other things" are the ones necessary to stabilise the wine in order to be able to send it without problems to America.

This divergence between the producers and the whole local population leads us to believe that the definition of quality that the producers have comes from their specific position in this industry and of their implication in the international wine trade. In today's environment, winery owners and directors themselves turn out to be intermediaries between wine worlds.

The goal of this paper was to identify the intermediaries in the wine world of Cirò Marina in Calabria. Through the analysis of the historical development of Cirò wine markets, we can see that many figures can assume the role of intermediaries. In some cases, these people are outsiders, and, in other cases, they are people from Cirò Marina. We first saw how, in the past, mule drivers and bullock cart drivers were in charge of the wine trade directed toward nearby town and villages. At the end of the nineteenth century, when a bulk wine trade started to develop with the north of Italy and France, it was foreigners who came to Cirò by train to buy the wine. This led to the appearance of the first local traders (*negozianti*) and wineries being built around the train station. Throughout the 20th century, emigration from Calabria facilitated the creation of markets for the wine of Cirò, recognised as such, in the north of Italy and in specific countries of Europe and America. Traders from this diaspora, from Cirò or elsewhere in Calabria, specialised in this activity until the establishment of the DOC Cirò which forced specific transformations. The wine now had to be produced and bottled in the territory of Cirò to have the right to bear the name "Cirò". From that moment, it was through representative agents that the producers started to sell their wine, especially at the national and international level. The representative can be met in wine fairs which are held locally, at the regional or the national level, Vinitaly for instance held each year in Verona, or in other countries. These representatives can also be reached directly on different markets. But as we have seen, the producer has become as much an intermediary who has to reach out to enter specific markets, as the representative who usually come from the places where he intends to represent a wine. As such, the producers themselves can be envisioned as occupying a role of intermediation in the wine world. This was observable in Cirò Marina through the discrepancy in the ways in which the producers and the rest of the population defined the quality of the wine.

Following our analysis, it seems difficult to identify and isolate the specific figure of the "intermediary" in the wine trade of Cirò: the people taking charge of the activity of intermediation, or who are from the production place, or who come from the markets where they sell the wine.

Accordingly, instead of trying to identify who the intermediaries are, it seems more appropriate to define and identify *activities* and practices that contribute to the intermediation of different wine worlds. Based on these *activities of intermediation*, we can then identify *categories of persons* related to these activities and their *consequences*. Like this, we can define the intermediaries of the wine world in a pragmatic way. If at first sight, the representative agents seem to occupy the role of intermediaries, they are rooted in the markets where they work and where they often come from. As I have demonstrated, the producers themselves participate actively in these mechanisms and are involved in the processes of intermediation. Through this approach, focussed on the activities of intermediation, it becomes possible to integrate other categories of persons into our analysis. Wine journalists occupy a role of intermediation because they themselves come from specific places where they are read, where they have an influence and where they play a role of intermediation. In the same manner, we could investigate the intermediation role of civil servants, or of the consumers themselves.

Sources

Archivio storico di Napoli, *Catasti Onciari*, voll. 6967-6970.

Catasto Agrario, 1929, fasc. 75.

References

Arlacchi P., *Mafia, Peasants and Great Estates, Society in Traditional Calabria*, Cambridge, Cambridge University Press, 1983.

Bevilacqua P., "Uomini, terre, economie", in Bevilacqua P. and Placanica A. (eds.), *Storia d'Italia, Le regioni dall'Unità a oggi, La Calabria*, Turin, Giulio Einaudi editore, 1985.

Calabria A., *The Cost of Empire, The Finances of the Kingdom of Naples in the Time of Spanish Rule*, Cambridge, Cambridge University Press, 1991.

Carchedi F. and Vitiello M., *L'emigrazione dalla Calabria. Percorsi migratori, consistenze numericheed effetti sociali*, Todi, Tau Editrice, 2014.

Caridi G., *Il latifondo calabrese nel Settecento*, Reggio Calabria, Falzea editori, 2000 (1990).

Dion R., *Histoire de la vigne et du vin en France des origines au XIXe siècle*, Paris, Flammarion, 1959.

Fournier V., "Le développement de l'industrie vitivinicole et les représentations du vin à Cirò en Calabre. Une anthropologie du particulier", thèse de doctorat, Montréal, Université de Montréal, 2005. Available online: https://papyrus.bib.umontreal.ca/xmlui/handle/1866/16874.

Lenormant F., *La Grande-Grèce. Paysages et histoire, 2 tomes*, Paris, A. Lévy, 1881.

Piseli F. and Arrighi G., "Parentela, clientela e communità", in Bevilacqua P. and Placanica A. (eds.), *Storia d'Italia, Le regioni dall'Unità a oggi, La Calabria,* Turin, Giulio Einaudi editore, 1985.

Pugliese G.-F., *Descrizione ed istorica narrazione, dell'origine, e vicende politico-economiche di Cirò, in provincia di Calabria Ultra 2,* 2 volumes, Cosenza, Edizioni Brenner, 1983 (1849).

PART III

Networks, Identity and Migration in the Wine World

Fruits of Their Labour: Networks of Migration, Knowledge, and Work in the 19th Century Cape Wine Industry

Chelsea Davis

When the British Empire took control of the Cape of Good Hope at the beginning of the 19th century, they inherited a nearly 150-year-old wine industry, one predicated upon a powerful Boer gentry and subjugated slave labour force. The Cape was a strategic chokepoint en route to Asian markets, offering a potential trade post and naval rest station. The colony also possessed advantageous opportunities for commodity export during a time when, as remembered by Mr. H. Cloete in 1831:

> England was marked with the most eventful crisis that any country ever exhibited; when every part of the Continent was closed to her trade, and the English palate was fast losing all recollection of Claret…and other standard wines of the British Tables, and the Vineyards of Spain and Portugal were destroyed by the horrors of war; it was then that the eyes of the British Government were first directed to this Colony as likely to supply that loss[1]…

In 1795, Great Britain attempted to take control of the Cape as "part of their general campaign to secure their hegemony over the world's seas in the course of their war with revolutionary France"[2]. The demand for

---

1 Mr. H. Cloete, in "Proceedings of a public meeting held at Cape Town on the 16th July 1831 to take into consideration the state of the wine trade &c., commerce, agriculture, and taxes, and the want of a legislative assembly", Cape Town, George Greig, 6.

2 Ross R., *A Concise History of South Africa*, Cambridge, Cambridge University Press, 2008, p. 37.

Cape wine even markedly increased between 1778 and 1815[3]. While the British Empire encouraged wine growing in its other colonies as a method of socio-cultural improvement[4], the Cape Colony inherited in 1806 had been growing and producing wine for years. Dutch surgeon Jan van Riebeeck arrived in the Cape of Good Hope in 1652, with the aim to produce wine for treating scurvy. By 1661, the first grapes were pressed into – albeit a very acidic and crude – but drinkable wine[5]. To transform this agricultural hobby into a viable commodity for export, the Vereenigde Oostindische Compagnie (VOC) sought skill and expertise from abroad. In 1688, the first group of French refugees sponsored by the Dutch East India Company arrived at the Cape, and by the end of 1691, there were 178 living in the colony[6].

Yet skill alone would not grow, harvest, and produce the grapes. That would require a large manual labour force. The indigenous population of Khoi living within the drawn boundaries of the Cape Colony actively resisted labour on wine farms, asserting their autonomy as cattle traders, though they would eventually become one faction of a growing labour population[7], manipulated with payments of tobacco, bread, and wine. By the end of the 17th and throughout the 18th centuries, the VOC imported slaves from other Dutch colonies in Southeast Asia, Madagascar, and Mozambique[8]. Slavery soon became a quintessential component to

---

3 Vink N., Boshoff W. H., Williams, G., Fourie J., and McLean L. S., "South Africa", in Anderson K. and Pinilla, V. *Wine Globalisation: A New Comparative History*, Cambridge, Cambridge University Press, 2018, p. 390.

4 See Dunstan D. and McIntyre J., "Wine, Olives, Silk and Fruits: The Mediterranean Plant Complex and Agrarian Visions for a 'Practical Economic Future' in Colonial Australia", *Journal of Australian Colonial History*, no. 16, 2014, p. 29-50.

5 Robinson J., "South Africa", *Oxford Companion to Wine*, Oxford, Oxford University Press, 1994, p. 897.

6 Coertzen P., "The Huguenots of South Africa in History and Religious Identity", *Dutch Reformed Theological Journal*, no. 52-1, 2011, p. 45.

7 Williams G., "Slaves, Workers, and Wine: The 'Dop System' in the History of the Cape Wine Industry, 1658-1894", *Journal of South African Studies*, no. 42-5, 2016, p. 895.

8 Rayner M., "Labourers in the Vineyard: Work and Resistance to Servitude during the Years of the Wine Farming Boom in the Cape Colony 1806-1824", Postgraduate Seminar on Comparative Commonwealth Social History, Crime, Deviance, and Control, London, University of London, 1983, p. 3.

Note: the importation of slaves from all over created a mixed race known as "coloureds". In the 20th century this would be deemed a racial class separate from

the functionality of Cape colonial society, with the number of slaves increasing from 350 in 1690 to 25,754 in 1798[9].

Historical writing about labour systems in South Africa tend to be dominated by discussions of slave labour at the Cape[10]. In fact, the most relevant and comprehensive histories of Cape wine are inextricably linked to the legacies of slavery. In her widely-cited dissertation "Wine and Slaves: the failure of an export economy and the ending of slavery in the Cape Colony, South Africa, 1806-1834", historian Mary Rayner revealed the systematic abuse endured by slaves on wine farms and suggested that the British enabled a legacy of racial discrimination to occur[11]. However, Rayner's work is limited in scope, as her studies do not extend beyond 1834, where, I would argue, there exists a broader tension between the introduction of skilled versus cheap, 'disposable' labour.

What is missing from the current literature on South African labour and wine is the *nature of work* in the vineyards. The 19th century wine industry at the British-controlled Cape of Good Hope would confront similar challenges as its 18th century Dutch predecessors. Not only did the Cape suffer the plight of distance from the metropole – shipping of vines, wines, and supplies, they also struggled to recruit labour for these vineyards. Who was most suited to *work* in the vineyard? To investigate that question and the relationship between skilled and 'unskilled' labour, this chapter will analyse the various types of labour on Cape wine farms, including the continuation of racialised labour systems, emigration of European labour, and the introduction of convict labour throughout the 19th century. Eventually, the increased circulation of people, technology,

---

black, native South Africans. It is used in this chapter as a term to describe all people of non-white ethnicity at the Cape, as it would have been used in the 19th century.

9 Viall J., James W., and Gerwel J., *Grape: From Slavery to BEE 1652-2011, Stories of the Vineyards in South Africa*, Cape Town, Tafelberg, 2011.

10 See Dooling W., *Slavery, Emancipation, and Colonial Rule in South Africa*, Scottsville, University of KwaZulu-Natal Press, 2007; Worden N. and Crais C., *Breaking the Chains: Slavery and Its Legacy in the Nineteenth Century Cape Colony*, Johannesburg, Witwatersrand University Press, 1994; Mason J. E., *Social Death and Resurrection: Slavery and Emancipation in South Africa*, Charlottesville, VA, University of Virginia Press, 2003.

11 Rayner M., "Wine and Slaves: The Failure of an Export Economy and the Ending of Slavery in the Cape Colony, South Africa, 1806-1834", PhD Thesis, Duke University, Microfilm Senate House Library, 1986.

and ideas brought on by the first era of globalisation would come to transform the nature of wine in South Africa.

Legacies of slavery and racialised labour

Upon Britain's early arrival to the Cape at the turn of the 19th century, wine was decreed as the most important agricultural commodity[12]. In this spirit, the colonial government established several initiatives – such as the Office of the Wine Taster, premiums for successful wine farming, and most importantly, preferential duties on colonial wine imported into Britain – to increase cultivation and improve production[13]. In July of 1813, "duties on [Cape] wine imported into Britain were reduced to a third of former tariffs"[14], meaning that in comparison to other continental wines, Cape wine received preferential treatment. This economic incentive spurred vine planting and cultivation, as well as overall production: "Wine output increased by 151 % between 1809 and 1823"[15] and wine exports into Great Britain increased from a mere 2,268 imperial gallons in 1806 to 1,062,936 gallons in 1817[16]. Between 1820 and 1824, "wine accounted for 72 % of the value of exports with Cape products standing third on the list of imported wines into Great Britain"[17]. In only a few years, wine had become the most valuable commodity at the Cape. But the short-lived wine boom would not have been possible without the violent and explicit exploitation of slave labour. The increased planting of vines which took place under Britain's early control, led wine farmers to disproportionately own more slaves than other farmers, with wine farmers in 1823 owning 18 % of the slave population – 21 families with 3,557 slaves between them[18]. The burden of work on slaves drastically increased, meaning the same slave who attended 6,534 vines in 1814 was forced to tend 11,137

12 Theal G. M., "Proclamation by Sir John Cradock", *Records of the Cape Colony, from March 1811 to October 1812*, vol. III, London: PRO, 1901, p. 214.

13 *Ibid.*, p. 281.

14 Viall, *op. cit.*, p. 102.

15 *Ibid.*

16 Henderson A., *The History of Ancient and Modern Wines*, London: Baldwin, Cradock, and Joy, 1824, Appendix B.

17 Rayner, *op.cit.*, p. 16 and 31.

18 Dooling, *op. cit.*, p. 82.

vines by 1823[19]. While such initiatives clearly amplified the burden for slaves, the nature of their work remained the same. Slaves were required to "clear the insects off of vines by hand, plant thousands of new vines, clean the casks, harvest and tramp the grapes, work in the household, make clothes, and build the gabled buildings"[20].

Initiatives to encourage wine synchronised with the passing of amelioration. After the prohibition of the slave trade in 1807 and prior to emancipation in 1834, the colonial government sought to appease both Boer settlers at the Cape and ardent abolitionists at home through amelioration – the improvement of slaves' working and living conditions. The government sought to "transform slaves into sober and self-disciplined workers, motivated by desires for self-improvement and personal gain" so "slavery would somehow wither away"[21]. Creation of posts such as the Office of the Protector of Slaves, among other ordinances, served to facilitate relations between slaves, freed blacks, and white settlers within the colonies. This would have included reports of abuse or mistreatment, petitioning for manumission, or complaints about living conditions. Amelioration was supposed to keep abolitionists at bay, decrease colonial violence, and improve economic efficiency on farms and plantations. The Boer slave-owning class felt betrayed by the British colonial government, as if insulted by the insinuation that their slaves and personal property were not already treated in the best conditions. The sjambok[22] "was not perceived by the colonists as 'violent', but merely 'necessary'"[23] and ultimately, the violent practices inherent to the institution of slavery persisted. In 1834, the British Empire mandated emancipation, followed by a four-year 'apprenticeship' period. This shattered the short-lived progress of the Cape wine industry, with Boer wine farmers unable – and unwilling – to adequately compensate their labour force.

Despite the newfound creation of a 'free' labour class, the nascent paternalism of slavery persisted. Wine farmers contracted a few coloured

---

19 Rayner, *op. cit.*, p. 83-84.

20 Viall, *op. cit.*, p. 42.

21 Rayner, *op. cit.*, p. 251-252.

22 This is an instrument made from hippopotamus hide and used as whip against slaves. To this day, the sjambok remains a constant reminder to the legacy of Cape slavery.

23 Dooling, *op. cit.*, p. 82.

See also on amelioration: Spence C.Q., "Ameliorating Empire: Slavery and Protection in the British Colonies, 1783-1865", PhD Thesis, Harvard University.

labourers to reside on the farms in dilapidated housing with meagre clothing and food provisions, while daily workers – often residing on separate mission stations – were paid as extra hands during harvest seasons. Cape wine farmers continued to operate within a racially-based dynamic of white master to coloured servant, and often complained at the notion that agricultural workers of colour deserved compensation. Records show a varying discrepancy in wages paid to vineyard workers. Some reports state that those who received board and lodging earned around 1 shilling per day, and up to 3 shillings per day during the busy seasons[24]. Other reports suggest that farmers could pay labourers "6d. to 9d. per day with food and a cottage and a small patch of garden ground, or at 1s. 6d. to 2s. per day without food or residence…with some labourers volunteering to forego a wage to receive food rations"[25]. These low wages were, without a doubt, racially motivated, as white vineyard labourers in Australia at the end of the 19th century were earning between 4 to 6 shillings per day *with* board and lodging[26]. This sentiment was echoed in the passing of the Masters and Servants Ordinance of 1842, which claimed to establish expectations for employers and employees, but in practice ultimately subjugated servants to harsh penalties and maintained the status quo of labour oppression and violence. The law's phrasing of 'master' and 'servant' reiterated social archetypes rooted in slavery. Even the construction of the vineyard reaffirmed white positions of power, with workers' houses being within sight – and under the umbrella of authority – of the wine farmer, with a Dutch slave bell tolling in the centre, commencing the start of the work day[27].

---

[24] "Report of the Select Committee Appointed by the House of Assembly to Take into Consideration His Excellency the Governor's Recommendation Concerning Immigration", Cape Town, Saul Solomon & Co., 1856, p. 95.

[25] "Report of a Commission appointed to enquire into the economic conditions of the Wine districts of the Cape Colony", Cape Town Government Printers, 1909, p. 6.

[26] Hahn T., "Viticulture in South Africa: A Scheme for the development of the Cape Wine industry", London, Trubner & Co., 1888, p. 22.

[27] Scully P., "Liquor and Labor in the Western Cape, 1870-1900", in Crush J. and Ambler C., eds., *Liquor and Labor in Southern Africa*, Athens, Ohio University Press, 1992, p. 60.

See also Scully P., *The Bouquet of Freedom: Social and Economic Relations in the Stellenbosch District, South Africa, c. 1870-1900*, Cape Town, University of Cape Town, 1990.

Wine farmers also continued to practice pre-emancipation methods of labour discipline, including violent corporal punishment. As late as 1889, a Report on the Select Committee on Masters and Servants Acts interviewed many farmers who felt that "the cat-o-nine-tails is the best instrument, and the man can never be injured with it"[28]. In these same hearings another farmer admitted "A master must use a different mode of dealing with those [native/coloured] servants than if he had European servants"[29]. The language here signifies the legacy of the master and slave relationship, as if race codified acceptability of violence. Other practices such as the dop system, which – prior to 1838 meant the provision of a crude wine[30] to slaves multiple times throughout the day – and after 1838, well into the 20th century, as a form of financial compensation, persisted. In addition to housing, clothing, and food provisions, Imperial Blue Books from 1854-1888 included "ordinary wine, brandy, and beer" as part of the *necessary* provisions required for agricultural labourers[31]. The 1893 Colonial Labour Commission interviewed several farm labourers from the Western Cape, who testified to consuming between five to six dops of wine – equivalent to around two bottles – per day. When asked if he preferred the wine or its monetary value, agricultural labourer Johannes Absalom explained, "I should accept the monetary value, but the farmer does not offer this alternative"[32].

Paying in wine – a practice which persisted late into the 20th century – fixed the underpaid and impoverished coloured labour force to the Cape's wine economy. Emancipation, followed by the elimination of preferential duties on colonial wines into Britain in 1860, brought the Cape wine industry to a screeching halt. Why would British consumers pay for Cape wine when they could purchase French products at the same cost? Overproduction and a low demand for Cape wines in the metropole exacerbated the oppression of the coloured labour force, who

---

28 "Report of the Select Committee on Masters and Servants Acts", Cape Town, W.A. Richards & Sons, Government Printers, 1889, p. 17.

29 *Ibid.*, p. 28.

30 Pamela Scully defines dop wine as "made of grape husks, the residue of the second pressing, water, and sometimes brandy…" in "Liquor and Labor in the Western Cape, 1870-1900", *op. cit.*, p. 59.

31 "Return of Wages &c.", Cape of Good Hope Imperial Blue Book, Cape Town, Legislative Council, 1858, p. 2.

32 "Cape of Good Hope Labour Commission", Cape Town, W.A. Richards & Sons Government Printers, 1894, p. 382.

being paid in wine served as the most cost-effective system of labour in Cape vineyards. The circularity of the relationship between the cost of production, the success of exportation, and the financing of a "deskilled labour force" ultimately hindered the integration of South African wine into the global market for years to come.

Emigration of expertise

After the emancipation of slaves, combined with the eradication of preferential duties on colonial wines, Cape agriculturists felt that there was only one method to rejuvenate the industry: "nothing is better calculated to revive and support Agriculture, wine and cattle farming than the importation of free laborers"[33]. Throughout the 19th century, there were many attempts to 'improve' the state of the colony – both economically and culturally – with an influx of European emigrants[34]. However, given that most wine farmers were of Dutch descent, the colonial government often faced resistance to a sudden invasion of British emigrants. A letter addressed to Rawson W. Rawson from the Colonial Office in 1857 stated, "a strong prejudice exists in the minds of almost the entire Dutch population of these districts against *English* emigrants"[35]. Moreover, a petition from 1862, signed by 60 prominent agriculturists from Groot Drakenstein, called for a suspension of British immigration "as they are wholly unsuitable for the agricultural wants of this colony; in fact, cannot be employed for that reason"[36]. This same petition even suggested acquiring non-white "cheap" labour from India, China, or other areas of Africa[37]. While this local predisposition certainly did not prevent colonial advocation of British emigration to the Cape, it did often determine geographic location for settlement upon arrival. British

33 Translation of "Memorial from Wine and Corn Farmers, addressed to General Sir George Napier", January 28, 1840, Western Cape Archives and Records Service, CO 4007-49.

34 "Minutes on Immigration", Government House letter, Cape Town, March 26, 1842, Western Cape Archives and Records Service, VC 248-6-22.

35 Colonial Office Letter, addressed to Rawson W. Rawson, Nov 26, 1857, p. 95, Western Cape Archives and Records Service.

36 "Petition of Landed Proprietors of Groot Drakenstein", Cape Town, Government Printers, June 4, 1862.

37 *Ibid.*

emigrants populated Eastern districts of the colonies, away from the wine-producing districts of the West. What British settlers also failed to possess, was years of expertise in vine culture. The concept of valuing viticultural knowledge and expertise was absolutely critical to the development of a sustainable wine industry in the Cape Colony[38]. Thus, the method to improving Cape wine was to actively recruit seasoned veterans from wine-producing areas of Europe. It was the hope of both local wine farmers and the larger colonial governments that in importing labour, they would be equally importing experience and technical expertise. When such goals were realised, it would establish a network of viticultural knowledge from the old worlds of wine to the new.

Germans were deemed the ideal candidates for emigration, given colonial perceptions about their proclivities towards agriculture and military prowess. In a period of border unrest, with frequent attacks from indigenous populations, the Cape government sought to bolster their defences with the settlement of able-bodied, militant Germans. It seemed an added bonus, and a natural fit, that such emigrants also came from a seasoned tradition of vine growing and winemaking. Among other British wine-producing colonies, the introduction of German expertise was essential to viticultural improvement and productivity. William Macarthur of New South Wales asserted that all landowners seriously interested in growing and producing wine *required* foreign assistance, and he was responsible for sponsoring some of the first German vinedressers to Australia[39]. Assumptions from Cape and Australian colonial governments drew upon early stereotypes of Germans as orderly, lowly, obedient inferiors – who fulfilled a Protestant work ethic in all endeavours, not least, the vineyard. An enclosure from July 6, 1858 to the Cape Colonial Government stated: "The [German] emigrants would be drawn from the very classes which a rising colony stands most in need of…the agriculturists from Silesia, Saxony, and Hanover, and the vinegrowers from the south. These latter…would be a most important acquisition for a colony whose climate is so favourable to the culture of the vine"[40].

---

38 See McIntyre J., *First Vintage: Wine in colonial New South Wales*, Sydney: New South Publishing 2012, p. 55 on concept of 'intelligent industry'.

39 Macarthur W., *Letters on the Culture of the Vine, Fermentation and the Management of the Wine in the Cellar*, Sydney, 1844, p. ix.

40 "Concerning German Immigration to the Cape", Sub enclosure 1, No. 1, on German Emigration to the Cape of Good Hope, July 6, 1858, p. 2, Western Cape Archives and Records Service, OPB 1-5.

Essentially, emigration agents would seek out German vinedressers, take cash payment from interested wine farmers, pay emigrant passage to the Cape of Good Hope, then deduct that passage money from their wages until their debts were paid to the wine farmer[41]. According to the 1891 Census, there were approximately 4,000 males and 2,500 females living at the Cape who were born in Germany, though it is unclear the proportion of these who specifically participated in wine production[42].

The colonial government was not alone in recruiting new labourers. Some wine farmers equally recognised the necessity of skilled labour in the vineyard. The Colonial Labour Commission asked wine farmer August Albrecht "How is it you are prepared to pay up to 3s. for a European who you will have to teach our ways of working, while you pay 2s. only to native agricultural labourers?" to which Albrecht responded, "The former will be more useful, he learns to work much more easily, and while the native may spoil your whole vineyard in the course of his education, the European will be apt in the course of a few weeks and can handle the scissors and pruning knife"[43]. Similarly, some Cape wine farmers sought agricultural assistance for vineyard labourers from Italy. Mr. J. Merriman, when asked by the Colonial Labour Commission what country of Europe would provide a 'good supply of labour' answered, "From the North of Italy, for one, Germany for another…My experience leads me to believe that you would get a very steady, industrious class of people from the North of Italy"[44].

Beyond skill was simply necessity. The Cape Colony – among other British colonies in the Commonwealth, like Australia – struggled to acquire mass immigration in the same scale as that experienced in the United States during the 19th century, due primarily to the plight of distance. Agricultural labour shortages became more frequent during the second half of the 19th century, given the migration of labour to mines. While the discovery of diamonds in Kimberley in 1871 and then

---

41 "Report of the Select Committee Appointed by the House of Assembly to Take into Consideration His Excellency the Governor's Recommendation Concerning Immigration", Cape Town: Saul Solomon & Co., p. 10.

42 "Diagram Showing the Birthplaces of the People, European or White, and other than European or White", Results of a Census of the Colony of the Cape of Good Hope, Cape Town, W.A. Richard & Sons, Government Printers, 1891.

43 Labour Commission 1893, *op cit.*, p. 106.

44 *Ibid.*, p. 147.

gold in 1886 increased the rate of global migration to the Cape Colony, it did not so easily translate into increased agricultural labour. In fact, many black and coloured labourers already in the colony abandoned agricultural work for steady consistent labour, far away from their homes, in dangerous diamond mines[45]. While vineyard work was characterised by short, seasonal contracts with little cash wages, mining offered a sustained income, in a booming town, with new economic opportunities – despite the obvious tolls on physical health.

Despite their complaints about labour shortages, many wine farmers in the Western Cape actively resisted the importation of European agricultural labour claiming such men would only work until they saved enough money to establish their own homesteads. Mr. Johannes D.J. Visser told the Colonial Labour Commission in 1893, "Germans are very good, but they will not work alongside of the coloured men. Moreover, as soon as they come here they want to start for themselves"[46]. Some Cape wine farmers suggested the importation of labour from Mozambique, in efforts to maintain a low-wage, racialised labour force, predicated on the concept that black labour from Mozambique was more "efficient" and "versatile" than local, free *white* labourers at the Cape. The tensions over recruiting viticultural labour demonstrate a variety of predispositions rooted in racism. In the Western Cape, wine farmers often rejected the global practice of employing a seasoned, expert, white European labour force in attempts to retain a cheap, non-competitive, easily controlled, coloured labour force. The 1875 Census estimates that approximately 94 % of the farm servant and agricultural labourer population – male and female alike – was of 'non-white' designation[47]. Such figures highlight both labour availability and the embedded racism present in the labour systems of the wine industry.

---

45 Leighton S., *Notes on a Visit to South Africa*, 1889, p. 29, Manuscript, National Library of South Africa Cape Town.

46 Labour Commission 1893, *op cit.*, p. 58.

47 "Results of a Census of the Colony of the Cape of Good Hope", March 7, 1875, Cape Town, Saul Solomon & Co., Printers, 1877.

Introduction of convict labour

The other attempt at quelling labour shortages on wine farms was to employ convicts from nearby stations. Tokai Convict Station was the ready and frequent supplier of convict labourers to wine farms in the Western Cape. For example, the government wine farm at Groot Constantia employed "a daily average of 27 men in trenching new ground for vines, manuring, pruning, and sulphuring vines"[48], while 19 other convicts were hired out to neighbouring farms[49]. Though male and female prisoners of all races were held at convict stations, the majority were men of colour. An 1894 report on convict stations revealed that in the two years it had been open, Tokai Prison had admitted 148 prisoners, of which 70 % were classified as non-white[50]. The term 'convict' was itself a social construct, codified to disproportionately prosecute men and women of colour, and readily applied to group a wide spectrum of 'criminals' into one category. Many of the men at Tokai in particular were non-violent offenders, often charged with public intoxication, especially after the passing of the Liquor Act of 1891. Farm work was deemed especially appropriate for 'inebriates' and with tragic irony, many faced employment on wine farms, where the provision of alcohol would have been readily supplied[51]. These men laboured in life – and death – for wine farms, with government bureaucrats such as Cape Viticulturist Baron Carl von Babo advocating for the use of convict human remains to fertilise vineyards. He wrote in 1888: "the bones obtained from the convict station were also, as in former years, burnt and crushed, and used as manure. But as the bones can best be used and their effect is most rapid if they can be put into the ground perfectly decomposed, we intend in future to ferment the bones by mixing them with urine and thus to decompose them in a cheap manner"[52]. Ultimately, the Cape wine economy valued convict labourers

---

48 "Reports on the Management and Discipline of Convict Stations, for the Year 1892", Cape Town, W.A. Richards & Sons, Government Printers, 1893, p. 2.

49 Pamela Scully, *The Bouquet of Freedom: Social and Economic Relations in the Stellenbosch District, South Africa, c1870-1900*. Cape Town: Centre for African Studies, University of Cape Town, 1990, p. 18.

50 "Reports on the Management and Discipline…", *op. cit.*, p. 18.

51 *Ibid.*, p. 25.

52 Von Babo C., "Viticulture in the Cape Colony", *Cape Agricultural Journal*, Cape Town, Government Printers, July 12, 1888, p. 68.

only for their utility in a capitalist system, as they were largely perceived by the colonial government and Cape gentry as disposable.

The environmental crisis of phylloxera in 1886 equally motivated the use of convict labour on local wine farms. Eradication measures to the vines included water submersion, fire-burning, and most often, chemical treatments with bi-sulphide of carbon[53]. To act quickly and quarantine the aphid from spreading to other vineyards, the government offered convict labourers to wine farmers in the Western Cape[54]. This practice yielded mixed results. Many wine farmers testified to the cost-effectiveness of convict labour: "the convicts do more regular and better work"[55], but much of the preference for convict labour over free labour, resided in methods of control. The actions and movements of convict labourers, being brought from the prison, could, in comparison to free coloured labourers in the Western Cape, be more easily restricted. Farmers believed that free labourers were responsible for carrying phylloxera from one vineyard to the next, despite the reassurance from Phylloxera Commissioners and Government scientists that this was most likely the result of the winged insect[56]. When asked by a Select Committee if there was a possibility free labourers were the ones spreading phylloxera, wine farmer Johannes Wynand Louw Hofmeyr responded, "Yes, decidedly. They make fun of it because they get extra work"[57]. The introduction of convict labour on phylloxerised vineyards, therefore, simply highlighted tensions between the white Boer wine farmers and free coloured labourers. In fact, because many of the men lived away from the farms, they were forced to dip their bare feet into the same chemicals used to destroy phylloxera. Colonial viticulturist Louis Peringuey, a French native who assisted in the eradication of phylloxera, testified in July 1889 that:

> when the work was over, [labourers] had to put their feet, with or without boots, into a bucket of bi-sulphide. This is dreadful, and those who happened

---

53 Known today as carbon disulfide.

54 Trimen R., "Report of the Phylloxera Commission", Cape Town, W.A. Richard & Sons, Government Printers, 1886, p. 66.

55 "Report of the Select Committee on Vineyards" Diseases Acts, Cape Town, W.A. Richards & Sons, Government Printers, 1889, p. 19.

56 Hofmeyr J. H., "Report of the Phylloxera Commission, with Minutes of Proceedings, Evidence, and Appendices", Cape Town, W.A. Richards & Sons, Government Printers, 1891, p. 25-26.

57 "Report of the Select Committee on Vineyards' Diseases Acts…", *op. cit.*, p. 20.

> not to have brought spare trousers are sprinkled with it...The disinfecting process with regard to these men is, in my opinion, scandalous. I certainly would not undergo anything of the kind myself, and yet, as painful as it is, the men have never refused to do it[58].

Similar testimonies affirming the continual – and forced – exposure of free labourers to harmful chemicals demonstrated a new method of labour oppression and racial violence[59]. Pieter Malan recalls, "I have often seen that the poison did not touch their feet. The men make such a strong and rapid rush past that many of them do not even get to the poison"[60]. On the one hand, Malan's frustration encapsulated a growing fear held by wine farmers that workers could spread phylloxera from one vineyard to the next. But his reaction, insistence upon literally poisoning the skin of coloured workers, illustrates an attempt to restrict the agency of free labour and reassert dominance of the white agrarian gentry over a coloured labour population.

The use of convict labour also increased tensions between Boer farmers and the British colonial government, as many farmers felt the steady, increased wage for convicts drove up prices for seasonal labour. Many wine farmers resisted the influx of convict labour, adhering to the notion that knowledge and experience were necessary components of labour on wine farms. Mr. Charles van Reenen, the farm manager at High Constantia argued, "From what I have seen of convict labour, they... have no practical knowledge...They would commence in the morning and would not be finished till the evening, but I would set one of my men to do the work in two hours"[61]. While this did not necessarily prevent the use of convicts on wine farms, it did alter the nature of work they were assigned. At the Cape, farmers eventually began to use convict labour *primarily* for farm work outside of the vines, such as digging trenches, clearing bushes, fixing roads, while leaving the pruning, trimming, and tending to the vines for more 'seasoned' experts.

---

58 *Ibid.*, p. 117.

59 According to the WHO, carbon bi-sulphide exposure can result in "central nervous system depression, coma, respiratory paralysis, and death". See "Carbon Disulfide", Concise International Chemical Assessment Document, *World Health Organization*, April 12, 2005, p. 15.

60 "Report of the Select Committee on Vineyards' Diseases Acts...", *op. cit.*, p. 10.

61 "Report of the Select Committee of the Legislative Council on Government Wine Farm", Cape Town, W.A. Richards & Sons, Government Printers, 1889, p. 47.

These seasoned labourers were most likely men and women of colour, who had for years built a repertoire of viticultural experience. Despite a lack of acknowledgment from the colonial government or white scientists in positions of bureaucratic power – who felt that only white European men of education possessed the knowledge and skill required to cultivate the vine, many coloured labourers in the Western Cape were the ones carrying out this work in real time. A case study of the cashbooks of Starke Brothers' farm Muldersvlei from 1895-1905 testifies to this. In these accounts, one worker named 'Julie' Dass[62] was employed every season to prune the vines at 2s. 6d. per day. In 1903 alone, 'Julie' pruned 26,500 vines. Similarly, the same 'Leah' was hired every year for grape pressing[63]. Such records confirm that not only were women hired during busy seasons on wine farms, but that men and women of colour were hired to conduct what is considered highly skilled technical work, usually reserved for 'white expertise'.

To conclude: this chapter places different viticultural labour systems of the 19th century Cape Colony into the same lens, in an effort to elucidate tensions between race, knowledge, and power. The 'old world' conception of viticultural superiority centred on the recognition of an *ideal labour force* – one that was white, European, and skilled. However, what this analysis demonstrates is that despite the global acknowledgement of an *ideal labour*, it did not so neatly fit within the constraints of *local practice*. The migration of German (and other European) labour to the Cape of Good Hope was not as pronounced as that experienced in the United States. Many wine farmers in the Western Cape balked at the notion of paying higher wages for white expertise, when they could maintain low wages for coloured labour, and still receive a consistent price for their wine. Even the use of convicts as an archetype of 'ideal labour' – one that could be more easily controlled during the phylloxera crisis – struggled to fit within wine

---

62 It is unclear from the accounts if Julie is male or female. Julie Dass is often listed in the 'daily labourer' sections, where mainly women are employed in the laundry and washing. However, it has not been determined if Julie is also short for 'Julian' or if this was simply a shortened English name assigned to a person of colour, common practice at the Cape.

63 "Starke Brothers Muldersvlei Cash Book Records 1892-1905", University of Cape Town Special Collections, Manuscript BCS291.

farmers' local expectations. Too often historical narratives overlook the viticultural knowledge and skill possessed by coloured labourers in the vineyards, ultimately whitewashing and recolonising South Africa's viticultural past. Reassigning agency to the individuals *doing the work* in the vineyard and assessing the facilitation of these networks within and outside the British Empire will force us to widen our scope of participants in the growing world of wine.

Rhinefarm and the German-American Market for 19th-Century California Wine

Kathleen Neils Conzen and Michael P. Conzen

When German immigrants Jacob Gundlach and Emil Dresel began developing their 300 acre Rhinefarm vineyard in California's Sonoma Valley in 1858, finding a market for the wine they would produce was likely the least of their worries. Their compatriots Charles Kohler and John Fröhling, the 1854 pioneers of California's commercial wine trade, had shown the profits to be made in quenching the thirst of Gold Rush California, and Rhinefarm's proprietors could focus their attention on the practical problems of growing wine to the highest standards they had known in Germany[1]. Two decades later, Rhinefarm was indeed producing some of California's most award-winning and expensive fine wines[2]. But

1 Sims L. (ed.), *Eva Hofmann Gundlach, Letters and Poems 1849-1874*, El Granada CA, Del Oro, 2016; Emil Dresel to Otto Dresel, 12/30/1861, Ellis Gray Loring Family Papers, Schlesinger Library, Harvard University, Cambridge MA; Pinney T., *The Makers of American Wine: A Record of Two Hundred Years*, Berkeley, University of California Press, 2012, p. 57-74. The original Rhinefarm purchase involved four partners and 400 acres; one partner soon sold his share to Gundlach, and a second took his 100 acres out of the partnership.

2 Hilgard E. W., Jones T. C. and Furnas R. W., *Report on the Climatic and Agricultural Features and the Agricultural Practice and Needs of the Arid Regions of the Pacific Slope*, Washington, D.C., Government Printing Office, 1882, p. 109-112; *San Francisco Bulletin* (SFB) 4/10/1882. "Fine wines" to Californians were those that commanded the highest prices, carefully made and matured from the best European varietals, and comparable in quality to superior European wines; by the turn of the century it was estimated that only 5 to 10 percent of California production merited this description, in contrast to ordinary "cargo wines" that made up the vast bulk of the trade; Bundschu C., "Fine Wines", *San Francisco Merchant* (SFM) 4/1/1887; Hotchkiss W. J., "The California Wine Industry", *Pacific Rural Press* (PRP) 12/14/1901.

like other California viniculturists, its proprietors by then were also directly confronting a painful marketing dilemma: with state production approaching 10 million gallons a year, California wine needed a national market. Yet most Americans were not wine drinkers, and those who were – mainly the more affluent – preferred status-signifying imported European wines over their domestic counterparts[3].

How then did producers find a market? Who indeed were the consumers of 19th century California wine, and how did it make its way to them? These are questions to which historians of California wine have paid relatively little attention. They have carefully documented winegrowers' marketing frustrations, the boom-and-bust cycles that this market situation helped generate, the adulteration and false-labelling of wine that it encouraged, and organised efforts to gain governmental support for the industry. As such, their historical narrative culminates in the 1894 organisation of the California Wine Association, a trust that soon controlled 84 percent of California's output, and stabilised the production and distribution of ordinary, if not fine, wines until Prohibition in 1920[4].

Yet a detailed look at the marketing efforts of Rhinefarm's proprietors suggests that this narrative requires a critical addition. The American marketplace by the mid-19th century did have a significant wine-drinking segment: its foreign-language-speaking population, including the French of Louisiana, small French and growing Italian colonies in major cities, and above all, the more than 5 million German-speakers driven to America over the course of the 19th century by economic and political dislocations in their homeland. At century's end they and their children comprised over 10 percent of the U.S. population, heavily concentrated

---

3 California State Board of Agriculture, *Report of the California State Agricultural Society for the Year 1911*, Sacramento, 1912, p. 191; Lender M. E. and Martin J. K., *Drinking in America: A History*, New York, Free Press, 1987; Murdock C. G., *Domesticating Drink: Women, Men, and Alcohol in America, 1870-1940*, Baltimore, Johns Hopkins University Press, 1998. Wine comprised about 4 percent of all U.S. alcoholic beverage consumption in 1869; Mendelson R., *From Demon to Darling: A Legal History of Wine in America*, Berkeley, University of California Press, 2009, p. 25.

4 E.g. Carosso V. P., *The California Wine Industry: A Study of the Formative Years*, Berkeley, University of California Press, 1951; Pinney T., *A History of Wine in America, Volume 1: From the Beginnings to Prohibition*, Berkeley, University of California Press, 2007; Simpson J., *Creating Wine: The Emergence of a World Industry, 1840-1914*, Princeton, Princeton University Press, 2011, p. 195-219.

in the nation's northeast quadrant and with an unusually large middle-class component[5]. As in Britain and the U.S., cost confined most wine drinking in 19th century Germany (except in the extreme southwest) to the middle and upper classes, but it penetrated more deeply into daily life and national culture. Despite the growing popularity of Bavarian beer, wine and a sentimentalised wine culture remained embedded in family and social settings, student life, and the cultural associations that nurtured German nationalism. Their wine-drinking habits accompanied Germans to America, and joined beer to lubricate the conviviality that lay at the heart of their ethnic culture[6]. By the mid-1850s city directories document the presence of a well-articulated German distribution system for imported European wines throughout urban America[7]. The success of Rhinefarm's proprietors in penetrating that ethnically segmented market system, we suggest, was key to their ability to survive and thrive as producers and sellers of fine California wines until Prohibition. Indeed, their experience likely reflects a broader pattern that illuminates the often-noted but seldom-explored dominance of Germans in the California wine trade throughout this period.

Rhinefarm origins

Jacob Gundlach and Emil Dresel, part of the large Gold Rush migration of Germans to California, brought deeper familiarity with the making and marketing of fine wine than most other pioneers of the California industry. Gundlach, born in 1818, came from a hotel, vineyard, and wine tavern-owning family in Aschaffenburg on northern

---

5 Conzen K. N., "Germans", in Thernstrom S., Orlov A., and Handlin O. (eds.), *Harvard Encyclopedia of American Ethnic Groups*, Cambridge, Harvard University Press, 1980, p. 405-25.

6 Tappe H., *Auf dem Weg zur modernen Alkoholkultur: Alkoholproduktion, Trinkverhalten und Temperenzbewegung in Deutschland vom frühen 19. Jahrhundert bis zum Ersten Weltkrieg*, Stuttgart, Franz Steiner, 1994; Conzen K. N., "Ethnicity as Festive Culture: German-America on Parade", in Sollors W. (ed.), *The Invention of Ethnicity*, New York, Oxford University Press, 1989, p. 44-76; Bungert H., *Festkultur und Gedächnis: Die Konstruktion einer deutschamerikanischen Ethnizität 1848-1914*, Paderborn, Ferdinand Schöningh, 2016.

7 As San Francisco's *Pacific Rural Press* observed 6/1/1872, "the German Rhenish, the most popular wine among all the real and constant drinkers of the Atlantic States", is shipped in large quantities direct from Germany to St. Louis, Cincinnati, Chicago, and other cities "to supply the demand of our foreign population."

Bavaria's Main river. He was trained for the wine trade there, in Bingen on the Rhine, and in the Pfalz, and spent more than two years with the Duc de Montebello's champagne house in Mareuil-sur-Aÿ before returning to the family business after his father's death. Economic, political, and romantic frustrations fuelled his 1850 emigration to San Francisco, where success as a pioneer brewer gave him the means to return to wine[8]. Emil Dresel, a year younger than Gundlach, though an academically-trained architect, came from a family that owned one of the Rhine's leading firms marketing the finest and most expensive of German wines, and he grew up absorbing the lore of the elite German wine trade in the old palace in Geisenheim that housed both the Dresel family and its business. His 1849 emigration followed the collapse of the family firm and the loss of his own government position in the aftermath of the 1848 revolution; after a crash course from a brother in vineyard planting and management, he emigrated with vine cuttings from Schloss Johannisberg to join another brother, Julius, in Texas. When their Hill Country vineyard succumbed to red ants, Emil left for California, where earnings as a lithographic artist paved his way to the Rhinefarm venture[9].

While Dresel managed the Sonoma vineyard, Gundlach in San Francisco handled marketing and shared the winemaking. From the outset, they aimed their wines at the top of the market, focusing on the dry Rhenish-style whites preferred by San Francisco Germans, and planting alongside California's Mission vines the Riesling, Traminer and other cuttings that Gundlach brought back from the Rhine on an 1858 trip to fetch his bride[10]. Gundlach's established beer distribution network and San Francisco wine depots provided local marketing for their first wines. But with the Civil War's end in 1865 and the rapidly

---

8 Conzen K. N., "Jacob Gundlach's German Years", in Sims L. (ed.)., *Gundlach's Diary: The Wine Legend's Account of His Dramatic Voyage to Gold Rush San Francisco*, El Granada CA, Del Oro, 2019, p. xvii-xxix. The authors are grateful to Lee Sims, Gigi Fernandez, and Jim and Jeff Bundschu for generous access to the Gundlach-Bundschu Winery Archive [GBA], Sonoma CA, and related family collections.

9 Dresel's background has been reconstructed from Dresel family correspondence in the Loring Family Papers, Schlesinger Library; from correspondence in the private Archiv Tenge-Rietberg in Rietberg, Germany; from Julius Dresel's 1880 manuscript autobiography in the private Dwyer Family Collection, Ft. Bragg CA; and from newspaper and other references. The authors are grateful to Carl-Philipp Lins and Rosita and Eugene Dwyer for generous access to their respective collections.

10 Sims, *Eva Hofmann Gundlach*; Bundschu C., "German Influences on Wine-Making in California", undated typescript, GBA.

improving quality of their wine, the partners set ambitious sights on the national market, reached by sail around the Horn or via Panama. Kohler & Frohling's bookkeeper, Charles Stern, had opened New York's first agency for California wine as early as 1861, and by 1867 the Rhinefarm Rieslings and hocks that it sold garnered particular praise in the New York press[11]. Dresel and Gundlach also had other contacts among Eastern wine importers, and soon enjoyed a reputation as particularly successful sellers of Sonoma wine, Gundlach boasting in 1868 that most of their production was already sold several years in advance to dealers in New York, Philadelphia, Boston, and New Orleans[12]. Thanks to its quality, much of their wine reportedly was made into champagne – by local producers using traditional methods, and with mechanical carbonation in the "California Champagne" houses that flourished in New York when French champagne prices skyrocketed during the Franco-Prussian war, and as phylloxera reduced both the volume and quality of French exports[13].

---

11 *Marysville Daily Appeal* 12/14/1860; C.L.B. (Charles Loring Brace), "The Vine Interest", *New York Times* [NYT] 12/10/1867.

12 F. W., "The Biggest Vineyard in the World", *Daily Missouri Democrat* 7/29/1869; Sims, *Eva Hofmann Gundlach*, p. 133. John Sattig, among New York's oldest German wine importers, was a Gundlach family connection who acted as New York agent for his brewery business, while Adolphus Oechs, founder of one of New York's most distinguished and long-lived German wine import houses, grew up with the Dresels in Geisenheim and likely worked for their firm at one point; his father was the manager of a leading Geisenheim wine estate. San Francisco coal dealer August Brecht, whose brother worked in Gundlach's brewery, opened a California wine wholesale firm in Philadelphia in 1866, and probably ordered the 11,000 gallons of 1864 Sonoma wine that Dresel and Gundlach shipped to Philadelphia that year; *Alta California* [AC], 2/3/1866.

13 Rühl K., *Californien*, New York, E. Steiger, 1867, p. 246; Schlagintweit R.v., *Californien: Land und Leute*, Cöln, Eduard Heinrich Mayer, 1871, p. 120; "Counterfeiting Trade Marks", AC 6/29/1867; "Grapes and Wine" and G. B. Crane letter, AC 1/20/1871. Clearly labeled "California Champagne" produced in New York by off-shoots of California firms provided a major market for growers, but so too did large-scale New York manufacturers of "bogus" champagne sold with falsified French labels. One of Dresel's brothers in Europe was part of an 1866 scheme with two French importers in New York to usurp the trade mark of Charles Heidsieck. A young wine merchant named August Werner, from a village near Geisenheim, appeared in New York about that time, and survived repeated charges of champagne counterfeiting to finally emerge as a reputable producer of "American" champagne in the later 1870s and became one of Rhinefarm's steadiest eastern customers for the next two decades; Browne H. B., *A Treatise on the Law of Trademarks and Analogous Subjects*, Boston, Little, Brown & Co., 1898, p. 466-467; *New York Herald* 7/27/1865,

Such long-distance shipments of wine in bulk to East Coast wholesalers left the partners vulnerable to both market swings and the chicanery of dealers who, as the common complaint put it, bottled the best California wine under foreign labels and sold only the trash as Californian. New York's fake wine industry enabled California wine to support itself in its infancy by tapping into the otherwise inaccessible elite American market for status-affirming European wines. But it was not a satisfying solution in the long run for growers concerned for the reputation of their product, and when Emil Dresel's unexpected 1869 death brought a new partner to Rhinefarm, with him came a renewed focus on the wine market's German immigrant segment.

Dresel willed his third-share in Rhinefarm to his Texas brother. Unlike Emil, Julius Dresel, born in 1816, had trained for the wine trade (including a year in the Champagne) and worked in the family firm, making lengthy sales tours to the Low Countries, northeast Germany, and Sweden before settling into the Geisenheim home office. In Texas his successful store selling wine to San Antonio Germans provided valuable insight into the retail side of the trade. When his 1870 arrival in Sonoma coincided with a market downswing, Julius drew on his accumulated wine trade expertise and the reputation of the old Dresel firm among German wine drinkers, and the following year made the first of what would be 13 annual transcontinental rail trips to sell directly to German-American dealers throughout the nation's northeast quadrant[14]. By the end of 1874, business was so good that Gundlach had to purchase additional older wine to fill all their eastern orders[15].

But Rhinefarm's unexpectedly large vintage that year, and the need for expanded capacity that it generated, also helped precipitate an amicable split between the two partners two years later, in the midst of a national depression, yet another wine market glut, and the discovery of phylloxera in their vineyard. Different family goals and financial circumstances influenced their respective choices. As early as 1870 the emergence of two separate California systems was evident: independent

12/10/1873, 6/7/1876; NYT 2/20/1878; "Champagne in New York", *Frank Leslie's Illustrated Newspaper* 4/27/1878, p. 133-134; "Advertising Werner's Champagne", *Printers' Ink*, n°30-12, 1900, p. 4-5.

[14] Dresel 1880 manuscript autobiography; Bundschu C., "Julius Dresel" typescript, GBA.

[15] Sims, *Eva Hofmann Gundlach*, p. 142.

grower-winemaker-marketers like Rhinefarm, and large San Francisco firms on the European model (like the old Geisenheim firm) that purchased wine from growers and absorbed the costs of preparing it for market[16]. Gundlach was already tending in the latter direction, having gradually disinvested from his brewery, and he had a new son-in-law, Charles Bundschu, a Mannheim-born relative who arrived in 1864 to keep Gundlach's books, moved on to meatpacking, and by 1876 was ready to join him in a San Francisco firm to prepare and wholesale premium California wines. Dresel, less financially secure, with a Texas-born son now starting medical education in Germany and eager himself to retire back to the Rhine, apparently balked at the costs and risk of Gundlach's scheme. He chose to continue making and selling his own wines with the aid of his other son, Carl, who would take over in 1891 when Julius retired to Germany and died later that year[17].

Marketing Rhinefarm wines: the Dresel strategy

The result was two differently structured firms grounded in the same Rhinefarm slopes, with two separate strategies for selling fine California wines to a predominantly German-American market. The chance survival of two Dresel copybooks of 1879 and 1880 outgoing correspondence, and address books from the 1890s, provides detailed insight into the Dresel strategy based on annual two-month selling trips (Map 1) through the heart of German America[18]. These tours, Dresel noted in 1880, "have been commercially necessary since 1871, and will always remain advantageous […] annually expanding for me the narrower circles in which every occupation has to move". Often traveling by night to save time and money, and staying in German hotels without the prepaid meals

---

[16] "The Queen City of the Pacific Coast", *Daily News* (London) 1/25/1870.

[17] Charles and Francisca Bundschu papers, GBA; Dresel manuscript autobiography; Bundschu, "Julius Dresel".

[18] Dwyer collection; GBA. Most Dresel records were lost in the destruction of the family's Sonoma home by fire in 1912. But these copybooks contained the first draft of the autobiography that Julius Dresel planned to finish in his retirement, and he apparently took them with him to Germany, and the son and daughter who were with him at his death passed them on to their heirs. Carl Dresel's 1890s address books, along with files of incoming correspondence and an 1899 copybook, were found by Jim Bundschu in the old winery on former Dresel land that his grandmother had purchased from Carl's widow in 1941.

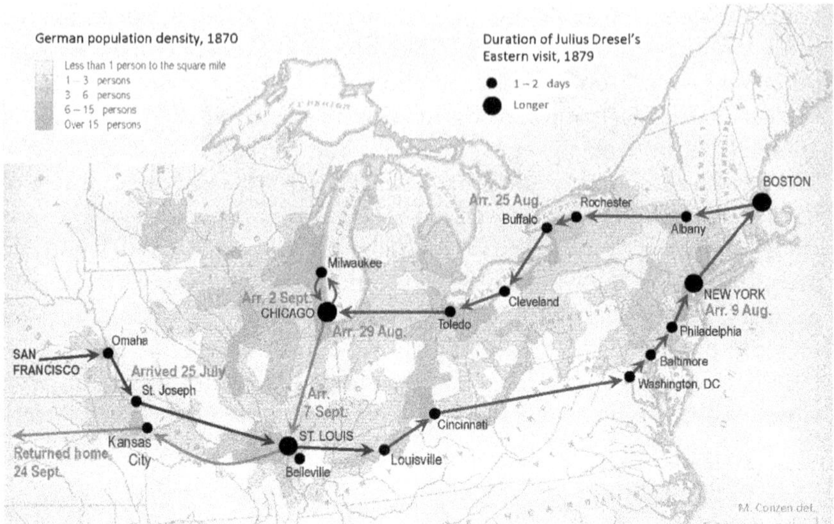

Map 1: Julius Dresel's 1879 Eastern Selling Tour. Sources: 1879 Dresel copybook, Dwyer Collection; Base map: Distribution of the German Element, in *Statistics of the Population of the United States*, Washington, D.C., Government Printing Office, 1872, p. 327

of their American counterparts, he toted sample vials from dealer to dealer each day, refilling them each evening from casks shipped by Carl to accommodation addresses along his route, and writing up the day's orders for Carl back in Sonoma to fill. His prices were high for California wine, but still, as he pointed out, significantly lower than prices of imported German wines, indistinguishable from them in quality, and guaranteed pure. Other California wine drummers were incredulous that he could survive selling only fine dry table wines. Riesling topped his list, followed by Gutedel (Golden Chasselas), Muscat, and white and red Zinfandel – the latter resembling a Burgundy some years, he noted, other years more like Bordeaux. He offered only unfined two- and three-year-old wine in casks; bottling and aging demanded more capital and storage than he could command, even as it meant that his wines were often purchased for blending or bottled under foreign labels[19].

---

[19] Description drawn from 1879 and 1880 copybook entries; quotation from draft autobiography, authors' translation.

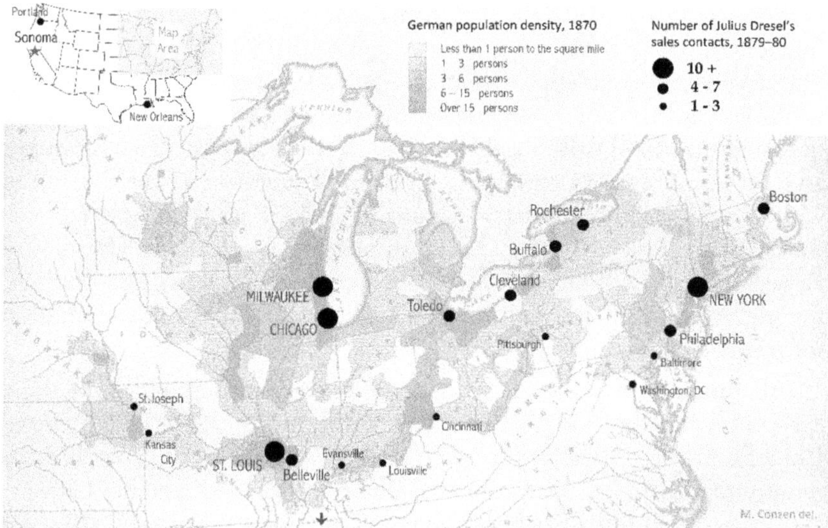

Map 2: Julius Dresel's 1879-80 Customer Contacts. Sources: 1879, 1880 Dresel copybooks, Dwyer Collection; Base map: Distribution of the German Element, in *Statistics of the Population of the United States*, Washington, D.C., Government Printing Office, 1872, p. 327

Dresel's list of 101 dealer contacts mirrored the nation's expanding German settlement system by 1880 (Map 2)[20].

At the top of the hierarchy were long-established wine importers in New York and Philadelphia, including off-shoots of Frankfurt and Mainz firms familiar to Dresel from Germany, whose wholesale reach was national. At the next level, every major city had large firms that combined wholesaling with retailing and often a tasting room or restaurant, imported wines directly from Germany, employed regional traveling salesmen, and served as foci for the local German community.

---

20 Collective biography of 101 firms compiled from on-line genealogical sources, censuses, city directories, newspapers, biographical compendia, and related sources. The list includes all dealers whom Dresel reported visiting in 1879, as well as those with whom he corresponded in 1880. It underrepresents his contacts during the first stages of his 1879 tour (Cincinnati, Louisville, Washington, Baltimore) and in Boston and Albany, when he was unable to copy his reports. It excludes a few private orders from individuals, as well as California contacts, since local sales were apparently recorded elsewhere.

Particularly in the Midwest, such firms were often also whiskey rectifiers (blenders), where their real money was made. In Cleveland and Toledo, Dresel encountered large German firms whose main interest in California wines was as blending stock to improve the quality of the "native" wine they manufactured from local vineyards. But other cities like Milwaukee and St. Louis were as renowned for their *Weinstuben* as for their beer, while post-fire Chicago's posh saloons offered elegantly appointed back parlours for wine drinkers[21]. Thus, alongside wholesalers, Dresel also visited specialised California wine retailers, wine taverns and gardens, restaurants, and grocers and druggists who valued his wine's reputation for purity.

All but five of the 101 firms on his list were German, and those exceptions proved the rule: a New York importer who had visited Rhinefarm on a California buying trip, a prominent French-Swiss restauranteur in New York, the ex-California owners of an elite Chicago saloon, an Irish-born Rochester manufacturer of sacramental wine and cordials, and a Boston purveyor of patent nostrums and medicinal wine. Language alone cannot explain his German focus; Dresel was fluent in both written and spoken English. Rather, he was selling German-style wines to Germans who were in the business of selling such wines to fellow German-Americans. Almost two-thirds of those on his contact list came from the wine-producing areas of southwest Germany. A few had German wine training, or relatives in the German wine trade, but most began their American careers as artisans, shopkeepers, or saloonkeepers, and moved into wine when they realised they could capitalise on homeland connections. Three-quarters of the group had arrived during the peak period of German immigration in the 1840s and 1850s, almost two-thirds as single men aged 16 to 22, the age range when Germans began and completed vocational training; older arrivals were often uprooted 48'ers like Dresel. The small number of American-born Germans (4), and childhood immigrants (8), is striking testimony to a segmented wine trade developed by immigrants for immigrants, and a measure of the generational challenge to sustain it that California wine would face.

Julius Dresel's particularly successful 1879 tour encouraged him to seek additional capital to continue replanting his vineyard with

21 "Will Repeal of Prohibition Bring Back Milwaukee's Oldtime Wein Stuben?", *Milwaukee Journal* 9/29/1933; "Take A Drink? Where You May Accomplish That Feat in True Artistic Style", *Sunday Times* (Chicago) 2/2/1873.

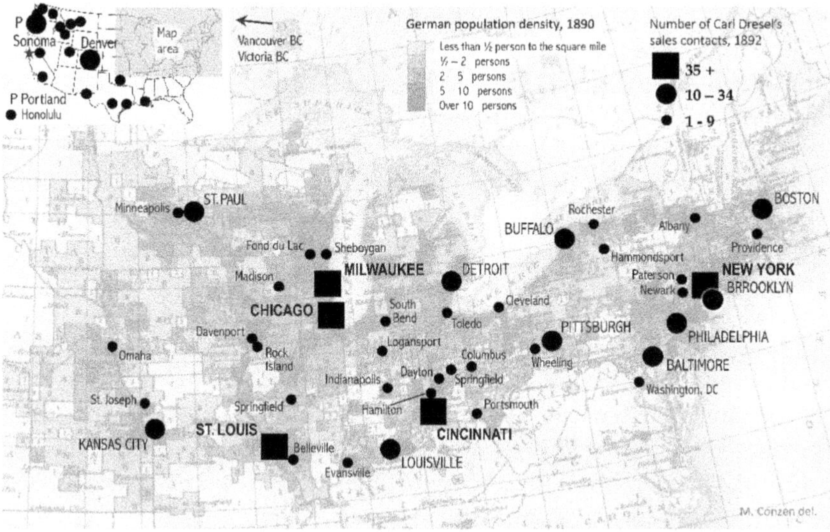

Map 3: Carl Dresel's 1892 Customer Contacts. Sources: 1892 Dresel address book, Gundlach-Bundschu Archive; Base map: Density of Distribution of the Natives of the Germanic Nations: 1890, in *Statistical Atlas of the United* States, Washington, D.C., Government Printing Office, 1898, Map 58

phylloxera-resistant rootstock, increase his cellar capacity, purchase more grapes, and add acreage. Carl took over the eastern trips in 1884, married Gundlach's daughter Rosie four years later, and further expanded production after Julius' 1891 departure.

But Carl's customer lists from the 1890s (Map 3) document the firm's continued reliance on the direct selling of premium wine in a segmented German market. His customer base remained deeply rooted in the German heartland of the northeast quadrant, and despite outliers in newer western areas where dealers were less apt to be German, 87 percent of Dresel's 621 dealer-customers in 1892 still had German names.

The Gundlach-Bundschu strategy

We lack comparable customer data for J. Gundlach & Co., the new premium wine wholesale house that Gundlach and Bundschu opened in basement wine vaults in downtown San Francisco in 1876[22]. But both its salesforce and its creative promotional efforts testify to the continued emphasis it placed on its German-American customers, even as it pursued an elite national market. Rhinefarm's own fine wines remained at the core of the firm's reputation, but its expanded San Francisco blending, bottling, and aging capacity and retail salesroom – soon augmented by additional cellars and then consolidated into the purpose-built Bacchus wine vaults in 1891 – enabled the firm to buy quality wines from throughout the state, market them aggressively both locally and nationally, and ship in glass as well as wood to insure the firm's reputation for quality[23]. Gundlach himself launched the new firm with an eastern tour in 1876, and Bundschu followed in 1878 and 1893, but normally they relied like other San Francisco wholesalers on constantly traveling salesmen, four in number by 1889, joined by Gundlach and Bundschu sons as they came of age. Almost all their traveling salesmen, as well as their agents in heavy-volume eastern cities, were German-speaking – except, tellingly, in New Orleans with its wine-drinking French population, where French-born agents tended their market until Prohibition[24]. When Gundlach's bachelor son Carl set up the firm's permanent New York agency in 1886, both his residence in the city's leading German hotel where visiting German celebrities stayed, and his membership in elite German clubs, spoke to the firm's continued cultivation of a German-American clientele; indeed, in 1891 he moved the firm's lower Manhattan cellars into a new Flemish Renaissance building whose very architecture proclaimed his wine's Germanic affinity[25].

---

22 Many of the firms's records, and most family papers, vanished in the 1906 San Francisco earthquake and fire; traces of the surviving early records, and most of those from the 1906-1920 period, disappear in the late 1920s.

23 "Mr. Bundschu […] goes in for nothing but high grade wines, and […] pays more for fine wines than any other firms on the coast"; *Sonoma Index-Tribune*, 4/23/1887. J. Gundlach wine purchases were regularly tracked in the California press, e.g. *Santa Cruz Weekly* 5/14/1881; *Sonoma Democrat* 9/24/1881; SFM 1/18/1884. The firm's development of European, Central American, and Pacific Rim markets lies outside the scope of this essay.

24 Liggett J. H., *The Industries of San Francisco*, San Francisco, Cosmopolitan, 1892, p. 150-152; directories for San Francisco and other cities; Bundschu papers, GBA.

25 AC 8/30/1885; NYT 2/29/1892; New York city directories, 1886-1912; *Das deutsche Element der Stadt New York*, New York, Otto Spengler, 1913, p. 123.

J. Gundlach & Co.'s initial San Francisco campaign was similarly focused on the city's German population. Gundlach's prominence in San Francisco German life and personal friendships with its German newspaper editors had long insured free publicity for Rhinefarm, but now splashy 1876 ads introduced readers of San Francisco's German press to the new firm and its Baby Bacchus logo (Fig. 1).

The logo, one of the first to be adopted by a California wine producer, recalled an image long familiar to German wine drinkers, but received less prominence four years later when the firm extended its advertising to the English language press. The promotional genius of Bundschu, who handled marketing for the firm while Gundlach focused on the wine itself, soon transformed their cellar glut into "California's largest stock of fine old cabinet wines". Bundschu experimented constantly with advertising aimed at different audiences, and though he developed a restrained, less explicitly Germanic aesthetic by the 1890s when others began to copy his florid imagery, he never fully abandoned the Baby Bacchus that invoked the firm's German roots. He also deftly used the

Fig. 1: Inaugural J. Gundlach & Co. advertisement, with Baby Bacchus logo. Source: *San Francisco Abend Post*, 16 October 1876

era's prolific local, national, and international exhibitions to shape his wine's appeal and affirm their quality. The firm's displays at San Francisco's periodic Mechanics' Institute Fairs moved quickly from conventional bottle pyramids in 1878 to increasingly elaborate stage sets influenced by the pageantry of German carnival and opera, culminating in the over-the-top spectacle of a two-story display inside a giant redwood tree that J. Gundlach shared with three other San Francisco wine merchants at the Chicago's World's Columbian Exposition in 1893. Thereafter his designs in both local and national settings retreated to a subtler classic mode more attuned to the tastes of elite consumers while still alluding to Bacchus' own Roman milieu – a style that the firm retained even after Bundschu's 1910 death[26].

These expositions yielded a wall-full of gold and silver medals for the firm's wine, along with praise for the "artistic" quality of its displays and free national publicity. But Bundschu also engaged in publicity stunts more directly aimed at German-American consumers. Thus in 1878 he sent a cask of Sonoma Gutedel to German Chancellor Otto von Bismarck, whose letter of appreciation for "California's liquid gold" received wide coverage in the nation's German-American press. He followed by sending a similar cask to German poet Viktor von Scheffel, author of highly popular drinking songs. Scheffel's two-stanza poem of thanks for "this echo of my songs [...] a child of California grapes" still featured in the firm's publicity 16 years later[27]. Even more enduringly, in 1887 the firm debuted Rodensteiner Traminer, a wine whose name invoked Scheffel's best-known drinking song celebrating the ride of Count Rodenstein's ghostly army through the night sky in search of a wine tavern still open at half past eleven. Rodensteiner, with its German-style label depicting Rhinefarm, was a wine designed for long, convivial German-American

---

26 Advertisements in California newspapers, directories, guides, and other publications, 1876-1919; newspapers reports of exhibition displays and awards; medal, photograph, and ephemera collections, GBA; SFB 8/30/1879. California's first successful wine branding and publicising has been attributed to Gustave Niebaum of Napa's Inglenook Winery in the mid-1880s; Sullivan C. L, *Napa Wine: A History from Mission Days to the Present*, San Francisco, Wine Appreciation Guild, 1994, p. 78-80.

27 SFB 11/15/1878; AC 12/7/1878; *Deutsche Correspondent* (Baltimore) 5/10, 8/30/1879; *Gedenkblätter zur Goethe-Schiller Feier veranstaltet von den Deutschen Californiens*, San Francisco, L. Roesch, 1895, p. 62.

gatherings, and along with similarly-labelled Riesling remained a staple of the firm until Prohibition[28].

But as the firm, renamed Gundlach-Bundschu after Gundlach's death in 1894, expanded the variety of wines in its inventory, it focused increasingly on the French and Italian-style reds favoured by elite American wine drinkers and newer immigrants from southern Europe. The new gravitas of the firm's aesthetic by the mid-1890s, evident also in most of its wine labels, matched Bundschu's growing authority within the profession. His regular circulars to the trade attracted national attention as authoritative reports on the state of California wine, and when San Francisco's eight largest wine wholesalers formed the city's Wine Dealers' Association in 1889, Bundschu became its first president[29]. But the solid customer base that the firm had developed with its commitment to premium wines helps explain why they were the only one of the Association's members to remain completely outside the 1894 wine trust, and how they were able to rebuild after the destruction of their wine vaults and a million gallons of their wine in San Francisco's 1906 earthquake and fire, and to dominate the wine awards at the city's great 1915 Panama-Pacific Exhibition. Even Carl Dresel now followed more closely the business path blazed by his Gundlach-Bundschu in-laws in bottling, branding, and publicising his wines, particularly after winning the grand prize at the 1904 St. Louis World's Fair. Both firms would close at the onset of Prohibition in 1920.

Any wine, historian David Hancock reminds us, is necessarily the outcome of "ongoing negotiations among producers, distributors, and consumers"[30]. Viewing 19th century California wine through the lens of the Dresel and Gundlach families moves its story centrally into the globalised networks of the Atlantic wine trade, and suggests the critical role of America's German immigrants in providing an outlet for the fine wines that ambitious California growers learned to produce. The tastes of German-American consumers shaped the kinds of wine that Rhinefarm's proprietors produced, the existing network of German-American wine

---

28 *San Francisco Chronicle* [SFC] 12/7/1887; Scheffel V.v., "Das Wilde Heer", *Fliegende Blätter* (Munich), n°26-609, 1857, p. 68-70; Label Album and bottle collection, GBA.

29 Rhinefarm Vineyard Map 1893, Label Album, GBA; SFM 12/10/1886; SFC 6/10/1887; SFB 10/6/1888.

30 Hancock D., *Oceans of Wine: Madeira and the Emergence of American Trade and Taste*, New Haven, Yale University Press, 2009, p. 104.

dealers offered them a distribution system, and German-American buying power helped both Rhinefarm firms play significant roles in the development of quality California wine in the 19th and early 20th century.

But can their experience illuminate the marketing of more ordinary California wines as well? Like Julius Dresel, many other California growers tried to free themselves from the control of New York wholesalers and untrustworthy agents by making their own eastern selling trips. But few had Dresel's persistence, and their frustrations fuelled the rise of the San Francisco wholesale houses to find markets for them[31]. Dresel encountered their traveling salesmen during his 1879 tour, when many of the eastern dealers whom he visited were already ordering wine from one or another of the San Francisco firms. By the late 19th century, as Bundschu would pointedly note, these San Francisco wholesale houses were predominantly German[32]. Of the ten members of the San Francisco Wine Dealers' Association by 1894 when the wine trust was formed, only one firm was not German, and that one was French[33]. Nativist resentment of these foreign-born wholesalers by California winegrowers exacerbated the market crisis that led to the wine trust[34]. Yet it was precisely these wholesalers' ability to tap into the national German-American market, with cargo wines as well as with fine wines, that likely helped account for their marketing success. The German immigrant market, this case study suggests, may have been as crucial in the emergence of 19th century California wine as was America's Italian immigration for its subsequent 20th century development[35].

This issue clearly demands more scrutiny. But whatever the case, the German immigrants who chose to consume California over imported

---

31 "Many of our largest vine-growers and wine-makers are now in the Atlantic States, making or looking for a market for their wines"; PRP 6/1/1872.

32 Bundschu, "German Influences".

33 PWSR 10/5/1891; *San Francisco Call Bulletin* 7/26/1894. The wholesale house headed by Arpad Haraszthy, an Austro-Hungarian, is included among the German firms; he self-identified as Hungarian, but his financing partners were German, and his father, pioneer winemaker Agoston Haraszthy, was the 1856 president of the elite *San Francisco Verein*; *Sacramento Daily Union* 10/4/1856.

34 E.g. SFB 7/24/1889.

35 Cinotto S., *Soft Soil, Black Grapes: The Birth of Italian Winemaking in California*, New York, New York University Press, 2016.

Fig. 2: "Bacchus in California". 1887 J. Gundlach & Co. Christmas card image. Source: *San Francisco Chronicle*, 7 December 1887

wine were clearly key actors in its story. Lower price for similar quality was a large part of California wine's appeal for these consumers, as was its relative freedom from the disruptions of war, poor harvests, and rumours of adulteration that plagued European imports. But consuming California wine also offered less tangible appeals to immigrants eager to preserve the best of the old world while celebrating their roles in the new. As San Francisco German poet Rudolph Thomann meditated over a glass of Gutedel on Rhinefarm's terrace, wine's successful transplantation to the new world offered a reassuring message that his own re-rooting in a new homeland would similarly thrive. Wine, asserted J. Gundlach & Co.'s 1887 Christmas image (Fig. 2), was among the civilising gifts brought by Germans to California – their own stake in the land[36].

[36] Thomann R., "Gutedel", in Zimmermann G. A., *Deutsch in America: Beiträge zur Geschichte der Deutsch-amerikanischen Literatur*, Chicago, Ackermann & Eyller, 1892, p. 170-171; "Bacchus in California", SFC 12/7/1887.

The Hunter Valley: Historicising a Multi-Form Wine-World in the Grape-Wine-Complex

Julie McIntyre and John Germov

The Hunter Valley in New South Wales is Australia's oldest continually producing wine region. This riverine valley is adjacent to the plain and river valleys of the Sydney district, where early experiments with wine growing accompanied the British invasion of Aboriginal lands to establish the colony of New South Wales from 1788. A few bottles of wine were made in the Sydney district as early as 1792. Between 1788 and 1821 New South Wales operated primarily as a military garrison, with labour for cultivation and construction provided by English and Irish convicted felons transported from England for a range of crimes. In this time, small acreages of winegrape vineyards were planted under official imperial auspices and variously at two or three of the fewer than a dozen nascent private estates trialling crops of introduced Eurasian plants for luxury goods. Until the 1820s, piecemeal attempts to produce wine relied on land grants and the importation of vine stock by agents of the British colonial administration. A small number of winegrape plantings occurred in the Hunter Valley from the late 1820s due to a wave of settler land privatisation by British authorities to seed capital investment in the colony. Small-scale winemaking in the region began in 1832 and therefore, as winegrape cultivation has not for some years been viable in the Sydney district, the Hunter is Australia's oldest wine region in continuous production[1].

This chapter presents our interpretation of multidisciplinary sources to historicise the commodity producing community of the Hunter wine region in the project Vines, Wine and Identity: the Hunter Valley, New

1 McIntyre J. *First Vintage: Wine in Colonial New South Wales*, Sydney, NewSouth, 2012, p. 175-196.

South Wales and changing Australian taste. Vines Wine and Identity was funded at the University of Newcastle for three years from 2014 by the Australian Research Council and the peak body for the Hunter wine growing community, the Hunter Valley Wine and Tourism Association (HVWTA). The second partner organisation was a major regional cultural institution in the Hunter Valley, Newcastle Museum. The project summary in the application to the Australian Research Council reads as follows.

> Australia is a leader in global wine trade and tourism, and Australian drinkers are shifting from beer to wine. Yet little is known about the regional communities that make wine, how wine production has shaped their identity, and how producers have changed national culture by creating a taste for their wines. This project explores these themes through an historical sociological study of Australia's oldest wine region, the Hunter. It traces intra- and transnational networks of people, knowledge and wine. This will in turn reveal elements of the power nexus in wine production, trade and consumption to provide critical new insights into Australia's change to a wine making and wine drinking country[2].

For the Hunter Valley Wine and Tourism Association (HVWTA) this was a legacy project and a quest to identify "historical capital" in the region's comparative longevity and durability, as an advantage in the wine marketplace, and for tourism[3]. For partner organisation Newcastle Museum, we curated the cultural heritage of a valued commodity community. The industry- and public-facing strands of the project are published in the book *Hunter Wine: A history*, and informed an exhibition by Newcastle Museum from August 2018 to January 2019.

As a historian and sociologist with a record of prior collaboration in wine studies, we perceived that the primary source material available to pursue Vines, Wine and Identity provided an opportunity to explore the extent to which a commodity community could be focal subjects of history. We aimed to treat members of the Hunter wine community as agents of their own history. This chapter discusses how some key source collections for the project contained multi-themed threads, enabling the

---

2 Australian Research Council Linkage Project application, LP146100140, Unpublished document, 2012.

3 Historical capital is a form of Bourdeusian extra-economic value, see McIntyre J., "Blank Pages, Brief Notes and Ethical Double-Binds: Micro Digitisation and the 'Infinite Archive' ", *Archives and Manuscripts*, vol. 44, n. 1, 2017, p. 5.

interpretation of historical action across multiple scales and structures, drawn from this source base. Our central research questions for the project were: why did wine growing begin in the Hunter and what was the basis of its continuity given that it is ahistorical to assume a commodity community is predestined either to emerge, or to endure[4].

Historians have not until now attempted to historicise a wine region through the actions of its commodity producing community, as agents of their own history, over time. Why did we not instead seek in Vines, Wine and Identity to define the Hunter wine region by classifying the characteristics and quality of the wine produced in the region? Why not foreground *wine* as a unit of study, rather than the people making it? Modern historians of empires and nation-states traditionally sought to locate geo-political entities within a competitive hierarchy appraising the achievement of modernity[5]. Surely histories of wine regions should seek to locate these product-based geo-economic units within a hierarchy of wine quality? The answer is that the source material that inspired the project did not lend itself to such an approach and would not have satisfied the project's aims. For the record, *Hunter Wine*, and the accompanying exhibition, refer to the many honours and prizes achieved by the Hunter region's wine producers and brands, as part of multi-scaled peer assessment of quality. We were certainly interested *as part* of our study to understand how Hunter winegrowers innovated forms of judging wines within their own community and how this changed over time[6]. But, historically, wine judging is not an objective and fixed, stable structure. Wine competitions confer "symbolic capital" through cultural consecration and are contingent on their social and cultural context[7].

---

4 The question of why plant wine grapes is initially addressed in McIntyre J. and Germov J., *Hunter Wine: A history*, Sydney, NewSouth, 2018, p 37-45. The whole of *Hunter Wine* is aimed at responding to the second question, which is a revisiting of the first across generations.

5 Curthoys A., and Lake M., "Introduction", in Curthoys A. and Lake M. (eds.), *Connected Worlds: History in Transnational Perspective*, Canberra, Australian National University E-Press, 2005, p. 5-17.

6 McIntyre and Germov, *Hunter Wine*, p. 79, 105-106, 110-111, 114-115, 165-168, 198, 205, 208, 219, 262.

7 Wei Z., "Understanding Classifications: Empirical Evidence from the American and French Wine Industries", *Poetics*, vol. 33, 2005, p. 179-200; Allen M. and Germov J., "Judging Taste and Creating Value: The Cultural Consecration of Australian Wines", *Journal of Sociology*, vol. 47, no. 1, 2011, p. 35-51.

Wine industry measures of quality provide insight into changing wine styles yet tell only a part of the story of regional wine history.

Our approach in Vines, Wine and Identity to the Hunter wine region as an entity within the global wine marketplace was closer to the difference between the world economy and world-economies, a framework to encapsulate space and time as extrapolated by Fernand Braudel in his exploration of the preconditions for modern capitalism. According to Braudel, as units or sets of study world-economies constitute the rhythms within a wider, macro-scaled world economy. The "movements" of these rhythms are either "periodic" (continuous) or "conjunctures" (episodes)[8]. Adapting a Braudelian approach, Vines, Wine and Identity historicised the Hunter wine region as a product of deep time affordances and 155 years of settler enterprise. *Hunter Wine* presented a wine-world with internal logics of geographic and economic expansion and contraction within a wider world economy. What this chapter offers that is new is a reflection on how our study of a regional wine-world contributes methodologically to wine studies as an international and interdisciplinary field of research.

A cross-disciplinary frame in space and time

Regional commodity development has its basis in the affordances of deep time formation of geological and geographical features. The Hunter Valley's geological boundaries are escarpments of the Great Dividing Range to the south, west and north and the Pacific Ocean shoreline to the east. Its soils are texture-contrast; sandy to clay. The Hunter's landscape promotes maritime moisture flow. Its rainfall occurs primarily in the summer months and the region is prone to storms[9]. Employees of the colonial administration of New South Wales named the valley's principal river, the Hunter, in the early nineteenth century. *Hunter Wine* charts the environmental, social and economic causes of a shifting loci of vineyards and wine enterprises in the region. This mobility of plantings, which took place in the main from the mid-valley's east to west, makes it impractical to see the Hunter region's history through geographical fixity.

---

8 Braudel F., *Civilisation and Capitalism 15th-18th Century, vol. 3, The Perspective of the World*, trans. Siân Reynolds, New York, Harper & Row, 1979 (1984), p. 21-31.

9 McIntyre and Germov, *Hunter Wine*, p. 26-37.

Place-product names or geographical indications are intellectual property in the global commodity marketplace. Australia's geographical indications for wine regions (GI) are relatively new. In the 1990s, Australian wines were increasingly labelled for place names, grape varietal names and the years of vintages[10]. Even so, Australian wine nomenclature retained vestiges of the European places from which Australia's British wine trade-inflected wine culture derived, such as Champagne. During bilateral trade negotiations the European Union insisted the Australian Government formalise place-name intellectual property, leading to the 1995 *Trade Marks Act* (Australian Commonwealth), known in the Australian wine industry simply as GI. The Act prohibited Australian wine from using European place names and introduced the definition of Australian geographical place names by co-ordinates. The GI's administering body, Wine Australia, does not prescribe wine production practices[11]. A study of the development and impact of the Hunter GI fell outside of the periodization of the Vines, Wine and Identity project and remains to be conducted.

At the outset of our study we determined that the precise temporal focus of the project would occur as the research progressed. It was intended that the year-dates for the Hunter wine region's origins, and the end point of the project research, would be determined in accordance with the Hunter wine-world's internal logics. This maintained the subjectivity of the Hunter's wine-producing community. As a result, *Hunter Wine* begins in deep time and pinpoints the inception of Hunter vine plantings in 1828[12]. The narrative end point of the book, 1983, reflects that year as a turning point in the Hunter's role in the emergence of a newly stratified Australian wine culture[13].

We would like to underscore that Vines, Wine and Identity was informed by geographic and economic perspectives, but could not be wholly framed in this manner and also meet the project aims. How do geographers view the Hunter wine region? A study completed in the late 1990s presents the region as unsustainable due to little rain during

---

10 McIntyre, J. and Germov, J., "Who Wants to be a Millionaire? I Do: Postwar Australian Wine, Gendered Culture and Class", *Journal of Australian Studies*, vol. 42, no 1, 2018, p. 65-84.

11 See https://www.wineaustralia.com/labelling, accessed 24 April 2020.

12 McIntyre and Germov, *Hunter Wine*, p. 1-18.

13 *Ibid.*, p. 230-266.

winter and spring, the frequency of rainfall and storms during the grape ripening season, susceptibility to mildews, soils of "undistinguished heavy clays" and unproductive business practices[14]. Be that as it may, the region remains in production, contributing around two percent per annum of Australian wine production, as discussed elsewhere. That said, the 2020 grape harvest, which would usually end in March, was a disaster due to smoke taint from widespread bushfires. Social distancing measures during the coronavirus pandemic also closed the tourism outlets on which much income now relies[15].

Whereas Europe's deep histories of continuous wine production in specific landscapes and ecologies has given rise to traditions of geographical specialisation and the naturalisation of supply chain patterns as structures associated with wine sensory characteristics informing geographers and geographical perspectives of history[16], this is not so in Australia. By comparison with Europe too, in Australia concepts of specialist wine locale arrived with immigrants of non-British ethnicity, or British men with some experience of European wine locales who expected to find such specialisations defined as part of a developing wine culture[17].

Although an early planted Australian wine growing region, the Hunter has limited land suitable for vines and other regions quickly eclipsed the Hunter in proportional output[18]. For this reason Hunter wine has not especially engaged economists and economic historians[19]. Nevertheless, economic perspectives were essential as a higher scaled context for the

---

14 O'Neill P., "The Gastronomic Landscape", in McManus P., O'Neil P. and Loughran R. (eds.), *Journeys: The Making of the Hunter Region*, Sydney, Allen & Unwin, 2000, p. 158 and 178.

15 On the primacy of tourism in the Hunter region and discussion of natural disasters see McIntyre J., Senese D. and Hull, J., "Fruit Forward?: Wine Regions as Geographies of innovation in Australia and Canada", in Van Luyn A. and de la Fuente E. (eds.), *Regional Cultures, Economies, and Creativity: Innovating Through Place in Australia and Beyond*, London, Routledge, 2019, p. 21-44.

16 See for example Dutton, J, "Geographical Turns and Historical Returns in Narrating French Wine Culture", *Global Food History*, vol. 5, no. 1-2, 2019, p. 113-131.

17 McIntyre J., Pierre M. and Germov J., "To Wash Away a British Stain: Class, Trans-Imperial and the Australian Wine Imaginary", in Dutton J. and Howland P. J. (eds.), *Wine, Terroir and Utopia: Making New Worlds*, London, Routledge, 2019, p. 42-57.

18 McIntyre and Germov, *Hunter Wine*, p. 283.

19 Anderson K., *The World's Wine Markets: Globalization at Work*, Cheltenham, Edward Elgar, 2004; Simpson, J. *Creating Wine: The Emergence of a World Industry, 1840-1914*, Princeton, Princeton University Press, 2011; Anderson K. and Pinilla V. (eds.),

Hunter's small comparative role in New South Wales and Australian wine production[20]. Australian wine industry aspirations preceded the collection of statistical data. Indeed, collection of statistics on New South Wales grape acreages and wine production began as an instrument of state encouragement for a wine industry when wealthy property owners with experimental vineyards were prominent in the colony's emergent legislature. Moreover, Vines, Wine and Identity could not be focused only on understanding the Hunter wine region within the guiding structure of a wine supply chain. A coalescence of Australian wine firms into an industry with supply chains did not occur until the 1860s[21].

Our interest in Vines, Wine and Identity, was to see the formation and continuity of wine production as Hunter wine became commodified, as Hunter wine production and distribution processes shaped and joined the flow of industry supply chains. To do this we sought to foreground community members as actors innovating and responding within an interconnected local, colonial/national and international system of structures and institutions encompassing production, distribution and consumption; known as the "wine complex"[22]. We were not the first researchers to reference the optic of production, distribution and consumption as the "wine complex". Others investigating wine-related topics in separate disciplines, and in separate national and transnational contexts, employed the term and the concept independently of each other. We became advocates, in 2013, of the value of thinking with the "wine complex" as a systems approach in the field of wine studies on recognising a pattern of logical interconnectivity among historical actors growing winegrapes, making wine, marketing, selling and drinking wine as a commodity in the research of others, as well as in our own inquiries[23]. An interdisciplinary wine complex frame suited Vines, Wine and Identity because the origins of Australian wine regions prior to the second half of the nineteenth century requires piecing together the preliminary and

---

Wine Globalization: A New Comparative History, Cambridge, Cambridge University Press, 2018.

20 McIntyre and Germov, *Hunter Wine*, p. 281-285.

21 See for example, McIntyre, *First Vintage*, p. 96-97, 102.

22 McIntyre J. and Germov J, "Drinking History: Enjoying Wine in Early Colonial New South Wales", in Eriksson S, Hastie M. and Roberts T. (eds.), *Eat History: Food and Drink in Australia and Beyond*, Melbourne, Cambridge Scholars Press, p. 120-142.

23 McIntyre J. and Germov J, "Drinking History".

recurring confluences of multidisciplinary factors: imperial, colonial, national, environmental, social, cultural, legal and economic[24].

The narrative progression in *Hunter Wine* as evidencing a system in action was based on multiple case studies conducted separately and then combined. Seeing the past as a conglomeration of connected, crossed or entangled histories is an approach to the unfolding of cultural know-how termed *histoire croisée*, 'a multiplicity of configurations according to logics that cannot be reduced to a process of linear evolution'[25]. Following practitioners of *histoire croisée*, our historical sociological approach to the industry- and public-facing threads of Vines, Wine and Identity entailed melding studies of synchronous time periods into a longer temporal flow, while also cutting-in and weaving through specialist academic studies conducted within discrete disciplinary areas on asymmetrical topics.

Sources and their interpretation

The primary source material for *Hunter Wine* constituted a multi-archival base across ten archive repositories, drawing from 13 discrete collections of family business papers, a further collection of family business papers held in private hands and two oral history series, one of these created for the project. Further, the primary source base encompassed statutes, commissions of inquiry, 22 historical publications, the *Maitland Mercury* and other newspapers, plus four key periodicals: the *Agricultural Gazette of New South Wales*, *NSW Government Gazette* and the *Statistical Register of New South Wales to 1900*[26]. Within this appreciable inventory, however, two collections of family business papers were formative in conceptualising Vines, Wine and Identity as focusing on the subjectivity of negotiating the formation and continuation of wine growing and wine business: Dalwood Records 1868-1902 and Wilkinson Family Papers 1836-1961[27].

---

24 See McIntyre, *First Vintage*.

25 Werner M. and Zimmermann B., "Beyond Comparison: Histoire croisée and the Challenge of Reflexivity", *History and Theory*, vol. 45, 2006, p. 47.

26 McIntyre J. and Germov J., *Hunter Wine*, p. 288-289.

27 State Library of New South Wales, Dalwood Vineyard Records 1868-1902, Mitchell Library Manuscript Collection (ML) 8051; State Library of New South Wales, Wilkinson Family Papers 1836-1961, Mitchell Library Manuscript Collection (ML) 532.

The Dalwood records are predominantly across the period when John Wyndham managed this family business, from 1868 to his death in 1887. There is correspondence with proprietor John Wyndham's wine agents at the closest ocean port. There are wine orders for personal use and retail in the colony's wine shops, and there is correspondence between family members about attempts and failure to secure new capital investment in the 1880s. Significantly too, the Hunter River Vineyard Association, established in 1847, came under the leadership of Wyndham in the final decade before its demise in 1876 due to failing membership[28].

The Wilkinson collection is in the main the work diaries of Audrey Wilkinson from taking control of his parent's mixed farm, including its winegrapes in 1892, aged 15, on the death of his father. Wilkinson learned wine growing from his father (who was employed in his younger years by John Wyndham at a property within the Dalwood enterprise). Audrey Wilkinson gained through the encouragement of his patrician and educated mother the lifelong habit of meticulous record-keeping of daily tasks from vine planting and pruning through to harvest times, fermentation temperatures, to neighbourhood bartering and technology exchange that sustained his property Oakdale during his lifetime to 1961, the year before his death[29].

Neither the Dalwood (Wyndham) nor the Wilkinson collections contain financial ledgers of a continuity that would allow quantitative analysis of capital investment and profit or loss, nor company meeting minutes or policy documents to evidence decision-making within the structures of a firm within an industry sector. The value of these collections to Vines, Wine and Identity was their qualitative evidence of threads requiring multiple forms of analysis of actors in a wine-world. Wyndham and Wilkinson were decision-makers for their own businesses and key influencers in the organisation of members of their commodity community through growers' associations.

John Wyndham self-avowed a lifelong interest in wine growing[30]. He dealt directly with wholesalers and retailers. He retained retail agents. He led the Hunter River Vineyard Association in the 1860s when the original inaugurators from 1847 had left the industry or passed away.

---

28 McIntyre and Germov, *Hunter Wine*, p. 132.

29 McIntyre and Germov, *Hunter Wine*, p. 129-130.

30 McIntyre, *First Vintage*, p. 208.

At the height of his wine enterprise in the early 1880s, the Dalwood on-site vineyard was 80 acres and grapes were purchased from at least two neighbouring properties with family ties. The on-site winery contained modern equipment, but there is no extant record of annual output.

Wilkinson's vertical integration extended a shorter depth along the wine supply chain than Wyndham. Wilkinson did not label his own wine or deal with customers, but shipped barrels in bulk by rail to Sydney merchants. He employed few hands outside of harvest and pruning seasons, relying often on two or three family members or neighbours, and usually performing these tasks alongside of his brother, uncle and other employees. Wilkinson made his wine rather than employing a winemaker and assisted neighbours to process their grapes. Wilkinson belonged to the Pokolbin and District Vine Growers Association from its inauguration in 1901. This association began in response to the market threat of wine flowing from other Australian colonies, and of increasing wine fraud, following the end of customs barriers between colonies. The new group filled a gap of many years in regional collectivism by growers, following the withering away of the Hunter River Vineyard Association[31].

One of many central threads through the Wyndham and Wilkinson papers is the difficulty of obtaining items on which depended the growing, making and trading of wine once a customer base emerged from the 1860s. In the remainder of this section, rather than only restate evidence from *Hunter Wine*, we present a new account of how working with the Wyndham and Wilkinson collections offers a pathway to multiform historical knowledge creation. Following this brief case study, we outline the critical wine studies perspective in Vines, Wine and Identity that is also illustrated through attention to the Wyndham and Wilkinson papers. And finally, we explain the organising principle resulting from the research in Vines, Wine and Identity that scaffolded *Hunter Wine*.

The cask problem as a case study

Casks are the coopered barrels of various sizes manufactured from timber and fastened with iron staves that stored all fermented wine, until the invention of stainless steel holding vats in the second half of the twentieth century. Although colonial Australian winemakers

[31] McIntyre and Germov, *Hunter Wine*, p. 196-197.

experimented with stone fermenting vats in the 1850s, and adopted concrete vat technologies from the turn of the twentieth century, timber casks were integral to linking the stages of grapes into wine, wine cellaring to sale quality, and wine to domestic wholesales and for export[32]. Because casks are organic, their wood imparts flavour qualities to the wine stored in them. The cask's effect on wine changes with use and reuse as wine infuses the timber grains. Australian timbers have chemical qualities that make them unsuitable for coopering into wine barrels. Some barrels and presses were made from native timbers. In 1869, John Wyndham sought Kauri pine planks to construct a wine press, but the lumberyard did not have stock of suitable quality and the manager recommended instead Richmond River pine[33]. Yet most casks in circulation were imported ones and frequently reused.

Early in 1887, wine shop owner Joseph Whitten ordered three quarter casks of "red wine" from John Wyndham in response to a newspaper advertisement[34]. Some weeks later, Whitten returned the casks, requesting that the bond paid on the casks in case of loss be credited to his account with Wyndham. Six months after the initial order, Whitten returned other casks and ordered a further "two or three [filled] casks in say a fortnight or thereabouts"[35]. This circulation of reused casks points to negotiations with suppliers themselves connected with other commodity chains. After the death of John Wyndham a manager unnamed in the records was employed in Wyndham's stead. In 1890 J.E. Cooke from Castlemaine Brewery sent an urgent purchase order for 500 gallons of "sweet red wine" from Dalwood, around the time of vintage in January, most likely to distil into brandy[36]. Six months later an exchange about emptied brandy barrels indicates freshly emptied ones were preferable, presumably as the timbers had not yet shrunk from dying out, but more could not yet be supplied to Dalwood[37].

---

32 McIntyre, *First Vintage*, see stone vats at Camden Park on p. 3 of colour section, and concrete vats at p. 142.

33 James Wolstenholme to John Wyndham, 15 October 1869, ML 8051/1/1.

34 Joseph Whitten to John Wyndham, 13 January 1887, ML 8051/1/1.

35 Joseph Whitten to John Wyndham, 16 June 1887, ML 8051/1/1.

36 Castlemaine Brewery (J.E. Cooke) to Dalwood manager, 6 January 1890, ML 8051/1/1.

37 Castlemaine Brewery (J.E. Cooke) to Dalwood manager, 4 June 1890, ML 8051/1/1.

John Wyndham had refused to sell wine to P.B. Burgoyne Limited, the main British wine importer with an agency in the Australian colonies, based at an office in South Australia. The agent, A.H. Nicholson, conducted tours to identify wines suitable for export to London to be blended and branded generically as Australian[38]. The manager who replaced Wyndham, following the latter's death, had no such qualms about losing brand identity for Dalwood wines. Nicholson, writing to Dalwood's manager in 1891, insisted "only very sound casks are used as the shipping people are particular and refuse all inferior casks"[39].

In February 1895, during the vintage at Wilkinson's Oakdale of grapes from his own and other vineyards, Audrey Wilkinson asked his uncle Lionel Stephen, a bankrupt winegrower who earned a living as a carrier, to take his horse-pulled dray on a series of errands. Wilkinson sent Stephen the short distance to another Wilkinson relative's vineyard and winery, Coolalta, "to try and borrow casks and to [neighbouring] Ashmans [owned by the Tyrrell family] for our vat head [a fermenting vat cover]"[40]. Wilkinson either walked or rode a horse the short distance to another neighbouring vineyard and winery, Drayton's, "to try and borrow casks but didn't succeed"[41]. In early March, Stephen returned to Coolalta with cases for grape picking and casks that had been borrowed at an earlier (unstated) date. A few days later Wilkinson and Stephen returned a wine press to another neighbour[42]. Hunter winegrowers did not establish co-operatives for winemaking yet community relations were vital, if not always fruitful, for business practices.

Ultimately Hunter producers, like others in a country without an industry providing oak timbers for casks, bore the cost of importing French or American oak barrels. The Wyndham and Wilkinson collections offer a close perspective on efforts to workaround the lack of casks and their subsequent cost to producers. Other topics or themes within the Wyndham and Wilkinson collections connecting these men as actors to institutions and structures at other scales include land purchases, vine plantings (varieties and planting styles) tied to predictions of consumer

---

38 McIntyre and Germov, *Hunter Wine*, p. 169-170, 172-174.

39 A.H. Nicholson to Manager of Dalwood Vineyards, Branxton, 24 December 1891, ML 8051/1/6.

40 Audrey Wilkinson, 1895 Diary, Entry for 27 February, ML 532.

41 *Ibid.*

42 Audrey Wilkinson, 1895 Diary, Entry for 12 March, ML 532.

markets, adaption of vineyard and winery technologies, the purchase and application of sulphur in vineyard and winery, modes of selling wine and transporting wine beyond the district, the formation and dissolution of industry associations, meetings with higher scaled industry representatives and meetings with bank managers. For this project, the Wyndham and Wilkinson collections provided depth and breadth that permitted attention to how these individuals negotiated the interplay of relationships in wine production, distribution and consumption, and also offered clues to others' practices shaping a wider wine-world identity.

The limits of historical agency

Taking individuals as its focal subjects over time and comparing the scant evidence that exists on their actions and reactions, *Hunter Wine,* by definition through source availability, concentrates on settler capitalists with small to medium-sized businesses. To understand individual settler pasts, we also accessed genealogical research. This assisted with dates and other data to triangulate with other evidence. Australian historian Tanya Evans has shown that genealogical publications, or family histories, once considered inferior to academic research, now offer a knowledge base for cultural histories of institutions and other historical forms that might otherwise be difficult to narrate[43]. Altogether from the 1820s to the 1980s, the characters for whom some historical agency could be discerned, and for whom short life course histories are offered in *Hunter Wine*, numbered close to eighty men and women. Seeing some family histories as legitimate source bases (some others proved unreliable in fact and argument when weighed against proven evidence), combined with primary sources on individuals such as Wyndham and Wilkinson, assisted in our narratives of wine-world patterns in synchronous time periods.

Still, commodity communities are part of societies as well as economies and geographies. As discussed at the first international meeting of wine studies scholars in 2016, critical attention is required to social groups traditionally excluded from histories of political economy: women, labourers and Aboriginal people dispossessed to obtain the land for settler

---

[43] Evans T., *Fractured Families: Life on the Margins in Colonial New South Wales*, Sydney, NewSouth, 2015.

enterprises including wine growing[44]. *Hunter Wine* is an intersectional history of a wine-world, recovering the roles of women, labourers and Aboriginal people where the historical record would allow it[45].

Theorising regional continuity across generations, over time

In *Hunter Wine*, synchronous sources covering short lengths of time became the basis of seeing patterns that, once laid end-to-end in a continuum, allowed a narrative of change and continuity across a longer timeframe. Hunter wine growing began as a pursuit of some of the colony's wealthiest settler capitalists on properties proximal to the major rivers and trading centres. By the 1880s, the main vineyards were clustered westward of the original sites due to environmental and social factors. Land reforms to encourage small-scale settlement and mixed farming, combined with the realities of a modest colonial market for wine led to regional industry stability until the 1920s. Across the mid-century, licencing regulations and social norms ceased to favour the convivial consumption of light wines, until reforms from 1955, with new social freedoms and a rising Australian middle class. The start and end years of each of these synchronous periods are presented in *Hunter Wine* as generations marking points of change but not breaks in commodity production.

The generation termed the Imaginers, from 1828-1846, covers the earliest planting of vines and the success of some property owners with small vineyard acreages within their larger enterprises to the initial shipment of wine from the Hunter to the Sydney goods market[46]. The Experimenters from 1847-1876, marks a period of German labour immigration and the span of the Hunter River Vineyard Association from inception to demise[47]. The First Wave Globalists were Hunter winegrowers at the core of a New South Wales wine market supplying

---

44 McIntyre J., "Wine Studies in the Humanities and Social Sciences: A Report on Symposia and the State of the Field", *Journal of Wine Research*, vol. 28, no. 2, 2017, p. 159-164.

45 McIntyre and Germov, *Hunter Wine*, especially p. 15, 26, 30-31, 44-45, 113-114, 136-157, 259, 270 (document image).

46 *Ibid.*, p. 46-101.

47 *Ibid.*, p. 102-135.

Sydney, and some other colonial centres, and exporting across colonial borders. In this generation, Hunter wine businesses sought to capitalise on wine shortages from the spread of phylloxera in European wine countries (the Hunter has no recorded phylloxera infestation) and were drawn into some exports by Burgoyne and other channels. John Wyndham is a key figure in this generation[48]. The Forgotten Generation (1901-1929) was clustered at Pokolbin, and this is the generation in which wine growing became embedded in Pokolbin, rather than other areas of the wider Hunter Valley. Audrey Wilkinson was a key figure in this generation. 1901 saw the inception of the Pokolbin and District Wine Growers Association in response to the need for a collective body, as federation of the Australian colonies led to inter-colonial free trade, the threat (actually realised) of South Australian wine substantially increasing supply in the Sydney market, and a rise in fraudulent labelling of wine. From 1916 until 1955, wine could not be served in a publically licenced pub, wine shop, club or restaurant in the (now) state of New South Wales after six o'clock in the evening, suppressing convivial wine culture for two generations of the wider community within the state[49].

Between 1930 and 1959, Hunter winegrowers contracted to fewer than a dozen vineyards and four winemakers. This was due to a glut in wine from government support in other regions of New South Wales, combined with a reduction in wine drinking culture resulting from temperance laws. These exogenous forces were exacerbated too by the economic collapse of the period, at its worst during the 1930s Depression, lacklustre consumer interest, and supply chain disruptions during World War II. The generation of Stoics is defined in *Hunter Wine* as ending in 1954, a year that marked a government inquiry report recommending a relaxation of licencing laws such as later closing in New South Wales, leading to the conditions for an upswing in confidence and industry investment from 1955[50].

The Renaissance Generation from 1955 to 1983, encompassed the rise in Australia's late twentieth century wine culture and the beginning of its increasing specialisation into newer varietal based wine styles. *Hunter Wine* traces the Hunter wine community's contribution to this

---

48 *Ibid.*, p. 158-183.

49 *Ibid.*, p. 184-213.

50 *Ibid.*, p. 214-229.

era. Although we termed the generation succeeding the Renaissance Generation as the Second Wave Globalists from 1984, the narrative of *Hunter Wine* ended in 1983. No source material was available to us to adequately present the period from 1984 within the project's duration. It remains for other historians to document beyond this time, to decide when the phase of second wave globalisation ended for the Hunter wine-world, and how this more contemporary history can be told[51].

Advancing wine studies: wine-worlds in the grape-wine-complex

Since the turn of the century, 'connected worlds' approaches in the English-speaking world have extended from transnational methodologies critiquing the racial inequalities of nation-states formed from the conquests of colonial empires, to critiques of capitalism as a global structure[52]. The wine complex informs a methodology aligned with these intellectual movements. In Vines, Wine and Identity we focused on the formative dynamics of human action by tracing evidence of individual and collective action and reaction that innovated and sustained, or disrupted, the development of wine industry and culture within Australia's economy and society. New critiques of capitalism include analysis of the hidden impacts on nature in commodity systems, such as Joshua Specht's history of the American cattle-beef-complex[53].

Wine, similarly, is the result of a *grape*-wine-complex. It is evident in so-called New World, or settler society, wine countries such as Australia that the grape-wine-complex is an amalgam of human processes dependent on extracting value from the diverse ecologies that host these vineyards[54]. The concept of a grape-wine-complex conjoins the interactivity of cultural agents and economic structures at work in the

---

51 *Ibid.*, p. 230-267.

52 Curthoys and Lake, *Connected Worlds*; and see, for example, Beckert S., *Empire of Cotton: A New History of Global Capitalism*, London, Penguin, 2015.

53 Specht J., *Red Meat Republic: A Hoof-to-Table History of How Beef Changed America*, Princeton, Princeton University Press, 2019.

54 McIntyre J., "Wine Worlds Are Animals Worlds Too: Native Australian Animal Vine Feeders and Interspecies Relations in the Ecologies that Host Vineyards", in Cushing N. and Frawley J. (eds.), *Animals Count: How Population Size Matters in Animal-Human Relations*, London, Routledge, 2018, p. 126-138.

processes of the wine complex over time, with the ecological context of grape growing. As we and other researchers seek to further understand modern and contemporary capitalism as an iterative and reiterative globalised structure, wine-worlds as units within a grape-wine-complex in world-economies, including Australia's, are significant for these inquiries.

Conclusion

JULIE MCINTYRE AND MIKAËL PIERRE

The chapters in this book highlight the evolution of the complex mechanisms of wine markets through the negotiations, collaborations and adaptations of actors in the processes of informing and reforming institutions of supply and regulation at local, national and international scales. Wine is a commodity produced, distributed and consumed through the intermediation of actors with varying modes of influence. Over time the intermediations of these individuals and groups have, by turns, informed and reformed the economic, socio-cultural and legal structures in which wine markets function. The contributions in *Wine, Networks and Scales* offer a broad analysis of the connections between producers, merchants, brokers, prescribers and consumers, from the late 17th century to the recent present. Wine is, indeed, an instrument of global history and contributors pay particular attention to the 19th century. This epoch marked a transitional period, when wine markets extended from Europe to all of the continents and regions of the world – the Americas, Africa and Oceania – during the macrostructural coalescence of globalisation.

Adaptation to markets is one of the key elements for which intermediations proved instrumental and new forms of intermediations emerged between the different actors of the wine industry from the 18th century. Disruptions in the late 17th century and throughout the 18th century in France led to the segmentation of the markets. Dishonourable merchant practices and predations necessitated a regulation system set by private socio-economic groups. A complexification of the market occurred in the second half of the 19th century, when the triumph of sparkling champagnes illuminated the importance of London agents as distributors of French wines. Despite instabilities and disputes deriving from asymmetrical information, these agents remained at the forefront of the marketing strategy of the Champagne houses to develop their branding and control the British market. In the same period, increasing intercontinental exchanges and international economic integration led to the emergence of new forms of competition between the Old World and the New World. This proved to be especially so between French wines and Australian wines competing on the British market during the phylloxera crisis. This Old World-New World competitive trade binary, stimulated by wine traders between Europe and wine countries Europeanised in the Modern Era, appears to be distinctive in the wine market, more so than other commodities on world markets. In the 19th century the apparition of sophisticated taste, the development of new products and the emergence of new producers worldwide contributed to the transformation of the wine sector through adaptation of new practices to control the market by merchants, trading agents or the winegrowers themselves.

Several contributions in this book show how wine proceeds from places of production to the hands of consumers through intersectional processes of intermediation, connecting actors in wine-worlds with other individuals or institutions that enable trade. The brokers in the United Provinces in the 18th century were instrumental in connecting buyers and sellers of wine. Though not always wine experts themselves, these brokers possessed an insider status in wine business that allowed them to play a key role facilitating transactions. In late nineteenth-century Italy, public institutions supported the wine sector to improve domestic production and compete more efficiently on international markets. The Italian State could thus intervene in the wine business as a part of a national strategy to obtain economic results. The *longue durée* analysis of the Cirò wine industry show the progress and diversity of intermediations. With the development of the DOC, representative agents and the producers themselves participated in the local wine industry as intermediaries to inform purchasers and consumers on the international scale about the characteristics of the wines of Cirò. Often neglected by scholars, wine cooperatives also have a role to play in this matter. In contemporary Alsace, wine cooperatives are at the centre of a debate between varietal wines that are best suited to international markets and terroir wines that are more adapted to the French market. This opposition has led to tensions with other wine-world actors (independent winemakers and traders) as a strategy advantaging *either* varietal *or* terroir styles' impacts upon the Alsatian wine sector as a whole, and the image of Alsace wines. In these cases, intermediaries shaped and are shaping the identity of the wine industry.

Identity is also at the centre of commodity production and distribution practices in the wine industry. Differences in race or ethnicity may mark inequalities in labour relations or a competitive advantage, or both. The clustering of wine market intermediaries by cultural identity or ethnicity is particularly noticeable in new wine-producing countries that emerged during the nineteenth century. In the British colony of the Cape, wine-farmers' exploitation of the cheap labour of convicts or coloured labourers, considered unskilled and disposable, complicates the vision of white European skilled workers as the "ideal labour force" in vineyards of the past. During the same period, in California, German migrants proved influential in shaping a new North American wine market by deftly orchestrating production, distribution and consumption suited to the German American community. In the Australian district of the Hunter Valley, the relative longevity and continuity of wine production and distribution has produced a distinctive regional wine-world identity. The Hunter wine region's identity evolved from origins in Aboriginal dispossession, British colonial aspiration, British-Australian settler toil and German indentured labour, followed by successive generations of persistence, adaptation and innovation, to the present.

The chapters of this book have focused on the intermediations occurring in this economic sector in different countries in Europe (France, Italy, Great Britain and the United Provinces), in the United States, in South Africa and in Australia. These examples are certainly new evidence of the diversity of interlinked processes in production, distribution and consumption of wine at work in the globalisation of the wine world, at least since the 19th century. A more complete global historical perspective requires future studies on other countries in Europe and in South America. New wine-producing countries like China could bring fresh perspectives to understand these intermediations in the current era of globalisation.

It is timely to consider the wine industry as other than a dehumanised structure and to perceive it instead as comprised of actors reacting and innovating in dispersed and varied socio-cultural contexts in space and time. As this book goes to press, the COVID-19 novel coronavirus pandemic has caused the most serious disruptions to the production of wine and the movement of wine through distribution channels, to consumers, since the end of the earlier global market era in the 1910s. This collection of studies on the agency of individuals and groups in the wine sector points to the dynamic responsiveness of the industry and the possibility of resilience and economic recovery in future.

Titres parus

Vol. 25 – Stéphanie Lachaud-Martin, Corinne Marache, Julie McIntyre, Mikaël Pierre (eds.), *Wine, Networks and Scales. Intermediation in the Production, Distribution and Consumption of Wine*, 2021.

Vol. 24 – Verónica González-Araujo, Roberto-Carlos Álvarez-Delgado, Ángel Sancho-Rodríguez (eds.), *Ethics in Business Communication. New Challenges in the Digital World*, 2020.

Vol. 23 – Didier Caveng, *L'éthique dans la finance. Les banques genevoises à l'épreuve des faits*, 2019.

Vol. 22 – Andre Tiran et Dimitri Uzunidis (dir.), *Libéralisme et protectionnisme*, 2019.

Vol. 21 – Dominique Desjeux, *The anthropological perspective of the world. The inductive method illustrated*, 2018.

Vol. 20 – Benoit Bernard, *Management Public. 65 schémas pour analyser et changer les organisations publiques*, 2018.

Vol. 19 – Dimitri Uzunidis (dir.), *Recherche académique et innovation. La force productive de la science*, 2018.

Vol. 18 – Jean Vercherand, *Le marché du travail. L'esprit libéral et la revanche du politique*, 2018.

Vol. 17 – Dominique Desjeux (dir.), *L'empreinte anthropologique du monde. Méthode inductive illustrée*, 2018.

Vol. 16 – Sophie Boutillier, *Entrepreneuriat et innovation*, 2017.

Vol. 15 – Arvind Ashta, *Microfinance. Battling a Wicked Problem*, 2016.

Vol. 14 – Jean Vercherand, *Microéconomie. Une approche critique : Théorie et exercices*, 2016.

Vol. 13 – Reseau de Recherche sur l'innovation, Blandine Laperche (dir.), *Géront'innovations. Trajectoires d'innovation dans une économie vieillissante,* 2016.

Vol. 12 – Societe Internationale Jean-Baptiste Say, Dimitri Uzunidis (dir.), *Et Jean-Baptiste Say… créa l'Entrepreneur*, 2015.

Vol. 11 – Faiz Gallouj, Francois Stankiewicz (dir.), *Le DRH innovateur. Management des ressources humaines et dynamiques d'innovation*, 2014.

Vol. 10 – Charlotte Fourcroy, *Services et environnement. Les enjeux énergétiques de l'innovation dans les services*, 2014.

Vol. 9 – Remy Herrera, Wim Dierckxsens, Paulo Nakatani (eds.), *Beyond the Systemic Crisis and Capital-Led Chaos. Theoretical and Applied Studies*, 2014.

Vol. 8 – Reseau de Recherche sur l'Innovation, Sophie Boutillier, Joelle Forest, Delphine Gallaud, Blandine Laperche, Corinne Tanguy, Leila Temri (dir.), *Principes d'économie de l'innovation*, 2014.

Vol. 7 – Michel Santi, *Capitalism without Conscience*, 2013.

Vol. 6 – Arnaud Diemer, Jean-Pierre Potier, Léon Walras. *Un siècle après (1910-2010)*, 2013.

Vol. 5 – Sophie Boutillier, Faridah Djellal, Dimitri Uzunidis (Reseau de Recherche sur l'Innovation) (dir.), *L'innovation. Analyser, anticiper, agir,* 2013.

Vol. 4 – Aurelie Trouve, Marielle Berriet-Solliec, Denis Lepicier (dir.), *Le développement rural en Europe. Quel avenir pour le deuxième pilier de la Politique agricole commune* ?, 2013.

Vol. 3 – Sophie Boutillier, Faridah Djellal, Faiz Gallouj, Blandine Laperche, Dimitri Uzunidis (dir.), *L'innovation verte. De la théorie aux bonnes pratiques*, 2012.

Vol. 2 – Faridah Djellal, Faiz Gallouj, *La productivité à l'épreuve des services,* 2012.

Vol. 1 – Abdelillah Hamdouch, Sophie Reboud, Corinne Tanguy (dir.), PME, *dynamiques entrepreneuriales et innovation*, 2011.

www.ingramcontent.com/pod-product-compliance
Ingram Content Group UK Ltd.
Pitfield, Milton Keynes, MK11 3LW, UK
UKHW020710041026
15590UKWH00002B/587

9 782807 614161